Rethinking Chronology
From Abraham *To* Solomon

By Applying Unused Texts

Rethinking Chronology
From Abraham *To* Solomon

By Applying Unused Texts

Setting Genesis, Job, Exodus, Joshua,
Judges, Ruth and 1 Samuel
into Old Testament Chronology

Brian Kuehmichel

© 2020 Brian Kuehmichel
Sheboygan, WI

Printed in the United States of America
All rights reserved. No portion of this book may be reproduced, stored in a retrieval system or transmitted in any form or by any means (electronic, mechanical, photocopying, recording or otherwise) without permission in writing from the copyright owner (author / publisher), except for brief written reviews.

ISBN: Paperback 978-1-7359782-4-6
EPUB Ebook 978-1-7359782-1-5

Unless otherwise indicated, Scripture quotations are from the King James Version of the Bible. Others are marked as follows:

AMPC – Scripture quotations marked (AMPC) are taken from The Amplified Bible, (AMP©), Copyright ©1954, 1958, 1962, 1964, 1965, 1987 by The Lockman Foundation. Used by permission. All rights reserved.

CJB – Quotations marked as (CJB) are taken from the Complete Jewish Bible, Copyright 1998 by Jewish New Testament Publications, Inc. Used by permission. All rights reserved.

CEV – Scriptures marked as (CEV) are taken from the Contemporary English Version©; (CEV©); Copyright ©1995 by American Bible Society. Used by permission.

CSB – Scripture quotations marked CSB, are taken from the Christian Standard Bible®, Copyright ©2017 by Holman Bible Publishers. Used by permission. Christian Standard Bible®, and CSB® are federally registered trademarks of Holman Bible Publishers.

DLNT – Scriptures marked as (DNLT) are taken from the Zondervan in the New Testament TransLine: A Literal Translation in Outline Format © 2002 Michael J. Magill, and by Wiph & Stock © 2008 Michael J. Magill. All Rights Reserved.

ESV – Scripture quotations marked (ESV) are from the The Holy Bible, English Standard Version® (ESV®), Copyright ©2001 by Crossway Bibles, a publishing ministry of Good News Publishers. Used by Permission. All Rights Reserved.

EXB – Scriptures marked as (EXB) are taken from The Expanded Bible. Copyright ©2011 by Thomas Nelson. Used by permission. All rights reserved.

NET – Scripture quoted by permission. Quotations designated (NET) are from The NET Bible®; (NET©), Copyright ©1996-2006 by Biblical Studies Press, L.L.C. http://netbible.com All rights reserved.

NIV – Scripture quotations marked (NIV) are taken from the THE HOLY BIBLE, NEW INTERNATIONAL VERSION®, (NIV®) Copyright ©1973, 1978, 1984, 2011 by Biblica, Inc.® Used by permission of Zondervan. All rights reserved worldwide.

With deep gratitude for God's help in understanding
and applying numerous concepts and texts that
demonstrated the unfailing accuracy of the Holy Scriptures.

Contents

List of Tables xii

Preface xiii

Foreword xv

SECTION I 1
    Setting Abraham to Solomon in Time 1
        Introduction 1
        Another approach 3
        Carefully framed conclusions 6
        Establishing a baseline 9
        Abraham 10
        Ishmael 11
        Isaac 12
        Jacob 12
        Jacob's children 15
            What we learned: 15
            Make a visual tool: 16

SECTION II 19
    When did Jacob's descendants intersect? 19
        Part 1: The children of Jacob and the
        intersections of their descendants 19

Joseph	20
Jacob's other sons	21
Lineage from Levi and Judah	23
Judah	24
Levi	26
"My covenant of peace"	30
The intersection of Aaron and Elisheba	33
Aaron	33
Elisheba	34
Naashon	36
What we learned:	37
Make a visual tool:	37
Genesis 15:13-16	**39**
Part 2: The children of Jacob and the intersections of their descendants	39
Examining three details	39
Strangers	42
Afflicted	43
Slaves	44
The fourth generation	46
Four hundred years - four ways	51
The meaning of Exodus 12:40	53
Exodus from Egypt	55
What we learned:	56
Make a visual tool:	56
When did the Pharaoh arise that "knew not Joseph"?	**59**
Part 3: The children of Jacob and the intersections of their descendants	59
The Scriptures gave enough information	61
That Pharaoh arose	63
What we learned:	64
Make a visual tool:	64
Can the book of Job be placed in time?	**65**
Part 4: The children of Jacob and the intersections of their descendants	65
Job's ancestry – Issachar to Job	65
Job's life span	66

Contents

        Esau to Eliphaz the Temanite 67
        Shuah to Bildad the Shuhite. 68
        Benjamin or Simeon to Zophar the Naamathite. . . 69
        Nahor to Elihu the Buzite 70
    Connecting Job to that pharaoh. 73
    Comparisons of wealth. 75
    Notable beauty compared 79
    Who wrote the book of Job? 80
    Using Job's own words. 84
    Answering unasked questions 86
        What we learned: 87
        Make a visual tool: 88

Can Rahab of Jericho be the wife of Salmon?. 89
    Part 5: The children of Jacob and the
    intersections of their descendants. 89
    Rahab and Rachab 89
    The expression "an old man" 94
    Jesse became "an old man". 95
    Life spans and birth ages 96
    Rahab of Jericho 96
    Other scenarios and calculations 97
    Perhaps another son 102
    Applying Mosaic law to the unique scenario of Ruth 102
    New Testament validation 108
    Narrowing Jesse's age. 110
    Unnamed Lineage 111
    Logical results 113
        What we learned: 114
        Make a visual tool: 115

When did the book of Ruth occur?. 117
    Part 6: The children of Jacob and the
    intersections of their descendants. 117
    The time for Ruth 120
        What we learned: 123
        Make a visual tool: 123

Contents

SECTION III 125
Connecting Joshua and Judges 125
- Background 125
- Joshua's estimated age 126
- What was Joshua's real age? 128
- The elders that outlived Joshua 130
  - What we learned: 134
  - Make a visual tool: 134

SECTION IV 137
Overview of Judges, Ruth and 1 Samuel 137
- Setting 137
- Comprehensive solution 138
- Using Scriptures carefully 140
- Introduction to Samuel 140
- The meaning of "judge" 142
- Judges as deliverers 144
  - What we learned: 153

SECTION V 155
Connections between Judges and 1 Samuel 155
- Simultaneous judges 155
- The divisions of 1 Samuel 157
- The beginning of 1 Samuel 159
- The keys 160
- The period of Eli and Samuel 161
- Who is Eli? 162
- The sons of Eli 165
- Notice and apply the details 167
- More about Samuel 169
- The man named Meraioth 172
- The early descendants of Meraioth 175
- Samuel was old 177
- Samuel died 180
- The reign of Saul 181
- Saul's time marker at David's birth 182
- Saul's age at David's birth 182
- Jonathan's age range 184

Contents

    Philistine rule during Saul's reign 185
    Saul's request of Ahiah marked time 186
    Saul's disobedience and rejection 187
    Saul's rage against David and death 189
    The alignment of numerous priests 190
    The lineage of the high priests 191
    The ark was taken 193
    "The light of Israel" 195
    Where was Jonathan? 197
    The period of Samson 199
    Samuel continued the worship of God 203
    Where was Samson? 204
    The Philistine forty-year oppression ended 205
    The placement of Jephthah 206
    Three hundred years 207
        What we learned: 209
        Make a visual tool: 210

SECTION VI 213
    The books of Judges, Ruth and 1 Samuel
    have a place in time 213
        Genesis through 1 Samuel 213
        Judges, Ruth, and 1 Samuel integrate 215
        Judges chapters 17–21 218
        Summary 219
        An invitation to study Holy Scripture 220
        Personal Thoughts 223
            What we learned: 224
            Make a visual tool: 224

INDEXES 225
    Names With Birth, Death and/or Event Year 225
    Name Index 229
    Major Event Index 234
    Brief Event Timeline 235
    Scripture Index 239
    Endnotes 251

List of Tables

Table 1　Jacob's age, [Abraham's relative year], mother and each child's age when Joseph was born 18

Table 2　The 4 required generations after Levi 47

Table 3　The calculated ages for begetting or birth, and of unusually long life spans to reach from Salmon to David 71

Table 4　The calculated ages if the ratio of 0.84 was used 71

Table 5　The results if Jesse was age eighty 81

Table 6　The life spans and birth ages to reach from Salmon to David when including Rachab as Salmon's daughter 84

Table 7　These judges were given and time periods summed 110

Table 8　The oppressions were given and summed 110

Table 9　Lists the time periods from the land division through Abdon and sums the total 113

Preface

This project was started as a means to organize and collate many diverse notes on time intervals in the Old Testament and put them in one place. They were scattered on various papers in file boxes, written on Bible margins, and held on small paper inserts inside of several Bibles. The plan was to add to this many parts that were retained in memory, especially emphasizing the time related material with "why" each piece fit or did not fit. This started small. Build a generic timeline to give an outline or structure to insert the time related data. Make the end material understandable to my children and grandchildren. Then write out separately the reasoning for various pieces.

In this portion of working through many notes the period of the birth of Jacob's sons became intriguing. The process of carefully noting minute details brought to light eleven sons born in seven years which gave a very narrow birth time to each of them, which Joseph in Egypt knew (Genesis 43:33). Later when Levi's 137 year age at death was given it yielded an exact year for his death. The same was true of Abraham, Isaac, Jacob, Joseph, Aaron, Moses, and many other individuals or events. Examining when Joseph died in Egypt prompted more inquiries. Can the time period of Israel in Egypt be resolved from Scripture alone? If so, how can this be accomplished?

The same questions came again with the puzzling statements about Joshua's death and the elders. What were the connections between Samuel's lineage and Eli's lineage since both were Levites? How did Samson or any judge fit with Eli, or Saul or any other person named in 1 Samuel? Out of this process and numerous requests for God's help to show how these fit together the answers to so many questions were obtained.

This document was formed and structured to explain in detail the reasoning and the time placement of the people named, including those across the period of the judges and 1 Samuel. Using Abraham's birth as a fixed starting point from which to proceed established more than 150 individuals in time. Some are only named at specific events. This method connected Abraham's lineage step by step into and out of Egypt by examining many named individuals up to, and some past, Solomon. This process connected God's promise to Abraham in Genesis 15:13-16 through his posterity to 1 Kings 6:1. These two key Scriptures bridged 879 complete years.

More questions surfaced during this study. Simple addition of the numbers of years given in certain parts of the text summed way too large to match the emphatic statement of 1 Kings 6:1. That verse stated the length of time that transpired from the day of the exodus from Egypt to the start of the temple under Solomon.

On the pages that follow those questions and many more are carefully asked and answered. Other unexpected details came to light as well. This book was the fruitful result of assembling this section of my notes for my family, asking hard questions, and accepting the integrity of Holy Scripture for its own answers.

Foreword

Rethinking Chronology from Abraham to Solomon supports those who believe God's words are really complete, established, true, and discernible and upholds those whose faith is in the living God helping man through His settled Word. The material affirms belief in the simplicity of God's word, its clarity of meaning, and ease of understanding. The intricacy of interconnected content presented in the text rebuts those who are seeking to find it somewhere or somehow in caves, clay jars, or in some not-yet-disclosed ancient archive.

Rethinking Chronology from Abraham to Solomon also stands in contrast to and separate from those who think the Holy Scriptures require individuals with approved credentials to decipher its message, who need to receive special training in ancient documents, and must attain a certain advanced or "critical" perspective (i.e. of doubt) from which to elucidate its understanding. Those individuals who hope to find or build the Scriptures believe man can help God settle His Word by their efforts. This began well over a century ago with the substituted text of Westcott and Hort proceeding through its derivatives while steadily implying and imposing the ideology that God did not preserve His Word amongst His own people, both Hebraic and Christian. That process is now in the twenty-eighth iteration (NA 28) and will never be finished for this reason: to believe God's Word had been settled at any point in the past made unnecessary their ongoing "scholarship" of searching for and "building" the Scriptures in centers of learning.

The endless citing of the work of others who may, or may not, believe the Holy Scriptures has become a circle of self-serving reinforcement that you cannot know anything for certain without promoting someone else first. Jesus taught with authority, not as the pharisees who constantly referred to the words of others. This material exercised the precept of Apostle Paul, that God has called the foolish of this world to confound the wise, and simply invites every Christian or interested person to use "the mind of the Spirit" to examine, evaluate and decide (Romans 8:27).

Rethinking Chronology from Abraham to Solomon accepted and used a completed platform of Holy Scripture held and preserved faithfully by God's people from the earliest disciples. This material returned to the *textus receptus* and its long-standing translation into English by unpaid but very capable men from notable scholars to broad-ranging layman under the watchful eye of the people of God.

The same text that has saved many souls, brought forth many small and large revivals in Europe and America, educated both the plowboy and milkmaid, developed great clergymen, evangelists, and civic leaders, and reformed secular society was carefully used in Rethinking Chronology. The words, terms, and phrases of the sacred Scriptures were accepted as God-given, and elucidated by their usage in other places of Holy Scripture. Many of the numerous connections with time for people and events that are disclosed and explained herein cannot be established by the contrived text of Westcott and Hort or its derivatives.

Rethinking Chronology from Abraham to Solomon did not accept as valid the perspective that the *textus receptus* and its historic translation into English had nothing to offer the modern academia. For those of you who read the Scripture plainly, simply, and straight forward the text had an amazing amount to say about chronology, when things occurred, how much time elapsed, and how old individuals were at various events. As both Jesus and Philip said, "Come and see." (John 1:39, 46)

SECTION I

Setting Abraham to Solomon in Time

Introduction

Distinct puzzles remain for the student of the Bible to resolve. Are we missing necessary interconnections between Abraham's descendants and others or just not recognizing them? Did the Scriptures tell us of any intermarriage between descendants of Levi and Judah? Did the New Testament offer information to help resolve some of these Old Testament puzzles?

What time placement was revealed in the book of Job? Who were those men who sat with Job? What year did the new oppressive pharaoh arise that enslaved the Israelites? How could Jochebed be both Levi's daughter and Moses' mother? What might that mean in relationship to time?

The long period starting from Joshua entering into Canaan as the appointed leader of Israel through the start of the reign of king David had very intriguing elements. What about Rahab of Jericho, did she marry Salmon or not? When did Joshua die? How long did the elders outlive Joshua?

Definitely puzzling elements included repeated statements, *"the people served the Lord all the days of Joshua, and all the days of elders that outlived Joshua"* (Joshua 24:31; Judges 2:7). Later, two identical expressions were given, *"and the children of Israel did evil again in the sight of the Lord,"* with one leading to eighteen years and the other to forty years of oppression (Judges 10:6-18 and Judges 13:1). The first statement of *"the land had rest"* was given in Joshua 14:15, *"And the name of Hebron before was Kirjatharba; which Arba was a great man among the Anakims. And the land had rest from war."*

The next use of "rest" was in Judges 3:11 with Othniel, Caleb's younger brother, as judge. The same was true for Ehud, Deborah and Barak, and for Gideon. No subsequent judge had that term applied. What did that mean?

Other details to notice were: the alternating reports of Israel's waywardness and deliverance each with varying duration (Judges 3:8–12:15), unusual expressions of an "old" or "very aged" man (1 Samuel 2:31; 17:12), the manner in which 300 years were given by Jephthah (Judges 11:26), and that, *"Samuel judged Israel all the days of his life"* (1 Samuel 7:15).

Then priest Eli was summarized stating that he had judged Israel for *"forty years"* (1 Samuel 4:18). Simple addition of the numbers of years given within Judges and 1 Samuel were way too large to match the emphatic statement of 1 Kings 6:1 which revealed that the 480th year was just begun.

Even when narrowing down this broad period of human history to the period of the judges and of Saul and David there remained many questions. Some riddles in this time period that have long plagued Bible students were these. Which judges overlap, how can this be supported by textual clues, and for how long did they overlap?

Where did Samson (Judges 13–16 chpts.) fit within the period of the judges? Where did Eli (1 Samuel 1:3) fit as judge and why was he a judge at all? When did the forty years of Philistine affliction (Judges 13:1) begin and end? When and how long did Samuel serve as judge (1 Samuel 7:15)? How many years really occurred from the land division before Jephthah began to serve? When did Abdon, the last judge given in series, die?

Numerous people over many years have struggled to take the various portions written in the text of Genesis through 1 Samuel which fit inside the longer time period reaching from Abraham to Solomon and completely make sense of them. Simple addition of various time periods stated within the text made the whole period too long. That sum did not match other texts that clearly gave a specific number of years from one important event to another.

From early Christian history up to the present, individuals have presented solutions that varied from thoughtful to speculative. Some solutions were narrow and only dealt with a small portion of this longer time period while some encompassed broader human history. These individuals delivered a solution that incorporated and appeared to harmonize with specific texts while other applicable texts were left hanging.

All Scripture statements about the people, events and time periods are equally valid since they came by inspiration through one supreme author. Not even one relevant word, phrase, or verse should be neglected, discounted, or ignored. This was quite important. Little details can help resolve many things.

What neglected events and/or Scripture texts can bring connections between what appeared to be disparate and unresolvable information? Can the marriage of a Levite to a Judahite make any helpful connections with time or individuals? Can the years from Abraham to Solomon be reconciled through application of unnoticed or under appreciated statements?

Another approach

The contextual approach to examine Scripture took verses in sequence and made sure that the meaning derived for various expressions was wholly consistent with the plain message of the text. This was specially indispensable with translators. They needed to choose words that conveyed what had been said inside of the original parameters of masculine, feminine, poetry, narrative, etc.

The topical approach sought out all of the pertinent Scripture statements to assemble every piece to explain the material at hand. This method was used across many generations to get the whole picture for God's plan of salvation for mankind, the process of substitution of Jesus' life for our life, of affirming his resurrection to support our future resurrection, etc. The topical approach took into account all relevant Scripture texts, phrases and words to obtain the comprehensive insight into God's wonderful working to redeem mankind from their bondage to sin and corruption and to bring all who will submit to the Lordship of Christ Jesus into His everlasting kingdom.

These two techniques were familiar to Bible students and scholars and have long been used in understanding other passages of Scripture including those teaching doctrine. Both were used here. But another method was obviously necessary.

Many struggled to resolve the data within the 400 years of Genesis 15:13-16 and the 479 years of 1 Kings 6:1. Their solutions were not integrating all of the peripheral textual facts for the intervening events. Nor did they incorporate all of those little essential details about the people involved.

Beside this, the writing style and manner of presentation used in this period of Israel's history was not familiar. For these and other reasons this extended time period from Abraham in Genesis through 1 Samuel up to Solomon needed another frame of reference, another starting point. Thinking about and approaching this material differently was necessary.

Used alone or together the contextual and topical approach was insufficient without looking for many more missing clues. This integrated approach required finding and applying relevant but unused Scriptures to help interpret terms, words, and phrases. Actively searching for word or phrase repetition, time related phrases and expressions, statements of actions, and seeking connections between individuals that were not easily obvious was necessary.

Many underappreciated Scripture terms, expressions, and details were found. When all three methods were applied with rigor, small to large details were revealed, explained, and applied to build upon various statements. The following essential topic provided one important clue.

When Apostle Paul wrote in his epistles, *"I was with you,"* (1 Corinthians 2:3) or its corollaries, *"I was present with you,"* (2 Corinthians 11:9) or, *"I was yet with you,"* (2 Thessalonians 2:5) these expressions certainly meant that his readers should connect his words and actions stated now in the letter to his words and actions in the past when he was among the Corinthians or Thessalonians as a missionary. This same approach was used by Christ Jesus on the last day of His human life. On that significant day Christ Jesus began to recite specific Old Testament material quite familiar to fellow Israelites.

These words were spoken while He was upon the cross, "*My God, my God, why hast thou forsaken me.*" Christ Jesus simply repeated words that were written much earlier in Psalm 22. These words told all of the observers of His crucifixion to note carefully everything that Jesus was experiencing because the entire scenario was foretold by prophet David.

Jesus had recited enough words from the beginning of that text so that every interested person could recognize it, find its words in a scroll, and study that Psalm. In the context of the struggle to breathe upon the cross, Jesus had emphatically pointed back to those previously written words. In that manner, as part of His last words, Jesus connected the crucifixion event to an earlier text (Matthew 27:46-50; Mark 15:34-37).

The person in the Old Testament that carried the same title, "son of God," as that of the Messiah presented in the New Testament was Samuel. That was what his name meant. And when prophet Samuel referred back to a former text in a manner similar to what Christ Jesus did then we should take serious note and study the passage carefully. To say it more crisply, when the Old Testament "son of God" referred back to a former written text in about the same manner that the New Testament "son of God" did we must take careful note of it. Then study it, and apply it well.

This repetition of former words was Samuel's special tool to get each reader to connect the subsequent text with prior text. Samuel used this method either to connect the second scenario in time with a former event or to have the reader substitute previous information into the text which conveyed time related details. When prophet Samuel referred to previous texts from the Pentateuch, Joshua, and Judges will be revealed and examined.

Sometimes the replication was by rewriting the longer text or at other times by a more subdued method when the author choose to use a specific phrase or meaningful word. The authors in Scripture that came after Moses used that specific type of repetition when they quoted former text and incorporated that text appropriately to mark an event in time. Together we will decipher the direct or subtle quotation of former texts when examining the accounts of Job, Judges, Ruth, and 1 Samuel and apply them.

Carefully framed conclusions

Various methods are used in which to gather information, collate the various pieces, and make sense of the information to a careful student of Scripture. Then conclusions can be made. The first focus used herein was to know the text. The second was to use available tools to seek out and expedite the search for all related information.

These were words, phrases, names, ages, years, events, word meanings, parallel uses of terms, etc. The third focus was to recheck facts and then assemble the pieces in one place. Then begin to synthesize the material into a meaningful set of data.

The fourth focus was upon assuring the reliability of various conclusions derived from the extracted textual information. The conclusions follow and proceed from the assembled information, discussion, and explanation of the texts involved. With all Scripture based statements used herein the source was either embedded within the text, within parenthesis as already demonstrated, or within square brackets.

The first method of deduction was the easiest because in one simple Scripture statement sufficient facts were presented from which to draw a firm conclusion. This was the case when the biblical text stated, *"And Abraham was an hundred years old, when his son Isaac was born unto him"* (Genesis 21:5). The conclusion was straight forward, Abraham was one hundred years old when Isaac was born.

The second method of deduction was used when two, three, or more verses must be assembled together to provide sufficient information to result in a conclusion. Then the process was a logic statement: if part one was true, and part two was true, then these statements joined together made possible a firm conclusion which, by default, also excluded false conclusions. The next paragraph will add to the conclusion statement about Abraham just made above.

> And the first came out red, all over like an hairy garment; and they called his name Esau. And after that came his brother out, and his hand took hold on Esau's heel; and his name was called Jacob: and Isaac was threescore years old when she bare them. (Genesis 25:25-26).

That also made a truth statement which can be made into a firm and reliable conclusion of age at birth or years between events. Start with Abraham at age one hundred for Isaac's birth, plus add Isaac at age sixty (threescore) for the birth of both Esau and Jacob. Then Abraham was 160 years of age when these twin brothers were born.

This was further confirmed because a later text said that Esau was a son in Genesis 27:5. By incorporating another or third text the statement that they were twin brothers became certain. We can proceed to a firm and reliable conclusion based upon sufficient facts. This showed how essential complete information gathering was before honest and wholly reliable conclusions were made.

Abraham was 160 years old when these twin brothers were born. Another valid conclusion was that Abraham had twin grandsons. To proceed to state that Abraham had fraternal twin grandsons required extracting more from those verses since only Esau was described like this, *"the first came out red, all over like an hairy garment."*

Both the first and second methods of deduction brought forward a very high level of confidence in the result because they restate or simply join together two, three, or more properly related truth statements. But not everything in the text of Scripture can be summarily drawn into a crisp, hard, absolute conclusion. Some pieces fall into what is known as the preponderance of evidence with a conclusion consistent with all relevant information.

This third method of deduction occurred when a large group of texts must be brought together. From those statements facts can be extracted (methods one and two), other relevant pieces of information applied, the collated material placed into a working structure or framework to make sense of it, complete a recheck that other pieces of information did not get excluded inappropriately, maintain a desire to go back and correct any prior assumptions, and then proceed to draw or redraw the best-fitting conclusion consistent with all pertinent facts. Vigilance was maintained to not exclude other biblical statements that placed various constraints or time limits upon the time range of the material under consideration.

Then a moderate to high level of confidence in the result or conclusion was held. This method of drawing a conclusion had decreased certainty. For some readers doubt could remain.

The fourth method of deduction followed the comprehensive gathering and sorting of information from method three. But because of the latitude of time for the birth of multiple children or for described events, even when connected with other peripheral information, the conclusion was less precise. From this carefully structured approach the most prudent conclusion was a time range in which that scenario fit.

The resulting time range had a moderate to high level of confidence, but the exact year was not determined. If two or more of these scenarios were chained together, the confidence level of the conclusion or time range was lowered a little even when the conclusion itself was logically derived, completely correct, and wholly consistent with the entire framework of biblical material.

This part of method three and four was worth repeating, to get reliable conclusions one must not reject, exclude, discount, or gloss over other pertinent biblical texts – relevant statements that in some manner limit or alter the scenario being researched. Fulfilling this carefully framed and rigid requirement provided the necessary information to discern the narrow birth period of Keturah's six sons, likewise for Jacob's first eleven sons and daughter, the length of the time period from Isaac to the exodus from Egypt, the meaning of Exodus 1:6, when the pharaoh[A] arose who enslaved the Israelites, the duration of Israel in Egypt, the scenario surrounding Salmon and Rahab, the narrowed birth time of Boaz, the placement of the book of Ruth, and much more.

Exodus chapter 1 also provided the details to obtain the twelve year time range for the Book of Job. It had placed Job's death prior to a specific event. This process of including unused texts also reconciled the time statements in the text from Joshua through the start of the reign of king David given in Judges, Ruth, and 1 Samuel.

[*Author's note: Please view each footnote for valuable information to help*

A. The term pharaoh is a title comparable to an emperor or empress, a king or queen, a caesar of Rome or raja(h) of India. This term was used in the Pentateuch with Abraham, Joseph, and Moses for three very different rulers. The same term pharaoh was used in later Scriptures to refer to other rulers of Egypt across the reigns of multiple kings of Israel and Judah from Solomon onward. The term pharaoh does not directly identify the person fulfilling this position of leadership and authority.

understand the text better.]

Each reader is invited and encouraged to 1) read contemplatively, 2) engage in thinking through the texts used, 3) examine carefully all computations and various conclusions derived from them, 4) identify the parenthetical statements and consider their applications, 5) grasp the words or phrases that indicated time and became substitutions for time, 6) explore the reasons to correlate pieces, and then, 7) recognize how all of these parts converged. Numerous large and small parts were necessary to explore to discern their proper import and potential impact upon the whole.

Establishing a baseline

When constructing a timeline, proceeding from Creation through David, the Biblical information was presented from Noah onward with increased complexity. Those facts given from early in Genesis about Shem's birth, later about Joseph's birth, and ending with Judah's offspring increased in length of material and in difficulty to unravel. Therefore, the necessity of comprehending and integrating a much longer and vastly more difficult word story problem (with many more people involved) in the period of the judges has hindered its resolution.

There must be a fixed starting point by which to add or subtract years to connect successive events in relationship to linear time. Abraham's birth year was exceptionally useful as a basic reference point and even worked with any conflicts about what year Abraham was born to Terah. The notation [A-xxx] was used. Starting from Abraham's birth 251 years was given by [A-251] and a time range by [A-238-239][B].

For example: the proximate birth period of Aminadab (Amminadab, [~A-387-415]) required the careful use of the account of Judah in Genesis 38–46 and the intersection of the marriage of Aaron with a descendant of Judah. It also used the long-term lineage of Judah (to prevent unnamed miracles of very late ages at births or exceptional life spans).

B. The numbers found in brackets such as [A-100] or [A-390-433] refer to the years since Abraham was born. Using Abraham's birth as an anchor made the placement of his descendants in time easier and connected the recorded events into a linear framework. This notation format simplified the addition and subtraction of years or time spans. It also enhanced the correlations between individuals who were in the same time period.

The examination process also incorporated the various statements about Aminadab's son Naasson (Nahshon, Naashon).

Naasson's birth occurred when Moses was about 10-30 years old [~A-435-455]. This son (Numbers 1:6-8; 2:3; 7:12, 17; 10:14; 1 Chronicles 2:10) was the leader of the tribe of Judah when Israel encamped around the tabernacle in their wilderness sojourn (Numbers 14:33-34; 32:13; etc.). Naasson will be fully examined later.

All of these pieces were necessary to place in time, as precisely as possible, each of the named descendants of Judah leading up to David. Then, among other details, the question about whether Salmon married Rahab of Jericho was answered. From here we step back in time to Abraham to build many necessary parts and develop some unique tools used later. When these are appropriately applied, the subsequent conclusions can be held with confidence.

[Author's note: Due to the complexity of material discussed in the subsequent text in this book become familiar with two of the indexes at the end of this book: Names With Birth, Death and/or Event Year, and, Brief Event Timeline. Place a bookmark by them to easily refer to relevant material to help refresh your memory in your journey through unfamiliar information and details.]

Abraham

Abram was a later born son of Terah with two older brothers, Nahor and Haran (Genesis 11:26-32; 12:4; 31:53, more details in SECTION II, Part 4. Nahor to Elihu the Buzite). When Abram was ten years of age (Genesis 17:17; 20:11-12, [A-10]) his half-sister Sarai was born. Later they married (Genesis 11:29-31).

After this God asked Abram and Sarai to depart from their homeland (Genesis 12:1; 11:27-32; Deuteronomy 7:7; 1 Chronicles 16:18-20) and go to the place God would show him (Genesis 12:1). God had promised that they would have offspring (Genesis 12:2). Terah died in Haran (Genesis 11:32) just before Abram departed Haran and entered into Canaan (Genesis 12:4).

Abram's age of seventy-five (Genesis 12:1-8, [A-75]) to enter Canaan became a significant time marker for his obedience to and worship of God (Genesis 12:4-8). Ishmael was born when Abram was eighty-six years old [A-86] (Genesis 16:11-16). Genesis chapter 17 detailed God's covenant with Abram who was renamed Abraham by adding a letter into the middle of his name, likewise for Sarai to Sarah. God reaffirmed his promise of offspring to both Abraham and Sarah in verses 4-9 and outlined the acceptance of the covenant, demonstrated by the circumcision of all males in Abraham's household and among his future progeny in verses 10-14.

Isaac was born when Abraham was one hundred years old [A-100] and Sarah was ninety (Genesis 21:1-5). The birth of these two sons became significant time markers in Abraham's life. Then at five years of age Isaac was both weaned and given essentially an inheritance party (Genesis 21:1-5, detailed more later) where he was declared to be the intended heir of all of Abraham's possessions. This was when Ishmael at age eighteen (in his nineteenth year) began to oppose Isaac (Genesis 21:8-10, [A-105]) who received the coveted position as the primary son.

Sarah died at 127 years of age (Genesis 23:1-2, [A-137]). Then Isaac married Rebekah after Eliezer sought her out in Haran (Genesis 24:67; 25:20). This became another marker in Abraham's life at 140 years of age [A-140].

Slightly later the same year Abraham married Keturah and through her conceived six more sons (Genesis 25:1-4). Some years later fraternal twin brothers, Esau and Jacob, were born to Isaac and Rebekah when Abraham was 160 years of age (Genesis 25:24-26; 27:5, [A-160]). After eight sons and 175 years Abraham died (Genesis 25:1-10, [A-175]).

Ishmael

Ishmael was born to Abram by Hagar, an Egyptian woman and servant of Sarai (Genesis 16:1), when Abram was eighty-six years of age and then renamed by God (Genesis 16:11-16, [A-86]). Ishmael was circumcised along with Abraham (Genesis 17:23-26) at age thirteen [A-99]. When Isaac was five years old [A-105] he was both weaned and given essentially an inheritance party (Genesis 21:1-5, detailed more fully later). At this event Ishmael was in his nineteenth year and began to oppose Isaac (Genesis 21:8-9). Subsequently, he was sent out from the camp of Abraham (Genesis 21:10-14).

Later Ishmael took a wife from Egypt (Genesis 21:21) and conceived twelve sons (Genesis 17:20; 25:12-16). He had a younger daughter (sister to his firstborn Nebajoth) who married Esau (Genesis 28:9; 36:3). At age eighty-nine he helped Isaac bury Abraham in the cave of Machpelah (Genesis 25:9, [A-175]). Ishmael lived to 137 years (Genesis 25:17, [A-223]).

Isaac

Isaac was born when Abraham was one hundred years old (Genesis 21:1-5, [A-100]), declared Abraham's heir at age five [A-105], married Rebekah at forty years of age (Genesis 24:67; 25:20, [A-140]), and at sixty years of age had the fraternal twin sons Esau and Jacob (Genesis 25:24-26; 27:5, [A-160]). At age forty Esau began his family (Genesis 26:34-35, [A-200]) while Jacob remained unmarried for many years. When Isaac considered that Ishmael died at 137 years (Genesis 25:17, [A-223]) and that he was almost 137 years old Isaac arranged to give a blessing to his oldest son (Genesis 27:1-4 [A-236]).

This was when Jacob obtained by subterfuge Isaac's blessing. Esau became overtly angry at Jacob and threatened Jacob's life (Genesis 27:5-41). After approval of Isaac and Rebekah, Jacob fled north into Haran to preserve his life and seek a suitable wife (Genesis 28:1-7; 31:41; 30:25–31:55). [See Jacob, below] [If married at age twenty, Rebekah was about 117.]

Isaac was 137 [A-237] and both Esau and Jacob were seventy-seven years old when Jacob met Laban and began to serve him. Laban was Rebekah's younger brother and Jacob's maternal uncle (Genesis 24:29; 28:2-5; 29:14-18, [A-237]). [Laban was about age 112, if five years younger than Rebekah (Genesis 22:23).] Joseph was born fourteen years later with Isaac at age 151 (Genesis 30:24–31:55; 30:24-25; 35:24; 37:3, [A-251]. [see Section II, Part 1. Joseph] Isaac died at 180 years (Genesis 35:27-29, [A-280]), five years older than the age of Abraham.

Jacob

Jacob was born [A-160] when Isaac was sixty years old (Genesis 25:24-26) and Abraham was 160 years old (Genesis 21:1-5). When Esau and Jacob were fifteen years old Abraham died [A-175]. Jacob was at age seventy-six to seventy-seven [A-236-237] when he obtained Isaac's blessing by subterfuge. Because of this Esau threatened Jacob's life (Genesis 27:5-41). With approval of Isaac and Rebekah Jacob fled north to Haran to preserve his life and seek a suitable wife (Genesis 28:1-7).

The account of Jacob's life threatened by Esau (Genesis 27:41–28:8) was the background for his flight northward to Haran. No age for Esau or Jacob was given during this episode in their lives. So this remained to be determined by integrating numerous verses, i.e. a lengthy word story.

The first and much shorter approach to solve this was by noting that Ishmael was fourteen years older than Isaac (Genesis 16:11-16; 21:1-5). Ishmael, Isaac's half-brother, died at 137 years of age [A-223] (Genesis 25:17). Thirteen years later when Isaac was 136 years old [A-236] and approached 137 years he thought that he was also near his own death and decided that he wanted to pass on a blessing to his firstborn son Esau (Genesis 27:1-4).

After Jacob obtained that blessing by substituting for him, Esau determined how he would punish Jacob thinking his father would soon die. Genesis 27:41 read this way. *"And Esau hated Jacob because of the blessing wherewith his father blessed him: and Esau said in his heart, The days of mourning for my father are at hand; then will I slay my brother Jacob."* Then Jacob fled north to Haran with his parent's blessing (Genesis 28:1-5) and arrived in [A-237].

The much longer and more precise approach was to follow the details of Jacob's life and experiences in Haran. Each validated the other method. After Jacob's flight into Haran his service to Laban was described in Genesis 29:20-28.

> And Jacob served seven years for Rachel; and they seemed unto him but a few days, for the love he had to her. ... And it came to pass in the evening, that he took Leah his daughter, and brought her to him. ... And it came to pass, that in the morning, behold, it was Leah: and he said to Laban, What is this thou hast done unto me? did not I serve with thee for Rachel? wherefore then hast thou beguiled me? ... Fulfil her week [7 days], and we will give thee this also for the service which thou shalt serve with me yet seven other years.

At the end of Jacob's time in Haran Genesis 31:38-41 stated this.

> This twenty years have I been with thee; thy ewes and thy she goats have not cast their young, and the rams of thy flock have I not eaten. That which was torn of beasts I brought not unto thee; I bare the loss of it; of my hand didst thou require it, whether stolen by day, or stolen by night. Thus I was; in the day the drought consumed me, and the frost by night; and my sleep departed from mine eyes. Thus have I been twenty years in thy house; I served thee fourteen years for thy two daughters, and six years for thy cattle: and thou hast changed my wages ten times.

As noted, Jacob served seven years before he received Laban's daughter as a wife (Genesis 29:18-21, 27-29). Since Laban was so greedy that he changed Jacob's wages ten times (Genesis 31:7, 41) he was not going to let Jacob marry until every last day of those seven years was completed. Hence, Jacob's emphatic words, *"And Jacob said unto Laban, Give me my wife, for my days are fulfilled, that I may go in unto her."* (Genesis 29:21). The term, *"my days are fulfilled,"* meant seven whole years of days.

Then through Laban's deception Jacob was given Leah first. After one more week (seven days) he was given Rachel (Genesis 29:20, 27-29). *"Fulfil her week, and we will give thee this also for the service which thou shalt serve with me yet seven other years."* In this way Jacob was leveraged to serve Laban *"seven other years"* for her again.

Joseph was born at the end of fourteen years of service to Laban as Scripture stated in Genesis 30:25, *"And it came to pass, when Rachel had born Joseph, that Jacob said unto Laban, Send me away, that I may go unto mine own place, and to my country."* [A-237 + 14 = A-251] After Joseph was born Jacob expressed he wanted to depart to Isaac. This only made the middle seven years [A-244-251] in which to receive eleven sons with Bilhah and Zilpah as additional wives. Shortly thereafter Jacob had a daughter named Dinah born to Leah. Laban urged Jacob to stay (Genesis 30:27-43).

Laban negotiated for Jacob to remain in Haran. Jacob served six more years to acquire his own livestock (Genesis 30:26-34; 31:41), *"Thus have I been twenty years in thy house; I served thee fourteen years for thy two daughters, and six years for thy cattle: and thou hast changed my wages ten times."* [A-237 + 7 + 7 + 6 = A-257]. Therefore, Jacob at seventy-seven years of age [A-237] began to serve Laban in Haran for twenty years (Genesis 30:24–31:55) from age seventy-seven to ninety-seven [A-237-257]. This was verified by examining Joseph's age before pharaoh when Jacob declared he was at the age of 130 years. [detailed in the next chapter, Section II, Part 1. Joseph]

Jacob went from eighty-four to ninety-one years of age [A-244-251] during those middle seven years. Joseph was born when Jacob was ninety-one years old [A-160 + 91 = A-251]. [see Section II, Part 1. Joseph] At age 120 Esau and Jacob buried Isaac [A-280] while Joseph was in Egypt.

Two years after the worldwide famine started Jacob went into Egypt at the age of 130 years (Genesis 45:6; 47:9, [A-290]). Then after seventeen years [A-290-307] Jacob died at age 147 [A-307]. He was embalmed, and buried in the cave of Machpelah by Abraham, Sarah, Isaac, and Rebekah (Genesis 47:28; 49:33; 50:1-14).

Jacob's children

To understand the birth times of Joseph's siblings and the implications of the record of their lives a lengthy discussion will be required. Numerous events in the Holy Scriptures have a simple beginning, but brought great consequences later.[C] Before proceeding further to establish the position of other individuals in time, the children of Jacob as well as the early descendants of Levi and Judah must be examined in the next section. From their record information can be extracted and multiple conclusions can be drawn which will ultimately help with firmly placing the time period of Job, the judges, the book of Ruth, and more.

What we learned:
1. Marking time by starting with Abraham's birth became a good

---

C. An example was Abraham's son Midian by Keturah whose later descendants included the Midianites who oppressed Israel and were defeated by Gideon (Judges 8:24). Another was Joseph who was sold into Egypt and later became the actual person who saved Jacob's family (Genesis 50:20). Saul's serious disobedience in not destroying king Agag (1 Samuel 15:1-35) brought a later descendant named Haman in the book of Esther who sought to destroy all Jews (Esther 3:1, 10; 8:3, 5; 9:24).

method to extend and connect time to the events that occurred throughout his lifetime and beyond.

2. This provided a way to place in time sequence the subsequent events, as given in the Scriptures, that occurred to Abraham's progeny.

Make a visual tool:

Each reader is invited to take a piece of paper, of business letter size (8 1/2" x 11" or 21.6 cm x 28 cm), and lay it horizontally (landscape). About 2.5 inches (6.35 cm) from the top draw a 10 3/4 inch (27.3 cm) long horizontal line with a straight edge or ruler from the left side to the right side with a very small margin (1/8 inch or 3 mm) to the end of the paper on each side. Then draw a vertical line upwards about 1/2 inch (1.2 cm) high at both ends of the horizontal line. [*The scale will be 1 inch (2.5 cm) is equal to 40 years.*]

Go to the far left side and label the short vertical line "Enter-Canaan" for when Abram entered Canaan. Then draw a shorter vertical line descending 1/4 inch (6 mm) below the horizontal line from that same place and label it "Abram-75" for Abram's age at entry to Canaan. Then from the far left side vertical line measure just over 3/8 inch (7 mm) to the right and draw a vertical line and label it "Ishmael" for his birth time. Draw a shorter vertical line descending 1/4 inch (6 mm) from that same place and label it "Abram-86" for Abram at age 86.

Measuring from the far left side vertical line draw another vertical line (above and below) 5/8 inch (1.6 cm) to the right of "Enter-Canaan" and label it "Isaac" for his birth, and also label it "Abram-100" for when Abraham was age 100. After this measure 2 1/8 inches (cm) to the right of "Enter-Canaan," draw another vertical line, and label it "Esau/Jacob" for the birth of Isaac's twins. Write one name on each side of that descending line, "Isaac-60" for Isaac at sixty years of age, and "Abram-160" for Abraham at 160.

Then starting again at "Enter-Canaan" measure 2 1/2 inches (6.35 cm) to the right, draw a vertical line, and label it "Abraham-died" for his death, and label it below "Abram-175." [*This material will continue using Abraham's relative age as a reference point.*]

From "Enter-Canaan" and measure just over of 3 11/16 inches (9.4 cm) to the right, draw the whole vertical line (above and below), label it above with "Ishmael-died" for his death, and label below "Abram-223" to mark the ongoing reference points. Almost 1/8 inch (2.3 mm) to the right of that Jacob entered Haran after he and Esau obtained their blessings from Isaac, label "Abram-237."

Begin again at "Enter-Canaan" and measure just over 4 3/8 inches (11.2 cm) to the right, draw the whole vertical line (above and below), label above with "Joseph" for his birth, and below "Abram-251." Jacob was age ninety-one and Isaac was 151 here, label as appropriate. Start at "Enter-Canaan" and measure to the right 5 1/8 inches (13 cm). Label it "Isaac-died" at 180 years of age and "Abram-280."

Start again at "Enter-Canaan" and measure to the right 5 3/8 inches (13.6 cm), label it "Enter-Egypt" *[Use a red pen, if possible, this is a major event referenced frequently.]* Below label this with both "Abram-290" and "Jacob-130" for Jacob upon entry to Egypt. *[This should be exactly half way across the whole horizontal line.]* Once more begin at "Enter-Canaan" and measure to the right just over 5 3/4 inches (14.7 cm), label it "Jacob-died" at 147 years of age, and below "Abram-307." This completed the most basic life events for Abraham, Ishmael, Isaac, and Jacob (Israel).

SECTION II

When did Jacob's descendants intersect?

Part 1: The children of Jacob and the
intersections of their descendants.

Noting the small granular details given in the Holy Scriptures about the children of Jacob was crucial. The early intersection of Levi's descendant with Judah's descendant offered us specific insights and even provided a method to obtain solutions to six difficult scenarios in the Biblical narrative. When these valuable details (shown here in Section II) were applied they provided a good way to resolve 1) the intended meaning of Genesis 15:13-16 and validate the length of the time period that Israel was in Egypt (Part 2), 2) show when a new pharaoh arose (Part 3), 3) establish the narrow time range for the book of Job (Part 4), 4) solve the inquiry, Can Rahab of Jericho be the wife of Salmon? (Part 5), 5) answer the question, When did the book of Ruth occur? (Part 6), and, 6) reveal more solutions to time related problems when applied to both the priest's and to David's ancestral lineage.

Difficult puzzles in the Biblical narrative were often solved through firmly establishing the time of birth for Jacob's sons. Data gathered about the early descendants of both Levi and Judah established boundaries to their births and lifetimes. Those scriptural limitations in turn affected a broader range of their descendants.

This careful gathering of information from the Old Testament narrative when integrated with unused and under appreciated Biblical texts resolved the first five distinct puzzles in Scripture listed above. These pieces of information revealed, reinforced, and emphasized the interconnecting and self-correcting cohesiveness of Holy Scripture. These were consistent with Jesus' words, *"the scripture cannot be broken"* (John 10:35), and Paul's words saying, *"O the depth of the riches both of the wisdom and knowledge of God!"* (Romans 11:33).

The Holy Scripture text was accepted as valid and a source of true information. That also meant accepting and engaging with any self-imposed boundaries given in the text. But accepting God's word as true did not necessarily mean applying miracles to enigmatic scenarios. Perplexing or difficult puzzles often needed a different perspective to understand and resolve them.

This brought some rather awkward pieces of information to bear upon the larger and smaller focus. The resultant effects were circumstances and events that were on the margin of quite unusual and that appeared possibly suspect. But the Creator of heaven and earth asked a powerful question relevant to all times and places, *"Is anything too hard for the Lord?"* (Genesis 18:14) and, *"Behold, I am the Lord, the God of all flesh: is there any thing too hard for me?"* (Jeremiah 32:27).

Joseph

Joseph was born [A-251] when Jacob was ninety-one years old [A-251 - A-160 = 91]. At age seventeen [A-268] Joseph was sold by his older brothers for twenty silver pieces as a slave and taken down into Egypt (Genesis 37:2-31). Joseph worked as the servant of Potiphar from age seventeen to twenty-seven (Genesis 39:1-19, [A-268-278]).

Then Joseph was falsely charged with attempted adultery and cast into prison for three years (Genesis 39:20–41:1, [A-278-281]). While there he interpreted successfully two dreams of court officials. Isaac died at 180 years [A-280] when Jacob was 120 years of age, so that made Joseph age twenty-nine [120 - 91 = 29] at Isaac's death. Isaac died while Joseph was still in prison in Egypt (Genesis 39:20; 41:1, [A-280]).

Joseph was called out of prison to appear before pharaoh, interpreted pharaoh's dream, and expounded a plan of action that was approved by pharaoh and his servants (Genesis 41:14-46, [A-281]). Then verse 46 stated that *"Joseph was thirty years old when he stood before Pharaoh king of Egypt."* He ruled Egypt during the first seven prosperous years and saved up provisions from age thirty to thirty-seven [A-281-288] before the seven years of famine that followed (Genesis 41:47-53, [A-288-295]).

Genesis 41:53 told us that *"the seven years of plenteousness, that was in the land of Egypt, were ended"* and verse 54 added, *"the seven years of dearth began to come."* Then under Joseph's leadership Egypt went through two years of famine to get Joseph at thirty-nine years of age (Genesis 45:6, 11, [A-290]). Genesis 45:6 was spoken in the context of Joseph disclosing his identity before his brethren. *"For these two years hath the famine been in the land: and yet there are five years, in the which there shall neither be earing nor harvest."*

Joseph sent his brothers with provisions back to Canaan to get Jacob and quickly bring all of their families into Egypt. Joseph at age thirty-nine welcomed his father, sister, brothers and all of their families into Egypt (Genesis 41:54-57; 45:6, 11, 24-28; 46:1-7; 47:7-10, [A-290]). Jacob's age can be aligned with Joseph's age.

Jacob stated his age before pharaoh in Genesis 47:8-9. *"Pharaoh said unto Jacob, How old art thou? And Jacob said unto Pharaoh, The days of the years of my pilgrimage are an hundred and thirty years."* Thus Joseph was born when Jacob was ninety-one years [130 - 39 = 91] and Isaac was 151 years old [A-251]. Two very different methods gave us Joseph's birth year.

Jacob appeared before pharaoh when Israel with sixty-six of his descendants joined Joseph's family to protect them from five more years of famine (Genesis 45:4-6; 47:9). At age fifty-six [A-307] Joseph and his brothers buried Jacob, age 147, in Canaan by his fathers. Egypt's elders with their entourage came along to honor Joseph and his father (Genesis 50:1-14). Joseph lived ninety-three years in Egypt [A-268-361], died at 110 years of age [A-361], was embalmed, and prepared for future transport to be buried in Canaan (Genesis 50:22-26; Exodus 13:19; Joshua 24:32; Hebrews 11:22).

Jacob's other sons

The length of the time period in which Jacob served Laban in Haran needed to be understood first. This information helped to confine and determine the birth year of the first eleven sons and one daughter conceived by Jacob. As a point of reference, the birth of Joseph will be used to get the relative age of each sibling because of the way the greater text was laid out with Joseph as the primary focus.

The placement of the ages of Joseph's siblings at this starting point can give us their ages when: Joseph was sold at seventeen, he was presented before Pharaoh at thirty, he was thirty-nine upon their entrance into Egypt, Jacob had died, or Joseph had died. Determining the siblings birth year set their year of death when given the boundaries for their lifetime, usually age at death. (See Table 1.)

Table 1. Jacob's age, [Abraham's relative year], mother, and child's age when Joseph was born is given. Each mother had thirty-nine weeks of gestation or 3/4 of a year from conception to birth. This made fractions for Jacob's age as father and the ages of the children compared to Joseph. Each mother has her own children one year apart. The birth of a child for the subsequent mother was given 3-4 weeks spacing from the prior mother. [39 weeks + 52 weeks + 52 weeks + 52 weeks + ~3 weeks + 52 weeks + ~3 weeks + 52 weeks + ~3 weeks + 52 weeks + ~4 weeks = 364 weeks = 7 whole years]

Jacob's age: [Abraham's year]	Mother:	Brothers & sister:	Age:	Citation:
about 84.75 [244]	Leah	Reuben ~	6.25	Gen 29:31-32
85.75 [245]	Leah	Simeon ~	5.25	Gen 29:33
86.75 [246]	Leah	Levi ~	4.25	Gen 29:34
87.75 [247]	Leah	Judah ~	3.25	Gen 29:35
87.81 [247]	Bilhah	Dan ~	3.19	Gen 30:4-6
88.81 [248]	Bilhah	Naphtali ~	2.19	Gen 30:7-8
88.87 [248]	Zilpah	Gad ~	2.13	Gen 30:9-11
89.87 [249]	Zilpah	Asher ~	1.13	Gen 30:13
89.92 [249]	Leah	Issachar ~	1.08	Gen 30:14-18
90.92 [250]	Leah	Zebulun ~	0.08	Gen 30:19-20
91 [251]	Rachel	**Joseph born**	0	Gen 30:22-24
91-92 [251-252]	Leah	Dinah ~	<=1	Gen 30:21
106-107 [266-267]	Rachel	Benjamin~	15-16 yrs. younger	Gen 35:16-18

Table 1 was derived from the textual account of Jacob, his four wives, and their offspring (Genesis 29:18–30:25). The standard period of thirty-nine weeks for maternal gestation and a short space between recurrent pregnancy was used so that the scriptural criteria was met regarding Joseph's birth at the end of Jacob's second seven-year period serving Laban (Genesis 30:25). This was immediately before Jacob and Laban negotiated the six-year period of service for the flocks and cattle (Genesis 30:25-43; 31:41).

Pregnancy can occur within two or three months after partum which could make some of these sons slightly closer together. Some could be slightly farther apart. Child spacing was set at twelve months apart for the same mother (Table 1).

For Leah to recognize *"that she had left bearing"* was about four months (Genesis 30:9). From Judah up to Zilpah's birth of Gad was about thirteen months. Judah to Issachar was about twenty-six months. Eleven sons were born within the seven years following Jacob's marriage to Leah (Genesis 30:25-31; 31:41). Dinah was born to Leah thereafter, with a maximum up to one year later.

Benjamin was born about fifteen to sixteen years later [A-266-277] (Genesis 35:16-18). See Table 1. Jacob's age could have been about one month earlier or later based upon the undisclosed spacing of the individual births for the same mother. But even this made little room for anything other than a minor adjustment of the birth times and the corresponding age of Jacob. This did not adversely affect any of the calculations used subsequently with Jacob's descendants.

The unusual, common, good, and bad were part of the experiences of Jacob, his children, and their descendants. The Scriptures faithfully reported the whole range of events. The ordinary, unusual, and the miraculous were all parts of God's providence in their lives.

Lineage from Levi and Judah

For the purpose of subsequent calculations note that Levi was more than four years older than Joseph. Use Joseph's birth year A-251 minus Levi's birth year A-246 to obtain five years in general terms. This method will be used for his other siblings.

Judah was more than three years older than Joseph [birth year A-251 minus birth year A-247 = ~4]. Levi was the ancestor of Aaron who began the high priest lineage because he was installed as high priest as described in Exodus 28, Exodus 40, and Leviticus 8. Judah was the ancestor of the Davidic lineage ultimately ending with Christ Jesus (Genesis 46:12; Ruth 4:18; Luke 3:23-38).

Joseph was born at the end of the second seven-year period [A-251], six more years transpired before leaving Haran. After departing Haran Jacob journeyed southward with his family. They dwelt at Shechem for about eight to ten years and then journeyed farther southward toward Isaac in Beersheba (Genesis 26:20-33).

Jacob's family departed from Shechem after Dinah's bad event and the retribution to the men of Shechem by Levi and Simeon. During this time period at Shechem Judah started his family (Genesis 38 chpt.), Dinah was violated, perhaps about age fourteen when Judah was about nineteen (Genesis 34:1-31). Simeon and Levi killed the men of Shechem about age twenty-one and age twenty respectively (Genesis 34:25, [~A-266]).

After departing Bethel Rachel gave birth to Benjamin while journeying southward near Ephrath (Bethlehem, Genesis 35:16-20, [~A-266-267]). She died before Joseph was sold (Genesis 37:2, [A-268]). About this time, probably between these two events, Reuben, Jacob's firstborn by Leah, laid with Bilhah his father's concubine (Genesis 35:22).

Only then was Rachel's firstborn, Joseph, promoted with a special coat, revealed his dreams, and was hated by his brothers. All this occurred before Jacob's group moved near to Isaac in southern Canaan (Genesis 35:27), arriving there about twelve years before Isaac died. This was when Joseph had probably first met Isaac (Genesis 35:27; 37:14). Then Joseph at seventeen years was sold into Egypt (Genesis 37:1-36, [A-268]). While Joseph was in prison about age twenty-nine his grandfather Isaac died at 180 years of age [A-280].

Judah Three sons were born to Judah [A-247-???], Er, Onan, and Shelah, with his wife (a daughter of Shuah who died early, Genesis 38:2, 12). Judah started his family with an early urge of libido with the bad and unusual given in detail. This can be shown by noting the following and taking the whole limited time period into account so that his son Pharez (Phares), also at an early age, had Hezron and his younger brother Hamul before entry to Egypt as stated in Genesis 46:12.

When did Jacob's descendants intersect?

When Judah was age twelve[D,E] [?A-259] Er was born (Genesis 38:2-4; 1 Chronicles 2:3). Onan was born early age thirteen (Genesis 38:2-4; 1 Chronicles 2:3) and Shelah was born late age thirteen (Genesis 38:5, [?A-260]). These births occurred while Jacob was still at Shechem.

Then about age thirteen Er married [?A-273] and died (Genesis 38:6-7; 46:12). Onan did not honor his older brother enough to raise up offspring, so that he also died early (Genesis 38:8-10) when Judah was age twenty-seven [?A-274].

After more than one year Shelah was not given to Tamar (Genesis 38:11-30) to raise up seed for his oldest brother [early in A-276]. This prompted Tamar to contrive a method to become pregnant. From this event Judah had conception with Tamar (Genesis 38:11-27).

Subsequent to this the twins Pharez (Phares) & Zarah (Zara, Genesis 38:27-30; 46:12) were born of Tamar (Thamar, Genesis 38:27-30) when Judah was about twenty-eight years old [late in A-276]. One of these two scenarios would follow from this. Scenario B was more much probable.

A) When Pharez [A-276] was about thirteen years old (Judah ~42) Hezron was born (Esrom, Genesis 46:12; Numbers 26:21, [A-289]). Then Hamul was conceived and born (Genesis 46:12, [A-290]) in the next year. (Judah ~43). Or,

B) When Pharez [A-276] was about fourteen years old (Judah ~43) Hezron and Hamul were born as twins [A-290].

Only if scenario B occurred with Hezron and Hamul born as twins, then Judah could have been about one year older from the birth of Er

---

D. The Jewish bar mizpeh recognizes the age of responsibility because of the potential for reproduction. But this was not the age of physical maturity. This was evidenced with Joseph at seventeen years when sold into Egypt and with David at the death of Goliath. There David was specifically called a "youth" and did not meet Israel's required age of twenty for war.

E. To correctly set ages for birth we must reconcile Genesis 38:2-5, "*And Judah saw there a daughter of a certain Canaanite, whose name was Shuah; and he took her, and went in unto her. And she conceived, and bare a son; and he called his name Er. And she conceived again, and bare a son; and she called his name Onan. And she yet again conceived, and bare a son; and called his name Shelah: and he was at Chezib, when she bare him,*" and reconcile Genesis 46:12, "*And the sons of Judah; Er, and Onan, and Shelah, and Pharez, and Zarah: but Er and Onan died in the land of Canaan. And the sons of Pharez were Hezron and Hamul.*" As stated in Genesis 46, Hezron and Hamul were counted in the persons entering Egypt so that they were born before this event.

through the conception of the twins Pharez and Zarah. In that second scenario Pharez was about one year younger and about age thirteen for the birth of both Hezron and Hamul. Carefully consider that this early age of successive generations occurred to match all the scriptural requirements (Judah to Er, Onan, and Shelah; subsequent conception of Pharez and Zarah, and later for Pharez to father Hezron and Hamul) within the limited time frame detailed in Scripture.

Hezron and his younger brother Hamul were both born before entry to Egypt because they were named and counted in the list given in Genesis chapter 46. Later in that same year Jacob took his family into Egypt [A-290]. Judah was shown as not fully four years older than Joseph who was thirty-nine when Israel entered Egypt with his progeny (Table 1). That meant Judah was about age forty-three when he brought his sons Shelah, Pharez, and Zarah along with the sons of Pharez (Hezron and Hamul) as infants into Egypt (Genesis 46:12, [A-290]).

Consider, too, that this early age scenario was the course of events that gave Judah an inside perspective into the heart of his father Jacob. Because Judah had such early births of Er, Onan, and Shelah it became possible that Er married early and died shortly thereafter. When Onan falsely took up marriage for the wife of Er he also died. Because Tamar was still quite young and apparently eager to have marital relations she sought Shelah as her next husband. Judah was reluctant to honor this with Shelah still so young, but probably not recalcitrant.

When Judah had Pharez and Zarah [~A-277] as later born sons and already had his first two sons die, he began to understand more fully how Jacob felt about the loss of Joseph. Remember here that Benjamin was born about [~A-266-267] and Joseph was sold in [A-268]. When Judah pledged himself as a replacement for anything that happened to Benjamin (Genesis 43:1-15; 44:18-34) he showed the love of a father, like Jacob had for his own sons. At that event Judah was already or very soon to be a grandfather to Hezron and Hamul.

<u>Levi</u> Jacob's third born son Levi [A-246-383, 1705-1568 BC, Exodus 6:16] was about five years older than Joseph [birth year A-251 minus birth year A-246 = ~5, Table 1] derived from the textual account of Jacob with his four wives (Genesis 29:18–30:25). Levi had a son Kohath

(Numbers 3:19; 26:59; 1 Chronicles 6:23) before entering into Egypt Genesis 46:8-27; Exodus 1:1-5). Levi was about age forty-four when he entered Egypt.

Not knowing when Kohath was born, anything from an early birth up to a late birth could be used. For simplicity, use the year of Joseph's ascension to authority in Egypt [A-281] when Levi was thirty-four and Jacob was about age 121. [Much later in this document the Levitical ancestry of Samuel is detailed. That also suggested around age thirty-three to thirty-four for Levi when Kohath was born.]

In turn Amram was born to Kohath (Exodus 6:16-18, perhaps about age fifty [~A-331], especially since Amram married his aunt Jochebed. She was Kohath's much younger sister and Levi's daughter, Exodus 1:5; 6:20; Numbers 26:59). At Amram's birth Levi was about age eighty-four [~34 + ~50].

Jochebed was explicitly given as Levi's daughter twice, "*And Amram took him Jochebed his father's sister to wife; and she bare him Aaron and Moses: and the years of the life of Amram were an hundred and thirty and seven years.*" (Exodus 6:20; Numbers 26:59). This detail must be incorporated.

If Levi had a late aged birth of his daughter, she was the right age for marriage with his grandson, Amram. Her age must also fit with the three births of Miriam, Aaron, and Moses. Levi at about ninety-three years of age [~A-339], had a late aged birth^F of his daughter.

F. After Sarah died at 127 years Abraham married Keturah. He conceived six sons with Keturah (Genesis 25). The last son, Shuah, was born when Abraham was about 147 years of age. Follow this for Abraham:

age 140	when Isaac married Rebekah (Genesis 24:67)
age 140.25	married Keturah (Genesis 25:1-2)
age 141.0	Zimran (Genesis 25:1-2) [~14.5 months average spacing to next sons]
age 142.21	Jokshan
age 143.42	Medan
age 144.63	Midian
age 145.83	Ishbak
age 147.04	Shuah

If eleven months spacing was used, then Shuah was born at Abraham age 145 and seven months, while twelve month spacing brought age 146. Abraham was at one hundred years of age for the birth of Isaac, Isaac at sixty years for birth of his twins, then add five years = Abraham at age 165. Shuah's birth with Abraham at age 147 plus eighteen years also equaled age 165. Shuah was eighteen to nineteen years old and capable of having been sent out (Genesis 25:6) on his own (same as Ishmael, Genesis 16:15-16; 21:8-14) when Esau and Jacob could also have had an inheritance party at five years of age, like the one given for Isaac. Abraham died later at 175 years. This gave us a ratio from the Scriptures of

This made Jochebed^G about eight years younger than Amram (about age 94) when Moses was born [A-425] or very late in [A-424] since Moses had died at age 120 (Deuteronomy 34:7) late in [A-544]. That was just over one month before Israel's entry to Canaan in Abib of [A-545].

For simplification we will use [A-425] hereafter. Jochebed was about 86 years old with an expected life span^H of 122 years or more. This was a close match to Sarah for birth age to life span.

The Scriptures were clear and specific about the early descendants for Judah and Levi. All details surrounding their circumstances were

---

84 percent of the male life span (147 years / 175 years = 0.84 or 84% of his life span) to use as a very reasonable maximum for paternal sexual reproduction and subsequent birth of a child. Consider Abraham's wife Sarah who died at 127 years. She also gave us a ratio from the Scriptures. This was at 71 percent of the female life span (90 years / 127 years = 0.708 or 71% of her life span) to use as a very reasonable maximum for maternal sexual conception, gestation, and birth of a child (Genesis 17:17). Sarah gave birth to Isaac at 71 percent of her life span. These ratios will be applied to scenarios later.

G. Early gestation by females before physical maturity resulted in shortened life spans as noted from various cultures around the world. A few years later in age for marriage and of subsequent gestation of children provided for a healthier and longer life for females. Completion of female growth and development before gestation of children provided for increased maternal health. This also made for a longer range of child-bearing years and factored into Israel's drastic population increase while in Egypt. Child bearing years for healthy women can reach above 65% of their life expectancy, but more commonly up to around 50%. [See footnote F.]

H. The best fit for Jochebed's birth was when Levi was about ninety-three to ninety-seven years old. Though this seemed unusual, men in general can successfully copulate at a later age than women can successfully conceive and gestate to birth. And this was when life spans were distinctly longer than at present. For Levi age ninety-three of 137 years was at sixty-eight percent [93 / 137 = 68%] and age ninety-seven of 137 years was at seventy-one percent [97 / 137 = 71%] of his life span. Jochebed at age eighty-six of an expected 122 year life span was at seventy-one percent [86 / 122 = 71%] to birth Moses. If her life span was the same as Kohath, then it was at age eighty-six of a maximum 133 year life span [86 years / 133 years = 65% of her life span]. If Jochebed was born four years later with Levi at age ninety-seven, then her age was at eighty-two of 122 years or at sixty-seven percent [82 / 122 = 67%] of her expected life span for Moses birth. The percentages were smaller for longer life spans.

This was comparable to Sarah's late age birth for Isaac, physically possible and workable. Jochebed was not able to have been born when Levi was about seventy years old. Then she was about twenty-three years older, about age 109, when Amram was about ninety-four years and distinctly outside of the Biblical template for a late aged birth. Amram at age ninety-four of 137 years was at sixty-nine percent of his lifetime (Exodus 6:20) [94 / 137 = 69%]. This meant a comparable late age of Levi for Jochebed's birth, for Amram to conceive, and for Jochebed to birth Miriam, Aaron, and Moses as shown was honestly tenable. This was within God's promise to Abraham in Genesis 12:2-3, "*And I will make of thee a great nation ... and in thee shall all families of the earth be blessed.*"

carefully incorporated. The valuable material presented in footnotes F, G, and H was applied and consistent.

Those ratios, presented in the Scriptures for both males and females, became powerful tools which helped solve multiple pieces. Each of these parts for Judah, Levi, and their early descendants must be faithfully accounted for and applied in any honest consideration of their lineages. However, another notable statement in Scripture must be examined which brought insight and confidence in this scenario.

> And the king of Egypt spake to the Hebrew midwives, of which the name of the one was Shiphrah, and the name of the other Puah: And he said, When ye do the office of a midwife to the Hebrew women, and see them upon the stools; if it be a son, then ye shall kill him: but if it be a daughter, then she shall live. But the midwives feared God, and did not as the king of Egypt commanded them, but saved the men children alive. And the king of Egypt called for the midwives, and said unto them, Why have ye done this thing, and have saved the men children alive? And the midwives said unto Pharaoh, Because the Hebrew women are not as the Egyptian women; for they are lively, and are delivered ere the midwives come in unto them. Therefore God dealt well with the midwives: and the people multiplied, and waxed very mighty. And it came to pass, because the midwives feared God, that he made them houses. (Exodus 1:15-21)

Many applied this to Jochebed. The expression, *"that he made them houses,"* meant that they were given a durable lineage like that meant with the expression, the house of David. This was necessary because Aaron was to become the initial patriarch for an enduring priesthood (Psalms 115:12). Another passage to incorporate was Numbers 25:6-14 which told of an event with Phinehas, son of Eleazar, son of Aaron.

> And, behold, one of the children of Israel came and brought unto his brethren a Midianitish woman in the sight of Moses, and in the sight of all the congregation of the children of Israel, who were weeping before the door of the tabernacle of the congregation. And when Phinehas, the son of Eleazar, the son

of Aaron the priest, saw it, he rose up from among the congregation, and took a javelin in his hand; And he went after the man of Israel into the tent, and thrust both of them through, the man of Israel, and the woman through her belly. So the plague was stayed from the children of Israel. And those that died in the plague were twenty and four thousand. And the Lord spake unto Moses, saying, Phinehas, the son of Eleazar, the son of Aaron the priest, hath turned my wrath away from the children of Israel, while he was zealous for my sake among them, that I consumed not the children of Israel in my jealousy. Wherefore say, Behold, I give unto him my covenant of peace: And he shall have it, and his seed after him, even the covenant of an everlasting priesthood; because he was zealous for his God, and made an atonement for the children of Israel. [See: vs. 14-15])

"My covenant of peace"

The full sense of the expression, *"my covenant of peace,"* was given when God explained His meaning when he added, *"he shall have it, and his seed after him, even the covenant of an everlasting priesthood"* (Numbers 25:11-13). This meant that Aaron's grandson was given a significant promise that had several components. First, God said Phinehas would have progeny from generation to generation. Second, that each generation would have one or more sons to carry on the priesthood.

Third, that priesthood would be everlasting, which was consistent with the third temple descriptions of priestly service given by Ezekiel. Fourth, that even in old age a son would be born to fulfill this promise of *"my covenant of peace."* Older age births reoccurred for Phinehas' descendants.

This *"covenant of peace"* for future descendants was rehearsed in part in Malachi 2:4-7. [See: The lineage of the high priests] Fifth, this "covenant of peace" proceeded to a unique person presented in the New Testament. Luke described him in the angel's words.

> And thou shalt have joy and gladness; and many shall rejoice at his birth. For he shall be great in the sight of the Lord, and

shall drink neither wine nor strong drink; and he shall be filled with the Holy Ghost, even from his mother's womb. And many of the children of Israel shall he turn to the Lord their God. And he shall go before him in the spirit and power of Elias, to turn the hearts of the fathers to the children, and the disobedient to the wisdom of the just; to make ready a people prepared for the Lord. (Luke 1:14-17)

Then Luke added this further description of John the Baptist in Luke 1:65-66.

And fear came on all that dwelt round about them: and all these sayings were noised abroad throughout all the hill country of Judaea. And all they that heard them *[i.e. the words of Zacharias regarding John]* laid them up in their hearts, saying, What manner of child shall this be! And the hand of the Lord was with him.

This further application of "my covenant of peace" was expanded in Luke 1:76-79 with Zacharias' prophecy. Zacharias spoke of his own son.

And thou, child, shalt be called the prophet of the Highest: for thou shalt go before the face of the Lord to prepare his ways; To give knowledge of salvation unto his people by the remission of their sins, Through the tender mercy of our God; whereby the dayspring from on high hath visited us, To give light to them that sit in darkness and in the shadow of death, to guide our feet into the way of peace.

John described himself saying, *"I am the voice of one crying in the wilderness, Make straight the way of the Lord, as said the prophet Esaias."* Later Jesus spoke in commendation of John when he began to speak unto the people concerning John in Luke 7:24-28.

What went ye out into the wilderness for to see? A reed shaken with the wind? But what went ye out for to see? A man clothed in soft raiment? Behold, they which are gorgeously apparelled, and live delicately, are in kings' courts. But what went ye out for to see? A prophet? Yea, I say unto you, and much more than a prophet. This is he, of whom it is written, Behold, I send my messenger before thy face, which shall prepare thy way before thee. For I say unto you, Among those that are born of women there is not a greater prophet than John the Baptist: but he that is least in the kingdom of God is greater than he.

Again Jesus spoke of John in Matthew 11:11-13.

Verily I say unto you, Among them that are born of women there hath not risen a greater than John the Baptist: notwithstanding he that is least in the kingdom of heaven is greater than he. And from the days of John the Baptist until now the kingdom of heaven suffereth violence, and the violent take it by force. For all the prophets and the law prophesied until John.

John's ministry started in Luke 3:2 when he labored to prepare men's hearts for their savior, the Messiah. Later John endured prison for a season (Matthew 4:12) until his early death (Matthew 14:1-2; Mark 6:14-19). Thus the duration of *"my covenant of peace"* reached from Phinehas, the original recipient of God's special promise, across a great many generations. It ultimately passed through Zacharias and Elisabeth and ended with John. They were each descendents of Phinehas with both Zacharias and Elisabeth described as a child of an Aaronic priest (Luke 1:5).

John's parents were both filled with the Holy Spirit in speaking their prophecies. (Luke 1:41-45, 67-79). John was described by the angel saying, *"he shall be filled with the Holy Ghost, even from his mother's womb"* (Luke 1:15). That made these three not only the last recorded individuals from the line of Phinehas, but also the ultimate recipients of that *"covenant of peace,"* as shown in the New Testament of Holy Scripture. And one more time there were three prophets in one family, very similar to Miriam, Aaron, and Moses.

After the end of their days the Levitical Aaronic priesthood was replaced (Hebrews 7:11) by Jesus. He became the *"one sacrifice"* for all people (Hebrews 9:11-14, 28). Jesus was resurrected to life again (Hebrews 11:24) to become *"the great high priest"* (Hebrews 4:14; 7:11-28; 9:14-15, 28) *"after the order of Melchisedec."*

In summary, in their older years a special gift was given to just one family, Amram and Jochebed, to conceive and birth three children, each of whom were declared to be prophets. These appellatives were given in Exodus 15:20 for Miriam, in Exodus 7:1 for Aaron, and in Deuteronomy 18:15; 34:10, Acts 3:22 and 7:37 for Moses. Aaron was born to Amram (about age 91, Exodus 2:1-8; 7:7 [A-422 or very late in [A-421] since he died at age 123 (Numbers 33:39) late in [A-544] about two months before entry to Canaan], and was three years older than Moses.

Miriam was born about five or more years before Moses to be sufficiently old to articulate her words to pharaoh's daughter in Exodus 2:1-7. If Miriam was born about [~A-420] with her death in [A-544] (Numbers 20:1), then she had around 124 years. This suggested a similar age for their mother Jochebed at death. This scenario of later age for three births by Jochebed was unexpected and completely disarmed pharaoh's daughter. She probably thought that this Hebrew "nurse" was an helpful old grandmother and neither Miriam's nor Moses' birth mother (Exodus 2:8-10).

The intersection of Aaron and Elisheba

Now briefly turn to Aaron who later became the first high priest of the tabernacle services. He was the descendant of Levi that intersected with Judah's lineage as stated in Exodus 6:23, *"And Aaron took him Elisheba, daughter of Amminadab, sister of Naashon, to wife; and she bare him Nadab, and Abihu, Eleazar, and Ithamar."* This time marker required research to understand its import. Aaron's marriage information was used to help resolve other event years, both earlier and later in time.

<u>Aaron</u> His birth to Amram [A-422-545, 1529-1406 BC, Exodus 7:7; Numbers 33:39] was three years before Moses (about age 91) [A-422] or very late in [A-421] since he died at age 123 (Numbers 33:39) late in [A-544] about two months before entry to Canaan (Exodus 2:1-8; 7:7). For simplification we will use [A-422] hereafter. Aaron married Elisheba, daughter of Aminadab, sister of Naashon (Nahshon, Naasson).

To establish when this occurred note that their first two sons, Nadab and Abihu, must be twenty-five years old at Exodus 28:1 to be included in the ceremony with Aaron and his sons (just the first two of four sons met the age criteria, Exodus 24:1, 9). Numbers 4:3, 23, 30, 35, 47 and

8:23-26 gave the required age limitations upon their service. The time periods of Judah's descendants must have Elisheba born soon enough to mature, marry, conceive, and birth both Nadab and Abihu to have both sons in the inaugural tabernacle ceremony.

Elisheba The time periods for the lives of Hezron and his descendants (son, grandson, great-granddaughter) must be set inside of constraining boundaries, so that the intersection of Aaron and Elisheba match Scripture requirements. These put limitations upon the time period for each successive generation and can be described as squeezing their lifetimes into narrowed parameters. Hezron's son Aram and grandson Aminadab cannot be born too early, so that the third generation was born too soon.

Neither can they be born very late in parental age and thereby force unnamed miracles of conception, nor can the births of Nadab and Abihu be forced into a later period of time. But this allowed for both earlier and later age for births within the general parameters already discussed above, i.e. Judah and Pharez with early age births and Levi, Amram, and Jochebed with modestly later age births. Plus there was the limitation of decreasing life spans.

Another limitation was that Elisheba was a sister of Naashon who was an ancestor of David. The time of the intersection of Aaron and Elisheba must work for both lineages plus meet the criteria of Numbers 1:6-8; 2:3 and 1 Chronicles 2:10 where Naashon was called *"captain of the children of Judah"* and *"prince of the children of Judah."* Aaron's marriage to Elisheba (from the tribe of Judah) lead to those Levitical priests that served in David's and Solomon's lifetimes and met various criteria that was given in 1 and 2 Samuel, and 1 Chronicles.

Judah was shown above to have been about four years older than Joseph (Table 1). Judah was about forty-three when he brought Pharez and Zarah (about age 14), and Pharez's sons Hezron and Hamul as infants, into Egypt (Genesis 46:12). Then Hezron, up to about fifty-six years old, had Aram (Ram, Ruth 4:19); Aram, up to about fifty-five, had Aminadab (Amminadab, Ruth 4:19); Aminadab, up to about fifty-five years, had Elisheba daughter of Aminadab.

Probably her birth was before or about [A-453-458], with Naashon

When did Jacob's descendants intersect?

(Nahshon, Ruth 4:20; Exodus 6:23) born earlier. Add about twenty-two years until Elisheba's marriage with Aaron, plus one more year to birth Nadab, plus two more to birth Abihu. Then add twenty-five years to arrive at the Levitical age for tabernacle service.

This set of estimated time periods summed to 216 years (56 + 55 + 55 + 22 + 1 + 2 + 25 = 216) with the twelve tribes of Israel living in Egypt only 215 years. In fact, 216 years reached to the beginning of the second year in the wilderness [A-506]. This addition of twenty-five years was required to meet the Levitical age for both Nadab and Abihu to become priests along with Aaron. This procedure was described in the inaugural tabernacle ceremony in Exodus 28, Exodus 40, and Leviticus 8.

Aaron's and Elisheba's third son Eleazar was not born as early as Joshua or Caleb (Aaron age 45) due to the scriptural statements in Numbers 1:18; 14:34-36; 26:4; 26:64-65; 32:11-12 and Joshua 5:4-6. Both Eleazar and Ithamar must have been less than twenty at the census in the second year and second month after the exodus from Egypt because they did not die in the wilderness (Numbers 1:1-18). Aaron was eighty-three at their departure (Exodus 7:7), minus nineteen or less years he was sixty-four years or older (Exodus 28:1; Numbers 3:2; 1 Chronicles 6) for Eleazar's birth. Ithamar was born one to two years after Eleazar.

This material showed that both Eleazar and Ithamar were not in the original ceremony installing Aaron with his sons Nadab and Abihu as priests at Exodus 28:1 (Numbers 3:2; Exodus 24:1-9). Eleazar and Ithamar became priests later, each at age twenty-five (per Numbers 8:23-26 and 4:3, 23, 30, 35, 47). This occurred before Nadab and Abihu had offered *"strange fire"* and died before the Lord (Leviticus 10:1-7; Numbers 3:4). Aaron died before entering Canaan (at 123 years in Mount Hor, Numbers 33:38). Eleazar and Ithamar were the promised fourth generation who entered Canaan.

The book of Joshua established that Eleazar was the high priest assisting Joshua with the land distribution before he died (Joshua 14:1; 17:4; 19:51; 21:21; 24:33). Since Eleazar was under twenty years old at the census in the second month of [A-506], then his birth time was no earlier than very late in the year of [A-486] to live through the wilderness. If Eleazar lived to 110 years like Joshua, then his life span was potentially from [A-~487-~597]. Since Eleazar's father Aaron died at age 123 perhaps he lived longer than this.

Note the words in Judges 2:10. This carefully said, *"also all that generation were gathered unto their fathers."* That gave an earlier death [<=A-590], of all who were born in Egypt like Joshua, before the first oppression came in [A-591, detailed later]. Thus Eleazar lived from [~A-487-~590] or ~103 years.

Naashon Let us briefly look at Naashon (Nahshon, Naasson), the brother of Elisheba, born to Aminadab (Amminadab). Numbers 2:3 stated that Naashon was a tribal leader, *"And on the east side toward the rising of the sun shall they of the standard of the camp of Judah pitch throughout their armies: and Nahshon the son of Amminadab shall be captain of the children of Judah."* Likewise the account of the dedication of the tabernacle spoke of Naashon, son of Aminadab as a tribal leader in Numbers 7:11-17.

> And the Lord said unto Moses, They shall offer their offering, each prince on his day, for the dedicating of the altar. And he that offered his offering the first day was Nahshon the son of Amminadab, of the tribe of Judah: And his offering was one silver charger, the weight thereof was an hundred and thirty shekels, one silver bowl of seventy shekels, after the shekel of the sanctuary; both of them were full of fine flour mingled with oil for a meat offering: One spoon of ten shekels of gold, full of incense: One young bullock, one ram, one lamb of the first year, for a burnt offering: One kid of the goats for a sin offering: And for a sacrifice of peace offerings, two oxen, five rams, five he goats, five lambs of the first year: this was the offering of Nahshon the son of Amminadab.

This was confirmed in 1 Chronicles 2:10, *"And Ram begat Amminadab; and Amminadab begat Nahshon, prince of the children of Judah."* Since Naashon was called a prince, his father Aminadab was no longer alive to be a tribal leader. To be considered a tribal leader Naashon was at least twenty years of age or more at the census in Exodus 28:1, and quite probably about fifty or more. He was old enough to go to war and most likely had matched the age of maturity for Levitical service which was twenty-five through fifty years of age.

When did Jacob's descendants intersect?

That material suggested that Naashon was born from [~A-435-455] and died around age ninety late in the wilderness. He did not die from old age, but from the penalty upon the Israelite congregation for unbelief. His ordinary life span was about 110-112 years and 80% of that was about ninety years and this was fully in the range to conceive Salmon near the end of the forty-year wilderness period Numbers 14:33-34; 32:13; Joshua 5:6; etc.). [See footnotes G and H]

This also meant that Aminadab was born earlier (Aram 29–54 years old) in which case perhaps Elisheba was older and closer to Aaron's age. These pieces gave a broader range of time in which Elisheba was born [~A-422–459]. This meant that Aminadab had an unknown birth year [~A-387–415] and died from ninety to 115 years of age before the time of the exodus from Egypt since he was not named as a prince of Judah.

What we learned:

1. The extremely narrow period in which Joseph's older brothers and younger sister were born.

2. The intersection of Aaron with Elisheba and how her birth time was affected by earlier and later events.

3. The earliest birth year for Eleazar and Ithamar.

4. The probable birth period placements for Naashon and Elisheba and for their father Aminadab.

Make a visual tool:

Take the timeline that was constructed earlier. About 1/8 inch (2.5 mm) to the left of Joseph's birth Levi and then Judah were born. Label as appropriate. Just to the right of Isaac's death (Joseph at age 29) he stood before pharaoh at age thirty. Label as appropriate. From the "Enter-Canaan" on the far left measure just under 4 7/8 inches (12.3 cm) to the right, draw the vertical line (above and below), label it above "Joseph-sold," and below "Abram-268."

Then just to the right of "Isaac-died" where Joseph was presented before pharaoh Kohath was most likely born. Label that "?Kohath-born." From "Enter-Canaan" measure just over 6 3/8 inches (16.3 cm), mark, label it "Amram" for his birth, and below "Abram-331." Measure just over 6 5/8 inches (16.7 cm), mark, label it "Jochebed," and below

"Abram-339," she was about eight years younger than Amram.

Joseph's death at 110 years measured 7 1/8 inches (9.7 cm) from "Enter-Canaan," label that "Joseph-died" and "Abram-361." From the same starting point measure just over 7 3/4 inches (19.6 cm), mark, label it "Levi-died," and below "Abram-383." For Kohath's death measure off just under 8 1/2 inches (21.5 cm) from "Enter-Canaan" on the far left, mark this "?Kohath-died," and below write "Abram-414." Then measure again for 8 3/4 inches (22.2 cm), label this "Moses," and below "Abram-425." Here Amram was about 94 and Jochebed about 86, label as appropriate.

If you have been careful, there will be 2 inches (5.1 cm) from Moses birth to the vertical line on the right. Label that "Exodus" above for Israel's departure from Egypt, draw the vertical line below, and label "Abram-505." The length of the line was 10 3/4 inches (27.3 cm) with a scale of forty years per 1 inch (2.54 cm). The time from Abram entering Canaan until the Exodus was 430 years. From Jacob at "Enter-Egypt" (labeled previously) to the Exodus was 215 years. Label if desired. For other measurements use Abram's relative age markers to add or subtract time intervals.

Genesis 15:13-16

Part 2: The children of Jacob and the intersections of their descendants.

The promise God gave to Abraham in verses 13-16 had a time delimited statement that must be considered when interpreting and applying the text to Israel's history. First, Abraham was told in verses 13-15 that his descendants would receive three kinds of experiences. The Scriptures revealed that each of the three types of events was fulfilled. Abraham's descendants were strangers in a land not their own, received affliction from others, and endured servitude to others. To bear this ominous future better, God encouraged Abraham with the statement that all of this was to end after 400 years.

To fulfill the statement regarding the fourth generation of Genesis 15:16 the lineage of Jacob must be established through Aaron, the high priest. But numerous other passages had a bearing upon this lineage and the timing of individual births. These were detailed and through this process the beginning of this 400-year period was confined and established while other starting dates for the 400-year period were shown to be unworkable. The length of this time period was critical because that determined exactly how many years intervened from Abraham's entry to Canaan up to the exodus from Egypt. This answer also showed how to interpret Exodus 12:40.

Examining three details

The statement spoken to Abraham by God in Genesis 15:13-16

detailed several aspects. First, *"thy seed shall be a stranger in a land that is not theirs,"* second, *"they shall afflict them,"* and third, *"and shall serve them."*

> And he said unto Abram, Know of a surety that thy seed shall be a stranger in a land that is not theirs, and shall serve them; and they shall afflict them four hundred years; And also that nation, whom they shall serve, will I judge: and afterward shall they come out with great substance. And thou shalt go to thy fathers in peace; thou shalt be buried in a good old age. But in the fourth generation they shall come hither again: for the iniquity of the Amorites is not yet full. (Genesis 15:13-16 KJV)

The text in Genesis 15:13 was translated as shown below. The CSB, ESV, NIV, and WEB gave the results revealed in the book of Genesis and early Exodus. None were consistent with the stranger, affliction, and slave sequence, as it was detailed in scripture, while some emphasized the severity of slavery. [Those marked by an asterisk * emphasized the 400 years of affliction.]

> * And he said unto Abram, "Know of a surety that thy seed shall be sojourners in a land that is not theirs, and shall serve them; and they shall afflict them four hundred years." ASV

> But I solemnly promise that your descendants will live as foreigners in a land that doesn't belong to them. They will be forced into slavery and abused for four hundred years. But I will terribly punish the nation that enslaves them, and they will leave with many possessions. CEV

> Then the Lord said to Abram, "Know this for certain: Your offspring will be resident aliens for four hundred years in a land that does not belong to them and will be enslaved and oppressed." CSB

> * Then the Lord said to Abram, "Know for certain that your offspring will be sojourners in a land that is not theirs and will be servants there, and they will be afflicted for four hundred years." ESV

Genesis 15:13-16

> Then the Lord told Abram, "You can be certain about this: Your descendants will be foreigners in a land that isn't theirs. They will be slaves there and will be oppressed for 400 years." ISV

> And he said unto Abram, "Know of a surety that thy seed shall be a stranger in a land that is not theirs, and shall serve them; and they shall afflict them four hundred years." KJV

> And he said to Abram, "You must surely know that your descendants shall be as aliens in a land not their own. And they shall serve them and they shall oppress them four hundred years." LEB

> * Then the Lord said to him, "Know for certain that for four hundred years your descendants will be strangers in a country not their own and that they will be enslaved and mistreated there." NIV

> * Then the Lord said to Abram, "Know of a surety that your descendants will be sojourners in a land that is not theirs, and will be slaves there, and they will be oppressed for four hundred years." RSV

> * He said to Abram, "Know for sure that your offspring will live as foreigners in a land that is not theirs, and will serve them. They will afflict them four hundred years." WEB

The Scriptures detailed all three types of events that occurred to Abraham's descendants starting with Isaac at age five: strangers in a land not their own, affliction from others, and some form of servitude to others. Following this paragraph are Scriptures under each heading: Strangers, Afflicted, Slaves. These were not brief transitory events, but they were recurrent or long-lasting. These groupings show how the Scriptures revealed that each category was fulfilled.

A definitive summary ended Genesis 15:13. God gave a time delimited period of 400 years for all three types of events to transpire from beginning to end. God concluded with another kind of affirmation (verse 16) delimiting the time duration by saying the fourth generation would leave this stranger–affliction–slavery condition and enter again into their promised land of Canaan. Both of these statements must be fully used to resolve when the beginning of this period did occur since the time of its beginning was disputed, but not the time of their ending at the exodus from Egypt.

Strangers

<u>Abraham</u>

Genesis 12:1 — Told to leave his homeland for another land, *"Now the Lord had said unto Abram, Get thee out of thy country, and from thy kindred, and from thy father's house, unto a land that I will shew thee."*

Genesis 17:8 — *"And I will give unto thee, and to thy seed after thee, the land wherein thou art a stranger, all the land of Canaan, for an everlasting possession; and I will be their God."*

Genesis 21:23 — *"Now therefore swear unto me here by God that thou wilt not deal falsely with me, nor with my son, nor with my son's son: but according to the kindness that I have done unto thee, thou shalt do unto me, and to the land wherein thou hast sojourned."*

Genesis 23:3-18 — Bowed to *"people of the land,"* and purchased *"a possession of a burying place amongst you,"* a burial cave and field

Hebrews 11:8-10 — *"By faith Abraham, when he was called to go out into a place which he should after receive for an inheritance, obeyed; and he went out, not knowing whither he went. By faith he sojourned in the land of promise, as in a strange country, dwelling in tabernacles with Isaac and Jacob, the heirs with him of the same promise: For he looked for a city which hath foundations, whose builder and maker is God."*

<u>Isaac's locations</u>

Genesis 21:5-10 — Lived with his father (locations shown just above)
Genesis 26:16, 27 — Philistines sent Isaac away
Genesis 37:1 — *"And Jacob dwelt in the land wherein his father was a stranger, in the land of Canaan."*

<u>Jacob's locations</u>

Genesis 28:1-5 — Isaac blessed Jacob that he may inherit the land upon which he was a stranger and then sent him to Padanaram unto

Genesis 15:13-16

Laban
Genesis 28:10; 29:4; 30:28; 31:1-16, 38-42 — Dwelled in Haran
Genesis 33:17-20 — Jacob bought land to live upon by Shechem
Genesis 37:1 — *"And Jacob dwelt in the land wherein his father was a stranger, in the land of Canaan."*
Genesis 46:1-7 — Lived in Egypt

Joseph's locations
Genesis 30:24–31:20 — Lived in Haran
Genesis 30:25–37:26 — Lived in Canaan
Genesis 37:36; 39:1 — Lived in Egypt

Jacob's sons locations
Genesis 30:24–31:20 — Lived in Haran
Genesis 30:25–37:26 — Lived in Canaan
Genesis 46:1-7; Exodus 1:1-5 — Lived in Egypt

Israel's descendants
Genesis 46:1-7; Exodus 1:1-14; 12:40-41 — Lived in Canaan and in Egypt
Exodus 1:12 — hated by Egyptians
Psalm 106:10 — *"And he saved them from the hand of him that hated them, and redeemed them from the hand of the enemy."*
Numbers 14:33; 32:13; Deuteronomy 2:7; Joshua 5:6 — Lived in the wilderness

Afflicted

Isaac's afflictions
Genesis 16:12; 21:8-9 — Ishmael mocking, Isaac age 5
Genesis 26:12-18 — Philistines had stopped wells
Genesis 26:16, 27 — Philistines sent away
Genesis 26:17-21 — Herdmen of Gerar strive with Isaac's herdmen over two wells
Genesis 26:34-35; 27:46 (28:9) — Esau's Hittite wives of the daughters of Canaan
Genesis 27:1-42 — Esau and Jacob conflict and death threat on Jacob

SECTION II Part 2.

Genesis 28:1-5 — Jacob's departure

Jacob's afflictions
    Genesis 27:1-42 — Esau and Jacob conflict and death threat on Jacob
    Genesis 28:10 — Jacob's journey alone fleeing Esau
    Genesis 29:24-26 — Laban's deception substituting Leah
    Genesis 30:28; 31:1-16, 38-42 — Laban changed Jacob's wages ten times
    Genesis 31:22-23 — Pursued by Laban and others
    Genesis 31:30 — Accused of thievery
    Genesis 32:6-8; 33:1-3 — Esau coming in haste with 400 men
    Genesis 34:1-2 — Shechem defiled Dinah
    Genesis 34:25-26, 30-31 — Simeon and Levi slaughter men of Shechem
    Genesis 35:11, 16-20 — Rachel's death after childbirth
    Genesis 35:22 — Reuben with Bilhah
    Genesis 37:31-32 — Deception by sons regarding Joseph
    Genesis 47:9 — *"few and evil have the days of the years of my life been"*

Dinah afflicted
    Genesis 34:1-2 — Defiled by Shechem

Joseph's afflictions
    Genesis 37:11, 19-20 — Hated by his brothers
    Genesis 37:23-24 — Placed in a pit
    Genesis 37:27-28; 40:15 — Sold to Midianite merchantmen
    Genesis 37:36; 39:1 — Sold in Egypt to Potiphar
    Genesis 39:7-19 — Falsely accused by wife of Potiphar
    Genesis 39:19-20 — Placed in prison by Potiphar
    Genesis 40:23–41:1 — Forgotten by chief butler in prison two years
    Genesis 46:29 — Separation from father and extended family, age seventeen to thirty-nine

Slaves

Joseph
    Genesis 37:27-28; 40:15 — Sold to Midianite merchantmen

Genesis 37:36; 39:1 — Sold in Egypt to Potiphar

All Israelites
Exodus 1:8-12 — Made slaves with taskmasters to afflict them
Exodus 1:13-14 — Made to serve with rigor–hard bondage, in mortar & brick, and all manner of service in the field
Exodus 1:15-22 — Limit offspring by command to kill and destroy male babies
Exodus 5:6-14 — Required to *"go and gather straw for themselves,"* and maintain the daily tally of brick

The Scriptures clearly revealed that each of the three types of events was fulfilled. Abraham and his descendants were strangers in a land not their own. That Abraham's early and later descendants received affliction from others, and then endured servitude to others was well documented. But the text in Genesis 15:16 also emphasized that the fourth generation would enter their land in Canaan. These translations emphasized the fourth generation.

> But in the fourth generation they shall come hither again: for the iniquity of the Amorites is not yet full. KJV

> And they shall come back here in the fourth generation; for the iniquity of the Amorites is not yet complete. RSV

> In the fourth generation they will come here again, for the iniquity of the Amorite is not yet full. WEB

God had encouraged Abraham that even though the duration of these experiences was long, the fourth generation, those afflicted in slavery, would enter the land in Canaan as promised. The years of the twelve tribes of Israel's sojourn in Egypt started with pharaoh making an agreement or covenant with Joseph regarding allowing Israel and his descendants to seek protection from the famine and dwell in Egypt (Genesis 45:17-21). The covenant entailed pharaoh providing Goshen as a place to dwell and by extension the provisions and protection of Egypt to maintain their well-being in exchange for Jacob's sons providing care for pharaoh's livestock (Genesis 46:33-34; 47:1-11).

Then Israel's family began carefully and effectively herding the livestock which provided a necessary service to pharaoh. And the reasoning probably went this way. If Joseph's service so richly benefitted Potiphar's household (Genesis 39:5-6), and his greater service blessed Egypt (Genesis 41:41–42:1; 45:4-8), then Jacob's family in willing service to pharaoh would benefit his household and Egypt, too. This two-way covenant, when broken by a later pharaoh, was part of the basis for the punishments upon Egypt and for Israel receiving the riches of Egypt as unpaid remuneration at their exodus from Egypt (Exodus 11:2-3).

The fourth generation

If Israel was in Egypt, which started in Genesis 45:16-18; 47:5-6, for 430 years with at least thirty good years and up to 400 bad years, the lineage of Levi across this time must be reconciled with the stated descendants. This family line went from Levi to Kohath (Numbers 3:19; 26:59); Kohath to Amram (Exodus 6:16-18); Amram to Miriam (Exodus 2:1-8; 7:7; Numbers 26:59), Aaron (Exodus 6:20; 7:7), and Moses (Exodus 6:20; 7:7; 1 Chronicles 23:13); and then to Aaron's sons: Nadab, Abihu, Eleazar, and Ithamar (Exodus 6:23; Numbers 3:2).

Exodus 28:1 stated, *"And take thou unto thee Aaron thy brother, and his sons with him, from among the children of Israel, that he may minister unto me in the priest's office, even Aaron, Nadab and Abihu, Eleazar and Ithamar, Aaron's sons."* This did not mean that all four sons were immediately inaugurated as priests, but this set the template that each in turn when they met the age criteria (Exodus 24:1; Numbers 8:23-26) was to be included. And in turn that each qualifying descendant by recorded lineage and birth year entered into service by passing through their cleansing period and inauguration ceremony as a priest (Leviticus 29:1-35; Leviticus 8).

Eleazar and Ithamar had done so as shown in Leviticus 10:1-16. Marred or maimed individuals were an exception. Leviticus 21:17-23 said this.

> Speak unto Aaron, saying, Whosoever he be of thy seed in their generations that hath any blemish, let him not approach to offer the bread of his God. For whatsoever man he be that hath a blemish, he shall not approach: a blind man, or a lame, or he that hath a flat nose, or any thing superfluous, Or a man that is

Genesis 15:13-16

brokenfooted, or brokenhanded, Or crookbackt, or a dwarf, or that hath a blemish in his eye, or be scurvy, or scabbed, or hath his stones broken; No man that hath a blemish of the seed of Aaron the priest shall come nigh to offer the offerings of the Lord made by fire: he hath a blemish; he shall not come nigh to offer the bread of his God. He shall eat the bread of his God, both of the most holy, and of the holy. Only he shall not go in unto the vail, nor come nigh unto the altar, because he hath a blemish; that he profane not my sanctuaries: for I the Lord do sanctify them.

This also meant that Israel was to keep a written record of their family lineage. All Levites and the descendants of Aaron showed their qualifications (2 Chronicles 31:16-19; Ezra 2:62) by ancestry and age to begin priest training or to end their formal service. All of this helped us understand that the records kept by the tribes of Israel reported what was true, so that others could rely upon their integrity. Their written records were valuable, pertinent, and accurate. We use these with confidence.

Suppose that Levi had Kohath (Genesis 46:11) as a newborn infant entering Egypt and noting that Moses was age eighty at the exodus from Egypt subtract from 430 those eighty years for 350 years remaining from Kohath's birth to Moses's birth. Exodus 6:18 stated that Kohath died at 133 years and Exodus 6:20 stated that his son Amram died at 137. Subtract from 350 both 133 and 137 and then eighty years were wholly unaccounted for [430 - 133 - 137 - 80 = 80].

That scenario required both Kohath and Amram to conceive the next generation on their death beds, which was completely unrealistic! This showed that far greater than eighty years, more likely greater than 135 years (factoring in the latest possible age to conceive and have a son), were unresolvable. The time span of 430 years in Egypt was unworkable. The same was true for 400 years in Egypt.

Consider an alternate start of the 430 years (Genesis 45:17-18; 47:5-6) at Mount Moriah when Isaac was offered to the Lord. Both the 430 year and 400-year periods end at the same point of the exodus from Egypt. If Isaac was thirty years of age at mount Moriah, then add thirty more years to Jacob's birth when Isaac was at sixty years of age (Genesis 15:13;

21:8-10, 21). This scenario had two generations (Abraham and Isaac) present to start the sojourn of 430 years and had three generations (Abraham, Isaac and Jacob) present to begin the 400 years of affliction (Exodus 1:8-13; 12:40) until the Mosaic Law was added (Galatians 3:15-17).

If so, the 400-year period started at Jacob's birth. He was 130 years old at entry to Egypt which then made the Israelites have 270 years in Egypt [400 - 130 = 270]. This scenario still brought conflict with other passages, and extremely late age births.

With this scenario if Kohath was born just before entry to Egypt, then he and Amram must have each been about 95 when they had the next generation [95 + 95 + 80 = 270]. With Levi's daughter Jochebed born when Levi was ninety-three years old (Part 1, Levi), then she was 141 years old at the birth of Moses. Levi was forty-nine years in Egypt before Jochebed was born [93 - 44 = 49]. With Moses at age eighty at the exodus, Jochebed's age at Moses' birth was 141 years [270 - 80 - 49 = 141]. Add more years if she was born earlier or vice versa.

In perspective, Jacob died at age 147 and Levi died at age 137. If Jochebed was born at Levi's maximum age for paternal sexual reproduction of a child at age 115 [115 / 137 = 0.84* or 84% of his life span; *see Footnote H in Part 1.], then Jochebed was twenty-two years younger [115 - 93 = 22] when she gave birth to Moses or 119 years [141 - 22 = 119] of a 133 year maximum life span. [Using the same age as her brother Kohath, 119 / 133 = 0.894 or 89% of her life span.] The argument for 270 years for the Israelites to dwell in Egypt, counting from Jacob's birth unto the exodus from Egypt, was completely untenable.

To fulfill Genesis 15:16 the lineage of Jacob must be established through Aaron, the high priest. [See Section II, Part 1. The intersection of Aaron and Elisheba] Levi (age 34-43) had Kohath (Numbers 3:19; 26:59; 1 Chronicles 6:23) before entering into Egypt (Genesis 46:8-27; Exodus 1:1-5). In turn Amram was born to Kohath (Exodus 6:16-18) about age fifty to fifty-nine, especially since Amram married his aunt Jochebed, Kohath's much younger sister and Levi's daughter (Exodus 1:5; 6:20; Numbers 26:59). Aaron was born to Amram (about age 91, Exodus 2:1-8; 7:7); and Eleazar was born to Aaron (age 64 or a little later, Exodus 28:1; Numbers 3:2; 1 Chronicles 6).

Genesis 15:13-16

Start with Kohath at age nine. Add forty-one to get to age fifty, add ninety-one for Amram, then add sixty-four for Aaron's age at the birth of Eleazar. Add nineteen more years for Eleazar at the exodus to reach 215 years [41 + 91 + 64 + 19 = 215, see Table 2].

Another text from Scripture that confined the fourth generation was given in Acts 13:16-20 (ESV & NIV). This period of *"about 450 years,"* began with Isaac at age five in Acts 13. The beginning 400-year period started when God *"chose the fathers"* as they dwelt in Canaan, proceeded through when God *"made the people great during their stay in the land of Egypt,"* and included the exodus from Egypt. Then for *"about forty years he put up with them in the wilderness,"* added six years *"destroying seven nations in the land of Canaan"* under Joshua's leadership, and took one more year when he *"divided their land to them by lot."*

Table 2. The four required generations after Levi who were in Egypt.

Born in Canaan,	entered Egypt & died in Egypt:	Levi,	Exodus 1:1-5
1st Generation,	entered Egypt & died in Egypt:	Kohath,	Genesis 46:11
2nd Generation,	born in Egypt & died in Egypt:	Amram,	Exodus 6:18
3rd Generation,	born in Egypt, died in journey:	Aaron,	Exodus 6:20
4th Generation,	born in Egypt & died in Canaan: Eleazar,		Joshua 14:1

This summed to a period of about 450 years (400 + 40 + 6 + 1 = 447) that ended after the division of the land by Joshua and Eleazar, the priest (Numbers 34:17; Joshua 13–19 chpts.; Acts 13:19). Some count the period of about 450 years beginning at Isaac's birth (5 + 400 + 40 + 6 + 1 = 452). Both 447 and 452 were *"about the space of four hundred and fifty years"* KJV and both fit with *"all this took about 450 years"* ESV and NIV.[I] Later

---

I. The 430 years (Exodus 12:40; until Law added, Galatians 3:15-17) began at Abram's journey into Canaan at age 75. Thirty years passed until Isaac was weaned. The 400 years reach from Isaac at age five with his affliction by Ishmael until the exodus from Egypt (Genesis 15:13; 21:8-10, 21; 45:17-18; 47:5-6 and the affliction of Exodus 1:8-13 until the Law Covenant was added, Exodus 23–24). From Isaac's weaning / inheritance party 185 years transpired up to entry into Egypt add 215 years in Egypt unto their exit, this summed to 400 years. When Apostle Paul (aka Rabbi Saul) spoke about this in Acts 13:16-22 and said it was *"about 450 years,"* (AMP, CEB, CEV, CJB, DRA, ESV, EXB, NET, NIV) he was speaking of two possible ways to derive that number.

As shown earlier, Apostle Paul used the term, *"about,"* and thereby acknowledged that others used either method of reckoning. The year of the exodus from Egypt was [A-505]

Apostle Paul (Rabbi Saul) addressed the early part of this time period, from Abram entering Canaan to the exodus from Egypt [A-75 to A-505 = 430], in Galatians 3:15-18 [30 + 400 = 430].

> Brethren, I speak after the manner of men; Though it be but a man's covenant, yet if it be confirmed, no man disannulleth, or addeth thereto. Now to Abraham and his seed were the promises made. He saith not, And to seeds, as of many; but as of one, And to thy seed, which is Christ. And this I say, that the covenant, that was confirmed before of God in Christ, the law, which was four hundred and thirty years after, cannot disannul, that it should make the promise of none effect. For if the inheritance be of the law, it is no more of promise: but God gave it to Abraham by promise.

Abram responded to God's offer recorded in Genesis 12:1-3. Apostle Paul said that God kept his pledge when Abram met the initial condition and entered Canaan. The relocation to Canaan was the evidence of Abram's acceptance of God's original offer or promise. Then Paul explained that adding the law covenant did not change the first covenant offered by God and ratified by Abram.

The text in Galatians 3:17 addressed the period from Abram entering the land of Canaan up to the event at Sinai and said the length was 430 years until the Mosaic law covenant was made, *"the law, which was four hundred and thirty years after."* This text was consistent with and meant the same duration of time as Exodus 12:40 which counted 430 years from Abram entering Canaan when their sojourning began in Abram's loins up through the day of departure from Egypt. Within two months from departure the twelve tribes were at Mount Sinai receiving the law covenant.

Genesis 15:13-16 measured off 400 years of time from Isaac's weaning / inheritance party and his affliction by Ishmael through the exodus from Egypt. Acts 13:16-20 started from either Isaac's birth or weaning and included: wandering in Canaan, entry into and departure from Egypt, journeying through the wilderness, entering and conquering Canaan,

---

1446 BC, the year of the land division to the eleven tribes was [A-552] 1399 BC.

and dividing the land. It covered "about" 450 years depending on the method of counting. It was 452 years from Isaac's birth or 447 years from his weaning and affliction by Ishmael through apportioning the land of Canaan to Israel.

Four hundred years - four ways

The Scriptures specifically incorporated the same 400 year-long time period through four separate methods to prevent any misunderstanding. All of these pointed to the same 215-year time limitation in Egypt, as detailed above. Two more pieces confirmed the 215-year time limitation: 1) Jochebed was both Levi's late daughter and Moses' birth mother, and 2) Eleazar and Ithamar entered Canaan as the fourth generation. There were six scriptural affirmations and confirmations consistent with each other. A seventh confirmation comes later.

The 400 years of Israelite affliction cannot fit three or four pharaohs with the same agenda. This span of years required at least five successive pharaohs with eighty year reigns or eight with fifty year reigns. All of this was highly improbable.

Using any later period than Abram entering into Canaan to start the 430 years (Genesis 12:4) and Isaac's weaning with affliction by Ishmael to start the 400 years (Genesis 15:13; 21:8-10) distorted plain Scripture texts, required unnamed progeny without ages for their birth, or multiple miracles for late ages at birth of children, etc. The simplest resolution was to accept all discussed texts as plain truth statements. Then no miracles of extreme old-age births were needed. All of this fit the marriage of Amram with Jochebed as written two separate times.

Amram and Jochebed, with older age births for Miriam, Aaron and Moses matched Psalm 105:37, *"He brought them forth also with silver and gold: and there was not one feeble person among their tribes."* And their family might be a fulfillment of Exodus 1:20-21, *"Therefore God dealt well with the midwives: and the people multiplied, and waxed very mighty. And it came to pass, because the midwives feared God, that he made them houses."* This older age birth also fit well with pharaoh's daughter who took up Moses as her own child and entrusted Moses to Jochebed's care. She did not expect this "nurse," a great-grandmother aged person, to be either Miriam's or Moses' mother (Exodus 2:8-10).

God had made this family special by 1) providing for older age births without any miracles, 2) establishing three sibling prophets (Exodus 7:1; 15:20; Deuteronomy 34:10; Acts 3:22; 7:37) and, 3) making the house of Aaron have sons through many generations, even in their seventh decade or later from Aaron through Zerahiah. Their progeny even reached well beyond priest Ezra (Ezra 7:1, 11). Psalm 115:12 agreed, *"The Lord hath been mindful of us: he will bless us; he will bless the house of Israel; he will bless the house of Aaron."*

Judah, his twins Pharez (Phares) and Zarah (Zara), and Pharez with his two sons, Hezron and Hamul, entered Egypt. Hezron's (1st generation) son Aram (2nd generation) had grandson Aminadab (3rd generation) and he in turn had Elisheba (4th generation) who married Aaron. Levi and Kohath entered Egypt where Kohath (1st generation) had Amram (2nd generation) who in turn had Aaron (3rd generation).

With Elisheba, Aaron had Eleazar and Ithamar (both 4th generation) who were less than twenty at the census in the second year and second month after the exodus from Egypt (Numbers 1:1-18). When Eleazar entered Canaan as validated in Scripture he fulfilled God's promise to Abraham, *"in the fourth generation they shall come hither again"* (Genesis 15:16). As noted before, the book of Joshua established that Eleazar was the high priest assisting Joshua with the land distribution before he died (Joshua 14:1; 17:4; 19:51; 21:21; 24:33).

Levi was forty-four years old upon entry into Egypt. He died at 137 years (Exodus 6:16) giving at least ninety-three or more years before Exodus 1:6, *"And Joseph died, and all his brethren, and all that generation."* *"All that generation,"* were those who entered Egypt with Jacob, including Hezron and Hamul as infants, Kohath, and others as named. After this Exodus 1:8-14 began. [See: Part 3. When did the new pharaoh arise that "knew not Joseph"?]

This detailed examination of information and placement of Jacob's early lineage made much better sense of Jochebed's age and marriage to Amram. This cannot occur when the text of Genesis was interpreted to mean that Israel was either 430 or 400 or even 270 years in Egypt. Only 215 years in Egypt made possible all parts of Genesis 15:13-16, the explanation given in Acts 13:16-20, and other properly incorporated texts!

Genesis 15:13-16

The meaning of Exodus 12:40

Exodus 12:40 read this way, *"Now the sojourning of the children of Israel who dwelt in Egypt was four hundred and thirty years."* But it should be understood in this manner, *"Now the sojourning, of the children of Israel (who* [had] *dwelt in Egypt* [awhile]*), was four hundred and thirty years,"* or at least punctuated in this manner, *"Now the sojourning, of the children of Israel (who dwelt in Egypt), was four hundred and thirty years."* This parenthesis and punctuation placed in Exodus 12:40 needed more material to fully explain.

Abraham entered Canaan, went to Sichem, Moreh, Bethel, and passed southward *"into Egypt to sojourn there; for the famine was grievous in the land"* (Genesis 12:5-10). He was described in Genesis 12:10-20 as sojourning very briefly in Egypt. After this the texts in Genesis (20:1; 21:22-23, 34; 26:1-3; and 35:27) describe both Abraham and Isaac sojourning in the area of Canaan. That Abraham and Isaac were sojourners and not yet owners of the land was evident from Genesis 23:3-18 when it was necessary to purchase from its present owners a field with a cave for burial.

Jacob had lived in Canaan (Genesis 25:26-28), fled north to Haran (Genesis 28:5, 7, 10) and sojourned with Laban (Genesis 32:4) and came back (Genesis 31:25; 33:17) to dwell in Canaan. That Jacob was also a sojourner was verified in Genesis 33:18-20 which recorded that Jacob purchased land to pitch his tent and build an altar to God. Later God directed Israel to enter Egypt (Genesis 46:2-4) where Jacob described his 130 years as a "pilgrimage," which meant he was a sojourner. Then the eleven sons of Israel spoke to Pharaoh in Genesis 47:4 saying, *"For to sojourn in the land are we come; for thy servants have no pasture for their flocks; for the famine is sore in the land of Canaan: now therefore, we pray thee, let thy servants dwell in the land of Goshen."*

This entire sojourn of Abraham, Isaac, Jacob, his sons, and their subsequent offspring began with Abram entering Canaan and after 430 years was completed with the children of Israel leaving Egypt. This was verified by the statements given in Hebrews 11:8-10 and in Exodus 6:3-5.

> By faith Abraham, when he was called to go out into a place which he should after receive for an inheritance, obeyed; and he

went out, not knowing whither he went. By faith he sojourned in the land of promise, as in a strange country, dwelling in tabernacles with Isaac and Jacob, the heirs with him of the same promise: For he looked for a city which hath foundations, whose builder and maker is God. (Hebrews 11:8-10)

And I appeared unto Abraham, unto Isaac, and unto Jacob, by the name of God Almighty, but by my name Jehovah was I not known to them. And I have also established my covenant with them, to give them the land of Canaan, the land of their pilgrimage, wherein they were strangers. And I have also heard the groaning of the children of Israel, whom the Egyptians keep in bondage; and I have remembered my covenant. (Exodus 6:3-5)

Now examine this important text, *"And as I may so say, Levi also, who receiveth tithes, payed tithes in Abraham. For he was yet in the loins of his father, when Melchisedec met him."* (Hebrews 7:9-10) If we take the reasoning of this statement as valid where the not yet conceived Levi paid tithes in Abraham, then we must also accept that the not yet conceived Israelites, *"the children of Israel,"* sojourned in Abraham, Isaac, Jacob, and the twelve sons down through their fathers before their own births.

Genesis 47:4, as shown above, stated the sons of Israel asked Pharaoh to "sojourn" in Egypt. At the end of this period in Exodus 12:40 Moses referred again to *"the sojourning of the children of Israel."* All of this material, from Abraham entering Canaan to the youngest person departing Egypt, detailed sojourning.

The focus of Moses was neither about how long Israel dwelled in Egypt, that was for just one-half of this whole 430 year period, nor was it pointing back to when Abram went briefly into Egypt, when his age was not given. Instead, Moses had summarized the long-term sojourning of Abraham and his progeny as focused by his first three words. Moses carefully said, *"Now the sojourning, of the children of Israel (who dwelt in Egypt), was four hundred and thirty years."*

Therefore, Exodus 12:40 meant that the whole period of sojourning from Abraham entering Canaan to the youngest infant who had left Egypt, was 430 years. Abram at age 75 at entry to Canaan, plus 430 years

Genesis 15:13-16

of sojourn reached year [A-505] at their departure.[1,2,3,4] [A-75 + 430 = A-505. For a further application of Exodus 12:40 see: Part 4. Answering unasked questions.]

Exodus from Egypt

The time placement of Abraham's descendants and the significant events that transpired as carefully recorded in the Scriptures were necessary to connect in a continuous sequence. This led to the correct year for the exodus from Egypt [A-505] relative to Abraham's birth year. From this event the text of 1 Kings 6:1 can begin at its proper time in the middle or 15th day of the first month, Abib, in the beginning of the year of Israel's exodus from Egypt.

> And Moses said unto the people, Remember this day, in which ye came out from Egypt, out of the house of bondage; for by strength of hand the Lord brought you out from this place: there shall no leavened bread be eaten. This day came ye out in the month Abib." (Exodus 13:3-4)

> Thou shalt keep the feast of unleavened bread: (thou shalt eat unleavened bread seven days, as I commanded thee, in the time appointed of the month Abib; for in it thou camest out from Egypt: and none shall appear before me empty:)" (Exodus 23:15)

> And they departed from Rameses in the first month, on the fifteenth day of the first month; on the morrow after the passover the children of Israel went out with an high hand in the sight of all the Egyptians." (Numbers 33:3)

From that day of departure on the 15th day of Abib the text of 1 Kings 6:1 began its counting of 479 complete years up to another 15th day of Abib. Then after sixteen more days, which was in the first day in the second month (Zif 1) of the 480th year [counting from Exodus 12:12-13], the temple construction began under Solomon. The texts of 1 Kings 6:1 and 2 Chronicles 3:2 read as follows.

> And it came to pass in the four hundred and eightieth year after the children of Israel were come out of the land of Egypt, in the

fourth year of Solomon's reign over Israel, in the month Zif, which is the second month, that he began to build the house of the Lord. (1 Kings 6:1)

Then Solomon began to build the house of the Lord at Jerusalem in mount Moriah, where the Lord appeared unto David his father, in the place that David had prepared in the threshingfloor of Ornan the Jebusite. And he began to build in the second day of the second month, in the fourth year of his reign. (2 Chronicles 3:2)

After the exodus event these were recorded in sequence: the duration of the wilderness journey, the long promised entry into Canaan, the conquering of the inhabitants, and the subsequent land division. From there the time of Joshua's death, the length of the period of the elders who outlived Joshua, the onset of and duration of the period of the judges leading up to the reign of David can be carefully examined and resolved. First, more will be revealed.

What we learned:
1. The full meaning and application of Genesis 15:13-16
2. The fulfillment of God's promise provided for 215 years with Israel in Egypt.
3. The marriage of Amram and Jochebed greatly impacted the interpretation and helped to establish how long Israel was in Egypt.
4. God's promise of the fourth generation from entry to Egypt to return again into Canaan was completely fulfilled.
5. God remarkably blessed Amram, Jochebed, and their family.

Make a visual tool:
Add to the timeline constructed earlier. Aaron was born three years before Moses. Aaron at age sixty-four was the earliest possible birth time for Eleazar and Ithamar. Measure from "Enter-Canaan" on the left 10 5/16 inches (26.15 cm) and end less than 1/2 inch (1.2 cm) to the left of "Exodus" on the far right, mark "Eleazar-born?", and "Abram-487 or >?".

Judah's grandsons Hezron and Hamul were born just before entry in

Genesis 15:13-16

the year of Israel entering into Egypt. Place them by "Enter-Egypt" (labeled previously). Label "Hezron, Hamul-born."

When did the Pharaoh arise that "knew not Joseph"?

Part 3: The children of Jacob and the intersections of their descendants.

Joseph entered Egypt when he was seventeen years of age (Genesis 31:1-36). At thirty years of age he stood before pharaoh (Genesis 41:1-57). He had interpreted the dream of pharaoh stating that God was warning him that seven good years and seven famine years were coming. Joseph was, therefore, thirty-nine years of age [30 + 7 + 2] when he spoke to his brothers in Genesis 45:6, *"For these two years hath the famine been in the land: and yet there are five years, in the which there shall neither be earing nor harvest."*

Levi was almost five years older than Joseph [birth year A-251 minus birth year A-246 = ~5; Part 1, Table 1] derived from the textual account of Jacob, his four wives, and their offspring (Genesis 29:18–30:25). Levi was about forty-four years of age when he entered Egypt with his father, sister Dinah, brothers, and their families. Exodus 6:16 stated that *"the years of the life of Levi were an hundred thirty and seven years"* [A-246-383, 1705-1568 BC].

Joseph [A-251-361, 1700-1590 BC] lived for 71 years with his extended family in Egypt. Joseph died and was embalmed after he lived for ninety-three years in Egypt. He had lived and served there from seventeen to 110 years of age [A-268-361, 1683-1590 BC] (Genesis 50:22-26).

Joseph died when Levi was about 115 years old, then he lived twenty-two more years. But Benjamin was about fifteen to sixteen years younger [born ~A-266-267] than Joseph and nineteen to twenty years younger than Levi. Benjamin was about ninety-four to ninety-five years old at Joseph's death. If Benjamin lived to about 120 years, then he died about two to three years later after Levi's death about [~A-386, ~1565 BC]. If Benjamin also lived to about 134 years, then add about fourteen more years with his death about [~A-400].

If Levi's death was the turning point, that gave about ninety-three years [137 - 44 = 93] in Egypt before the Scripture in Exodus 1:8-14 began. Then the Israelites had experienced about ninety-three or more good years and endured about 122 or less years of slavery in Egypt for a total of 215 years from their entry to their Exodus. These facts were necessary to consider to help establish the time period for the pharaoh that enslaved the Israelites.

During the life of Joseph, Egypt so valued Joseph's service that when Jacob died (Genesis 49:33–50:14) the Scriptures reported that *"the Egyptians mourned for him threescore and ten days."* Then the text added that when *"Joseph went up to bury his father" "with him went up all the servants of Pharaoh, the elders of his house, and all the elders of the land of Egypt."* It was strange to conceive as possible, and even harder to imagine, that Joseph was forgotten before he died or that he was devalued while his brothers still lived. Even then those elders in Egypt who had lived as children through the famine certainly knew about Joseph and his service to Egypt.

The Egyptian elders were up to thirty-seven years younger than Joseph, if they were born when the years of famine began. If Egypt's elders also lived to about 110 years, then they surely knew who Joseph was and would honor his service to them and Egypt until they all had died within thirty-seven years after Joseph's death by [A-398, 1553 BC]. The exodus from Egypt was in [A-505] 1446 BC[5,6] and the difference was about 107 years. That gave the period of Israelite slavery, at a maximum, about 144 years at Joseph's death, 122 years at Levi's death, and down to 107 years at the death of the last Egyptian elder as described. Probably their slavery was even shorter.

For another pharaoh to arise who *"knew not Joseph,"* (Exodus 1:1-14) this event must have been near or after 1553 BC. According to

Wikipedia's list[7] of pharaohs and their respective time periods this was Khamudi of the Fifteenth Dynasty [about 1674-1535 BC] from the Hyksos people (now understood to be opportunistic Amalekites post exodus) whose rule was about 1555–1544 BC. Possibly that new king that arose deposed or destroyed the current leadership of Egypt and assumed rule. Then this event occurred a little earlier in time.

Apepi[8] ruled about forty or more years just before Khamudi. That rule started a little before Joseph's death and encompass the thirty-seven-year period after his death. Others propose that Ahmose I[9], a Theban prince, king of Egypt (suggested reign 1570-1546 BC), founder of the 18th Dynasty, who began the New Kingdom was the best candidate.

Another asserts that Amenhotep IV / Akhenaton[10] fit this ruler. These rulers and their dating were given according to the best of men's current knowledge. The Egyptian timeline is now undergoing significant revision and shortening and those pharaohs who accurately match the time period from around 1553 BC to the 1446 BC exodus from Egypt will be adjusted accordingly. [11,12,13,14,15]

The Scriptures gave enough information

The Holy Scriptures really did give us enough information to correctly discern when another pharaoh arose who *"knew not Joseph."* Three specific texts gave us parallel information. These were Exodus 1:6-24, Psalm 105:22-27, and Acts 7:15-21.

This information can be collated and interwoven by placing the texts side-by-side in three columns and then align the matching statements to get the complete picture. These can be briefly listed as: entry, death of Jacob and sons, their placement in the tomb at Shechem, [simultaneous] population growth, Egypt hated and feared them, another pharaoh arose who dealt treacherously with Israel, command to destroy infant boys, and both Aaron and Moses arrived.

The parts to specially note were always given in the same sequence: death of Jacob and sons, population growth, another pharaoh arose, and the command for the destruction of infant Israelite boys. Added caveats came in Acts 7:20, *"in which time Moses was born,"* and in Exodus 2:1-2, *"And there went a man of the house of Levi, and took to wife a daughter of Levi."*

SECTION II Part 3.

And the woman conceived, and bare a son: and when she saw him that he was a goodly child, she hid him three months." Exodus chapter 2 followed behind the introduction of the pharaoh and his policies and supplied expanded information about their impact upon one family and one very influential life.

This sequence was a vital key. Exodus chapter 1 clearly stated one additional, potent, illuminating phrase which allowed for an accurate resolution of this time period. The words of Exodus 1:6 were these, *"And Joseph died, and all his brethren, and all that generation."* The phrase *"all that generation"* meant that the last of those who journeyed with Jacob and his family, who were born beforehand and who entered Egypt, had died.

The lineage of Jacob through Levi and through Judah was clearly shown (in Section II, Part 1.) and both will be applied again here. In Genesis 46:12 Hezron (Esrom, [A-289-290]) was born and then Hamul was born [A-290] before entry into Egypt. Hezron was shown to be just about or under one year of age and Hamul was a newborn infant, unless they were twins in which case they were both newborn.

Hezron and Hamul were two of the individuals specifically meant by Exodus 1:6 because there was a clearly discernible birth year for them, the year of entry to Egypt. Their births were pressed into an exceedingly narrow range by the timing of the births and events surrounding Judah's family. With Hezron and Hamul born within a year of their entry [A-290], add their expected life span to the year of entry to discern which year they died.

The son of Jacob was Levi who died at 137 (Exodus 6:16), the son of Levi was Kohath who died at 133 (Exodus 6:18), the son of Kohath was Amram who died at 137 years (Exodus 6:20) as the third generation counting after Jacob. The son of Jacob was Judah, the son of Judah was Pharez, the sons of Pharez were Hezron and Hamul (both third generation) who entered Egypt. Both family lines had sons who entered Egypt, i.e. Kohath through Levi and Hezron and Hamul through Judah. The stated age for Kohath of 133 years at death was also the expected life span for Hezron and Hamul. This was certainly within the right margin since the parallel third generation through Levi was Amram who lived to 137 years.

Abraham's relative age at their entry to Egypt was [A-290], add 133 years to reach the relative age of [A-423]. Simple arithmetic will give us an answer to when this pharaoh arose. The year of the exodus from Egypt was 215 years after entry or [A-505; 290 + 215 = 505]. Subtract eighty years from that to get Moses' birth year (Exodus 7:7) [A-425, 1526 BC] and likewise subtract 83 years to get Aaron's birth year (Exodus 7:7; Numbers 33:39) at [A-422, 1529 BC]. This simple method showed that just one year after Aaron's birth Hezron and Hamul died at the expected life span of 133 years [A-423] (Exodus 1:6).

That Pharaoh arose

Then after Hezron and Hamul died this oppressing pharaoh arose in [A-424, 1527 BC], broke covenant with Israel, made his edict of slavery, and within that year added his edict to cast out the Israelite baby sons (Exodus 1:8-16). Aaron was not described in the Scriptures as having been under jeopardy of life at his birth. But baby Moses was presented as being under this edict carried out in Exodus chapter 2, rehearsed in Psalm 105:26, and detailed again in Acts 7:18-21.

Psalm 105:26 stated clearly that Aaron and Moses were sent at this time, *"He turned their heart to hate his people, to deal subtilly with his servants. He sent Moses his servant; and Aaron whom he had chosen."* Stephen stated the same thing in Acts 7:18-21.

> Till another king arose, which knew not Joseph. The same dealt subtilly with our kindred, and evil entreated our fathers, so that they cast out their young children, to the end they might not live. In which time Moses was born, and was exceeding fair, and nourished up in his father's house three months.

Therefore, beginning later in [A-424] 1527 BC the Israelites endured less than eighty-one years of slavery, oppression, and abuse before the exodus from Egypt in Abib of [A-505] 1446 BC. Recall that Moses was born after that pharaoh arrived, fled Egypt at age forty (Exodus 2:11-15; Acts 7:29-30), and returned at age eighty (Exodus 7:7). From late [A-424] to the very beginning of [A-505] was plainly just eighty years.

Parts 1 through 3 in Section II have been developed by participating with confidence under the inner cohesion and internal explanatory consistency (self-elucidation of words, phrases and expressions) of

SECTION II Part 3.

Scripture. Through this the length of time Israel was in Egypt was firmly resolved, the year the new pharaoh arose was established, the duration of Israelite slavery was determined, and Holy Scripture has been validated as accurate in minute detail. Many of these expressions were "hidden" in plain sight, not by any form of secrecy, but by a presentation foreign to so many Bible students and scholars.

A corrected history of Egypt is requisite to discern which pharaoh arose against Israel. Then he made his edicts to enslave Israelites and cast out the Israelite baby sons. This would help scholars discern the identity of the subsequent pharaoh in that dynasty who rejected Moses' request eighty years later on behalf of God to *"let my people go"* (Exodus 5:1). It is technically possible for that pharaoh to be the same person, if he started at age twenty-five he would be at age 105 eighty years later.

What we learned:
1. The meaning of the expression, *"and all that generation."*
2. When the new Pharaoh arose that *"knew not Joseph."*
3. The Israelites endured eighty-one years of slavery, oppression, and abuse before the exodus from Egypt.

Make a visual tool:
Add more to the timeline. Aaron was born three years before Moses in [A-422 or very late in A-421 since he died at age 123 (Numbers 33:39) late in A-544 about two months before entry to Canaan]. Measure 8 11/16 inch to the right from "Abram-75" and mark it "Aaron-born" and "Abram-422." (Hezron and Hamul died at 133 years of age in the year [A-423].) For Moses' birth measure 8 3/4 inches (22.25 cm) from "Abram-75" and label it "Moses-born" and "Abram-425."

The year before that Pharaoh arose who *"knew not Joseph."* Place in smaller text a label "Pharaoh-arose" and below place "Abram-424." Or place these labels farther away from the horizontal timeline or make a text box with the information and draw a short line toward the positions of "Abram-423" and "Abram-424."

Can the book of Job be placed in time?

Part 4: The children of Jacob and the intersections of their descendants.

The book of Job recorded various kinds of statements about facts, ages, comparisons, and relatives. The author of Job named people by including information about their lineage, except for Job. Then the visit and conversations of four named individuals was described. This was followed by reporting on additional visitors who gave to Job gifts which helped him to restart again.These and other specific facts gave enough information to narrow down to a specific person the individual that fit with all of these pieces.

Each relevant fact, age, comparison, comforter, and relative is given consideration in this chapter. Their named lineages are examined. Plus the ratio for late aged birth to life span when carefully applied is shown to derive valuable results. All of these pieces fit with one person who lived during a specific time period and descended from Abraham.

Job's ancestry – Issachar to Job

Issachar, son of Jacob, was born an older brother to Benjamin (23rd generation) through Leah in [A-249]. He was at age forty-one at entry to Egypt [A-290]. Genesis 46:13 listed these, "*And the sons of Issachar; Tola, and Phuvah, and Job, and Shimron,*" (as part of the 24th generation). The text in 1 Chronicles 7:1 gave Issachar four sons and listed Job's other name as Jashub. He had some sisters, too (Job 42:11). When applying Genesis 46:26, with Isaachar starting early to have children, Job was born in the maximum possible range of [~A-270–288]. This was because Job had both older and younger siblings born before entry to Egypt.

The words in Job 15:10 were spoken by Eliphaz to Job, "*With us are both the grayheaded and very aged men, much elder than thy father,*" i.e. older than Job's father. This was especially true, if Issachar and Job were only twenty-one to thirty-nine years apart. Note also the character of Issachar, which was displayed by Job, which came through to his descendants as given in 1 Chronicles 12:32. "*And of the children of Issachar, which were men that had understanding of the times, to know what Israel ought to do; the heads of them were two hundred; and all their brethren were at their commandment.*"

Job's life span

If we use Job's maximum birth range [~A-270–288], then when Job was at seventy years of age for the book of Job that was across [A-340–358]. When the age of seventy was doubled and then added to his original seventy years, as some do (using Job 42:12-16), then Job was 210 years at his death [70 + (2 x 70) = 210; ~A-480–498]. This later time period was from twenty-five years down to seven years prior to the exodus from Egypt in [A-505].

But if we apply other verses more carefully from Job 42:10 and 13 to Job's age of seventy years, only seventy more years are added. Then Job was 140 years at his death when applying the same maximum birth range [70 x 2 = 140; A-410–428]. Levi died in [A-383] at 137 years (Exodus 6:16). Benjamin died at the latest about [~A-400], if he had up to 134 years of life.

Kohath (24th generation) the son of Levi, died at age 133 about [A-414]. If Kohath was not about nine years of age at entry, which was presented earlier as a reasonable proposition, but was only an infant, then he too died 133 years later at [A-423] like Hezron and Hamul. The slightly longer 140-year life span of Job was consistent with these stated ages and ancestry.

There was one more verse, that others have neither considered nor implemented, which must be applied to be careful and get truly reliable results. Exodus 1:6 said this, "*And Joseph died, and all his brethren, and all that generation.*" Previously this text was shown to specially apply to all of those who had entered into Egypt. Now that text included Joseph's eleven brothers, his sister Dinah and all of their children.

Upon taking the carefully stated order of this text into account, it made perfect sense. Joseph died at 110 years, probably at the youngest age from his hard experiences. Next his siblings died (23rd generation) followed by their children, all of those from the twenty-fourth generation. Then Hezron and Hamul (25th generation) who had entered Egypt as infants died. That clearly meant Job (from the 24th generation) had already died. This made Job's death at 140 years of age occur before Hezron and Hamul died last in [A-423].

When the maximum birth range for Job was applied that meant Job's death occurred somewhere during the time frame of [A-410–428]. Since Exodus 1:6 in the preceding paragraph showed that Job died before [A-423] the time range for his birth was narrowed to [A-270–282]. Thus the time period for the book of Job, when Job was at seventy years of age, was also narrowed by more than five years to a smaller maximum range of twelve years [A-340–352].

The best fit was [A-347] when using biblical numerology]. This was shortly after Amram's birth time [~A-331] and just after Jochebed's birth time [~A-339] as detailed in the footnotes F, G, and H for Section II, Part 1. In contemporary time this twelve-year period for the book of Job was from 1611 through 1599 BC.

Who were the individuals that sat in front of Job?

To get pearls divers go deep in water for clams and oysters, to get diamonds miners tunnel deep into the earth. The satisfaction for the toil of diving and digging comes from the priceless nuggets brought up from the depths. Nothing brought better results, more satisfaction, and increased joy like mining in Scripture.

Some of the following textual information was presented earlier and was easily connected to more individuals. With freshly mined information added to previous material new connections were established. Working with a concordance or suitable search engine as the tool in one hand, the Spirit of God guiding our heart and mind, and the text of Scripture as the inexhaustible depths, lets go digging!

Esau to Eliphaz the Temanite Together we can examine some of

Abraham's descendants starting with his firstborn grandson through Isaac. As presented earlier, Esau was born in [A-160] (Genesis 25:24-26). He was also known as Edom (Genesis 25:30; 36:8). Esau at age forty married Adah who was the daughter of Elon the Hittite (Genesis 26:34; 36:1-8; 1 Chronicles 1:34-37). They had a son Eliphaz (23rd generation from Adam) most likely born around late [A-200] or early [A-201].

After Jacob returned to Isaac Esau moved from Isaac's area eastward and lived in mount Seir along with Seir's family (Genesis 36:6-8, 20-30). *"Thus dwelt Esau in mount Seir: Esau is Edom."* [See Jeremiah 49:8] Seir was part of the territory of Uz as stated in Lamentations 4:21, *"Rejoice and be glad, O daughter of Edom, that dwellest in the land of Uz."*

Eliphaz had five sons, *"Teman, Omar, Zepho, and Gatam, and Kenaz,"* (24th generation, Genesis 36:11) with Teman born around [~A-230-240]. Teman in turn had a son born about [~A-267] named in the book of Job (Job 2:11a, Eliphaz the 25th generation and grandson to the first), *"Now when Job's three friends heard of all this evil that was come upon him, they came every one from his own place; Eliphaz the Temanite."* This Eliphaz, a son of Teman (Temanite), and a grandson of Eliphaz and great-grandson of Esau as Scripture laid out, fit well for a general age of seventy-three to eighty-five years since he spoke first in Job 4:1.

<u>Shuah to Bildad the Shuhite</u> Next examine Abraham's last born son, Shuah [A-147] (21st generation). Shuah possibly had an unnamed son born around [~A-207] and then a grandson Bildad (23rd generation) born about or before [~A-267]. That was the same time period as Benjamin's birth and generation twenty-three like Jacob's sons. But it was still very probable that Shuah was a father to Bildad near age 120 of an 150-160 year life span [<0.84 ratio]. In order for Bildad to be named a Shuhite (Shuahite) he must have been either a grandson or a son of a Shuah or have lived in an area named Shuah. The only contemporary Shuah was the son of Abraham.

Shuah was the last son of Abraham and lived under God's blessing to Abraham with a longer life span. The seven year world-wide famine which brought Israel into Egypt occurred near Shuah's time of death. He probably was the last son of Abraham to die which was about the end of the famine in [A-295] or a little later, somewhere around age 150-160, longer than his eldest brother Ishmael's 137 years and shorter than Isaac's 180 years.

Another useful connection with Shuah was given. The text of Genesis 38:12 clearly named him when it said, "*And in process of time the daughter of Shuah Judah's wife died.*" Judah [A-247] had married once and started at a very young age to begin his family with his son Er [A-259]. Judah's wife was a later born daughter (22nd generation) with Shuah around age ninety-eight to one hundred [~A-245-247].

Possibly, Judah's wife could have been one more generation, a granddaughter. The best fit in Holy Scripture was almost always the shortest route which meant that Bildad was most likely the son of Shuah. Shuah's daughter was the preferred person to have been a wife to Judah.

Bildad, as the second person listed in Job 2:11 and the second speaker recorded in Job 8:1, was near or over the age of eighty years. Eliphaz the Temanite and Bildad the Shuhite were both carefully described by lineage which helped place their ancestry with confidence. The same was not true of Zophar the Naamathite. Perhaps Zophar's ancestry came from a third branch of Abraham's growing tree of descendants.

<u>Benjamin or Simeon to Zophar the Naamathite</u> Benjamin (23rd generation) was about age twenty-four at entry to Egypt [A-290]. His birth year was less certain, but extremely close to [A-266-267]. Genesis 46:21 gave the "*sons of Benjamin: Belah, Becher, Ashbel, Gera, Naaman, Ehi, Rosh, Muppim, Huppim, Ard.*" This many sons born to Benjamin before entry into Egypt fit best with multiple wives as mothers since no statement of twins were given.

Naaman was born the fifth son (24th generation) with an estimated birth time about [~A-285], born before entry to Egypt. In turn Naaman could have had a son born named Zophar and be called the Naamathite (25th generation, [~A-302 or greater]). With this lineage his age was thirty-eight to fifty years when he spoke as the third person in Job 11:1. But if Zophar (as the 24th generation) was a direct son of Benjamin born after entry to Egypt in [A-291] and not listed in Genesis 46:21, then he was about forty-nine to sixty-one years of age when sitting before Job.

Next, consider that in Genesis 46:10 Simeon's fifth son was Zohar (also 24th generation). Zohar was the birth name and perhaps another name was given, Zophar (with additional letter(s) placed in the name). They derive from two Hebrew words, H6714 and H6691 respectively with the central letters changed.[J] Possibly Zohar was renamed or also known as Zophar with a similar sounding name.

That was quite like Abram renamed Abraham, Sarai renamed Sarah, and Job who was also known as Jashub. Each had different letters placed in the center of their names. This was also true of Joshua (aka, Jehoshuah, 1 Chronicles 7:22-27; Numbers 13:8, 16), of Solomon who had two names (2 Samuel 12:24-25), and of others.

If Simeon [A-245] started his family at age seventeen and had a son each year, then his fifth son Zohar could have been born as early as [A-266-267] and have been age eighty before his cousin Job. To descend from Simeon and then called the Naamathite, Zophar needed to live by a place named Naamah. A village named Naamah was listed in Joshua 15:41 which belonged to southern Judah near to or inside the older territory named Uz. If Zophar the Naamathite was neither from Benjamin nor from Simeon, then he had no identifiable ancestry. More discussion about Zophar will follow later.

Nahor to Elihu the Buzite Last of all a fifth and younger man named Elihu spoke in Job 32:2. Chapter 32:4 said exactly this, *"Now Elihu had waited till Job had spoken, because they were elder than he [was]."* Elihu added in Job 32:6, *"... I am young, and ye are very old; wherefore I was afraid, and durst not shew you mine opinion."* He was at least thirty to thirty-five years of age because they were not considered adequately wise less than thirty years of age (Genesis 41:46; Numbers 4:3, 23, 30, 35, 47; 2 Samuel 5:4; Luke 3:23).

His expanded name was given in verse 2, *"Elihu the son of Barachel the Buzite, of the kindred of Ram."* Ram may fit the shortened spelling of Aram from Genesis 10:22-23, *"The children of Shem; Elam, and Asshur, and Arphaxad, and Lud, and Aram. And the children of Aram; Uz, and Hul, and Gether, and Mash."* Plus note the text of Genesis 22:20-22.

J. Zohar came from Strong's number H6714. The Hebrew characters צֹהַר are transliterated to Tsochar. It is patronymically from צַחַר (H8487). Zophar came from Strong's number H6691. The Hebrew characters צוֹפַר are transliterated to Tsowphar. It is from צָפַר (H6852). Both are from https://www.blueletterbible.org.

Can the book of Job be placed in time?

> And it came to pass after these things, that it was told Abraham, saying, Behold, Milcah, she hath also born children unto thy brother Nahor; Huz his firstborn, and Buz his brother, and Kemuel the father of Aram, And Chesed, and Hazo, and Pildash, and Jidlaph, and Bethuel.

That made Elihu's lineage harder to determine. He was possibly a descendant of Shem through Aram through an unknown Buz through a Barachel. Much more likely, he was from the lineage of Nahor, Abraham's older brother (20th generation), through Buz (21st generation) and then Barachel (22nd generation), dwelling in the larger territory of his near kindred of [A]Ram (Genesis 22:21; 1 Chronicles 1:17). In either case of lineage Elihu was living inside or right beside the land of Uz to be connected with Job.

Abram's brother Nahor (20th generation) by age 105 or so had Huz, Buz [~A-88–91], Kemuel, and their siblings (21st generation). This connection with Elihu provided another purpose for and fit well with the inclusion of the news about Nahor's family given in the text in Genesis 22:20-24. This information surfaced right after the event on mount Moriah [~A-117].

In turn by age 115 Buz had Barachel (22nd generation), and that by age 105 Barachel had Elihu (23rd generation) [~A-88 + 115 + 105 = 308 years, + 35 for Elihu's estimated minimum age = ~A-343]. The book of Job transpired during [A-340–352]. This scenario fit Nahor, if he was only a few years older than Abraham's age, especially when beginning his family quite late like Abraham.

Genesis 11:26-29 suggested that for Nahor to marry Haran's daughter, Haran was a much older firstborn son of Terah. Verse 29 said that both Abram and Nahor took wives suggesting that they were closer in age and married nearer the same time frame. If this was correct reasoning, then Elihu was kindred to Abraham, like Moab and Benammi (22nd generation) were through Lot (21st generation), the descendant of Haran (20th generation, Genesis 12:5; 19:35-39; Deuteronomy 2:9). Elihu as a great-grandson of Nahor matched his description (Job 32:2-7; 33:1-6).

Elihu's words fit with and made complete sense of the statement given in Genesis 31:53, *"The God of Abraham, and the God of Nahor, the God of their father [Terah], judge betwixt us."* This descendant of Nahor still carried the knowledge of God and expounded it well before Job and the other three comforters (Job 32–37 chpts.). The divergent lineage of Elihu descending from Nahor and dwelling in a different area from Abraham's family for many years accounted for Elihu's different style of speaking in chapters thirty-two through thirty-seven from that of Job, Eliphaz, Bildad, and Zophar, as noted by various Old Testament commentaries.

How old were the men in front of Job?

Here Job 32:6 must be examined. *"And Elihu the son of Barachel the Buzite answered and said, I am young, and ye are very old; wherefore I was afraid, and durst not shew you mine opinion."* Elihu called all three of the men *"very old."*

He was not referring to Job who merely responded to the three comforters, Eliphaz, Bildad, and Zophar, who had each made assertions about Job. Without further material from the scriptures this expression, *"ye are very old,"* was too broad and vague. When this expression was given in 1 Samuel 2:31 and 17:12 no specific age was given.

But the meaning of this term was explained in 2 Samuel 19:32, *"Now Barzillai was a very aged man, even fourscore years old: and he had provided the king of sustenance while he lay at Mahanaim; for he was a very great man"* [of wealth]. Barzillai's carefully stated age established that this expression, when used in the Scriptures, meant the person had reached or exceeded eighty years. Barzillai revealed that reaching eighty years of age qualified him for the descriptive title of a "very old" or "very aged" man.

If we take Elihu's statement from Job 32:6, *"I am young, and ye are very old,"* as meaning that all three comforters were *"very old,"* then Elihu gave us distinct, precise, and useful information. He conveyed that the age of these three men was at or exceeded eighty years. If these three men sitting before Job were born slightly earlier to their fathers, each still entirely fit into the framework detailed above. The approximated birth times for Eliphaz and Bildad needed little or no adjusting.

With Elihu's statement applied to this scenario, only if this Zophar was Simeon's son, then he was eighty years old. Zophar could not have been more than sixty-seven years old as Benjamin's son. Taken altogether this suggested that Eliphaz and Bildad fit with and were correctly identified by their reported ancestry. The material considered above suggested that Zophar's ancestry was less certain, but fit best with Simeon.

One more age was directly given in Elihu's words in Job 32:6 when he said, *"I am young."* That term *"young"* meant Elihu was half the eighty-year ages of the other comforters and that he was forty years of age. This distinct Biblical expression, *"young,"* will be explored more fully with Joshua later. When applying the twelve year range for the book of Job, Elihu was born from [A-300 to 312]. When Job's best fit was applied Elihu's birth year was [A-307].

If this assembly of lineages and inferences was correct, then all four of Job's comforters were fully connected to Abraham. Either they were Abraham's descendants or his relative with all of the men not so distantly related to each other. Elihu fit best through Nahor as the 23rd generation.

Did you notice the generation level of Abraham's descendants? Adam was counted as the first generation from God. Eliphaz the Temanite was 25th generation, Bildad the Shuhite and Zophar the Naamathite were both 24th generation with Elihu in the 23rd generation? This was remarkable since Miriam, Aaron, and Moses were 26th generation.

Connecting Job to that pharaoh

Between Part 3 and Part 4 in Section II enough information was presented to connect the pieces of information between the material in the book of Job, his experience, when Job died, and that pharaoh who arose who *"knew not Joseph."* You as a reader have the same body of Scripture texts and various details laid out above. You are invited, even encouraged to study the texts, assemble the facts, collate and organize those pieces into a workable and meaningful structure, and then draw a fitting conclusion, all by yourself. Please ask God's help first, then give this a try.

In the case that you are not able to do so, here it is. The premise of Satan in his statement to God was that Job served God just for pay and not for any other reason (Job 1:9-10). Satan also asserted that if the pay was removed, Job would remove himself from God (Job 1:11). God proceeded to show to Satan via the harsh and calamitous experiences Job received that this was simply not true. But what was true was that Satan was convinced that men serve God (or gods) for pay!

Behind the scene that was obvious to us Satan had seventy or so years in which to orchestrate the rise to power of this pharaoh. This was specially verified by the text of Exodus 7 and 8 that spoke of the "magicians" and "sorcerers" that served a later pharaoh in that dynasty. They were worshipers of Satan because of what they said in Exodus 8:19, *"This is the finger of God."* The magicians and sorcerers directly emphasized that this "God" was not their god.

As just detailed above, Job only lived seventy more years after the end of his experience. Job had died somewhere in that twelve year window before Hezron and Hamul died in [A-423]. [Author's best fit: ~A-417 or ~1534 BC.] Then in [A-424] that pharaoh arose to power through Satan's application of belief that men serve God (or gods) for pay. Through those servants yielding to him Satan endeavored to work his will, opposed the plans and purposes of God, and especially sought to destroy Israel as God's witness. This pharaoh was one of many men and women Satan manipulated to insert into positions of power and authority that he might have influence within the governments of this world.

This specific pharaoh started a dynasty of Egyptian rulers that enslaved, oppressed, and mistreated the Israelites (Exodus 1:10-14). On top of that, this pharaoh even demanded the death of their male infants in Exodus 1:22, *"And Pharaoh charged all his people, saying, Every son that is born ye shall cast into the river, and every daughter ye shall save alive."* At this time Moses was born as one of those first male children under that edict (Exodus 2:2; 1:6-24; Psalm 105:22-27; Acts 7:15-21). Moses, in accord with that edict, was *"cast into the river,"* not to die, but wholly entrusted into the providence and loving care of the Most High God (Exodus 2:3; Acts 7:20-21).

In the ultimate twist, God used one of those first children to be under that edict. Moses, a condemned child, but kept alive in faith was cast into the river–a form of baptism into death, taken up–a preview of the resurrection, preserved, and even highly educated in that same pharaoh's household (Exodus 2:1-11). Eighty years later God carefully engaged that same Moses to bring about the removal of that dynasty.

After the multi-part series of confrontations and opportunities for repentance carefully detailed in the book of Exodus God stopped the progression of that dynasty and its schemes by the death of pharaoh's firstborn son (Exodus 11:5; 12:29-30). Then God destroyed both that pharaoh and Satan's work when that pharaoh was drowned in the sea with his whole army (Exodus 14:9-28). These things connected the book of Job directly to that pharaoh who arose who *"knew not Joseph."*

Comparisons of wealth

Three additional details were necessary to consider in this time placement of Job. The first significant piece of information was in Job 1:2-3 where the text said, *"there were born unto him seven sons and three daughters ... [plus] ... his substance also was seven thousand sheep, and three thousand camels, and five hundred yoke of oxen, and five hundred she asses, and a very great household."* The statements of Job's character, his amount of children, and the details of his wealth as described by livestock provided the introduction to the man named Job.

The closing phrase in the third verse gave a statement of comparison, *"that this man was the greatest of all the men of the east."* Then the text further supported this comparison by describing the feasting of his sons and daughters in turn, perhaps a monthly rotation or birth anniversary. This expression of comparison to *"the men of the east"* urged the question, compared to whom?

Prior to Abraham no person in the Scriptures was described by wealth, only he had this original epithet. Abraham had 318 trained servants (Genesis 14:14) and described himself as rich (Genesis 14:23) by age eighty-five. His son Ishmael was promised to be blessed, fruitful, multiplied, and begin a great nation with twelve princes (Genesis chpt. 17).

God promised to Abraham that nations and kings would come from him (Genesis 17:6). When the Philistine Abimelech had taken Sarah by entering Abraham's camp and carrying her away (Genesis 20:2-3), he restored his breach by giving unto Abraham these items: sheep, oxen, men and women servants, plus 1,000 pieces of silver (Genesis 20:14-16). This kind of restoration and degree of generosity of gifts to secure forgiveness was never done toward a poor man, but only granted for a leader of great wealth and significant power (Genesis 21:22).

Later in life when Abraham had acquired more and was 140 years of age (Genesis 24:1) the text stated, almost in an offhand manner, *"the Lord had blessed Abraham in all things."* This blessing, as suggested in the previous texts, was immense. Abraham finished his years dwelling in the plains of Mamre Genesis 13:18), by Beersheba (Genesis 21:30-32), and Hebron (Genesis 22:19; 35:27, Kirjatharba), which were separate names for parts of the same area. Here he secured a burying place for 400 shekels of silver (Genesis 24:16).

This wealth was emphasized when Isaac moved westward to Gerar when the second famine in Canaan came (Genesis 26:1, 6). Isaac, after Abraham had died, was described as exceedingly wealthy (Genesis 26:12-14) to the point of envy by the Philistines. Isaac was sent away eastward (back toward Mamre, Hebron, Beersheba) because he was viewed as a threat with his vast array of servants (Genesis 26:16, 27). A while later the Philistine leaders came from the west to make a treaty (Genesis 26:26-31) with Isaac while he lived by Beersheba in the east (vs 32).

All of this was shown to reveal the background to compare to the statement of Job's wealth. If Job acquired this wealth during the lifetimes of Abraham or Isaac, he certainly was not mentioned nor matched their stated wealth. Since Abraham (Genesis 24:50) and later Isaac (Genesis 25:5, 11) were so described this highly suggested Job came after these two great men.

Jacob's growing wealth was quite evident in Jacob's gift to Esau (Genesis 32:13-15). Then Jacob came to live nearer to Isaac before his death. After Isaac died the great wealth of Isaac was portioned and added to that already acquired by Esau (Genesis 32:6) and Jacob (Genesis 32:3-5).

The two camps of Esau and Jacob when added to that of Isaac was too much for the land to bear. They were separated by Esau when he took his family and property and moved farther eastward into the area of mount Seir (Genesis 36:1-8). Thus the Scriptures stated that there were three men of significant wealth living in the east at the same time, but Job was not mentioned there.

Four successive men of great wealth were described, all in one family line. Jacob remained and dwelled in southeastern Canaan for some years before the third famine in Canaan arrived. This famine was in all lands, extended worldwide, and greatly affected everyone (Genesis 41:56-57). This famine diminished both Jacob's wealth and that of Esau's family. After two years of famine (Genesis 45:11) Jacob and his growing family removed from Canaan and went down into Egypt [A-290]. They were sustained there and grew until the promised year of deliverance came (Genesis 15:13-16, [A-505]).

When Job was recognized as Jacob's grandson through Issachar, that he returned from Egypt into southeastern Canaan after the famine ended, practiced the faith and conduct of Abraham, and thus was an inheritor of Abraham's extended blessing we can truly understand the statement of Job's wealth. For in turn Abraham, Isaac, and Jacob were promised such a blessing to their progeny (Genesis 28:12-15; 30:43–31:1; 31:16; 32:28). Isaac, Jacob, and Issachar carried on God's description of Abraham which in turn extended to Job.

> For I know him, that he will command his children and his household after him, and they shall keep the way of the Lord, to do justice and judgment; that the Lord may bring upon Abraham that which he hath spoken of him." (Genesis 18:19)

Jacob's sons' wealth was started at Shechem (Genesis 34:27-29). Jacob was given a further blessing of prosperity at Bethel (Genesis 35:11-12, 15). Under the lineage and faith of Abraham plus this last promise from God (as just cited), Job was blessed when he dwelled in Canaan in that same land in the east (Job 1:3).

The sons of Esau were these (Genesis 36:9-14): by Adah: Eliphaz; by Basemath: Reuel; by Aholibamah: Jeush, Jaalam, and Korah. From Eliphaz came Teman, Omar, Zepho, Gatam, and Kenaz. From Reuel came Nahath, Zerah, Shammah, and Mizzah. These were called dukes or tribal leaders (Genesis 36:15-17). The grandsons (24th generation) and great-grandsons of Esau (25th generation) along with later descendants of Abraham by Keturah, who also dwelled in the east (Genesis 25:6), were some of the actual individuals to whom Job was compared in Job 1:3.

These men and any others, *"all the men of the east,"* were juxtaposed for wealth and status at Job's age of seventy years. They, of course, included Eliphaz, Bildad, Zophar, Elihu, and other significant men, i.e. their near kinsmen. At this time period [A-340–352] Job was plainly described as *"the greatest."*

Though not explicitly stated as a comparison in the text, another or second comparison was made when Job had died at the end of his 140 year life [A-410–422]. Job had acquired over the next seventy years, *"fourteen thousand sheep, and six thousand camels, and a thousand yoke of oxen, and a thousand she asses [plus] seven sons and three daughters"* (Job 42:12-13). This second direct comparison was implied since that text carefully restated the number of sons, the number of daughters, and the details of his wealth again. At age 140 God had doubled the amount of possessions, doubled the total number of his children, and doubled the years of life Job had recorded at age seventy.

Abraham's family descending through Isaac had demonstrated as a portion of their blessing somewhat increased life spans compared to others in their same generation level from Adam. Eliphaz, great-grandson of Esau, was born sometime before [A-267] (25th generation) at age eighty or more was sitting in front of Job. But seventy years later from this Eliphaz had died and the wealth of his son(s) was compared to Job at his death.

Bildad (23rd generation), a son of Shuah, was born before [~A-267]. Bildad was also age eighty or more before Job and seventy years later had died, so that Bildad's son(s) were compared at Job's death. [age 80 + 70 years = 150 years] Zophar the Naamathite (24th generation) was suggested to have been born before or in [A-267] and age eighty when he sat before Job. Adding seventy more years, Zophar died before Job at age 140 [A-410–422] with any of his sons compared to Job.

Elihu, son of Barachel, was the youngest man before Job. He was born from [A-300–312] with the best fit birth year in [A-307] and generation twenty-three from Adam. He was at age forty before Job and with seventy more years probably still alive.

Only Elihu remained to directly compare to Job's wealth and status at Job's death. Others were the near kinsmen to Eliphaz, Bildad, and Zophar along with any more significant men of the east living at Job's death. Under the umbrella of God's blessing upon Abraham and his progeny through Isaac, Job had increased more in seventy years starting over from the pieces of money and earrings of gold given to him by his family and acquaintances (Job 42:11) than Elihu had amassed in his 110 years.

Notable beauty compared

The third significant comparison to consider given in the book of Job was written in the third from the last verse. Job 42:15 affirmed, *"in all the land were no women found so fair as the daughters of Job."* Only eleven times post Noahic flood was a specific woman called *"fair," "very fair," "fair to look upon," "very fair to look upon,"* or similar terms in the Scriptures. Sarah (Genesis 12:11, 14), Rebekah (Genesis 24:16; 26:7), a Philistine woman (Judges 15:2), Absalom's daughter Tamar (2 Samuel 14:27), Abishag a Shunammite (1 Kings 1:3-4), Vashti (Esther 1:11), Esther (Esther 2:7, 17); Job's last three daughters, Jemima, Kezia, and Kerenhappuch (Job 42:14-15), and the unnamed woman from Song of Solomon (Songs 1:15-16; 2:2, 10, 13; 4:10; 5:9; 6:10; etc.) were described as beautiful or very fair to behold.

Five of those ten named females were easily connected to Abraham and his progeny. Additionally, Job's three daughters were connected in this chapter. Remarkably, eight of ten "fair to look upon" women were connected to Abraham's family line.

That Vashti was a later descendant through Esau, through a son of Keturah, or even through Nahor from whom Rebekah came was possible, but unable to be determined. The last unnamed woman from the Song of Solomon was best understood, not as an ordinary person, but as the composite bride of Christ (2 Corinthians 11:2). Even then this bride was counted as a part of the offspring of Abraham by faith in God's promises (Romans 4:12-13, 16).

The meaningful comparison of Job to contemporary men of the east and the details of the beauty of Job's daughters were consistent with and more fully explained by the information given in Genesis and the ongoing narrative of Abraham's progeny. Job's lifetime was determined by the additional information given in Exodus. All of this when put together, i.e. the significant preponderance of evidence, pointed to Job as the son of Issachar. The whole array of information about Job's lineage, his comforters' lineages, his direct comparison to the men of the east, and the beauty of his daughters connected Job to Abraham and thus to God's blessing upon Abraham and his offspring.

If a comparison was made and there was no knowledge of the identity and circumstances of the people made in the comparison, then the comparison had vastly diminished or even no tangible meaning. Either the book of Job was fully connected to the ongoing narrative of God working through Abraham and his descendants or it stood alone with little or indiscernible meaning to some of its terms, expressions, and lineages.

Who wrote the book of Job?

The book of Job was given in two distinct parts. One part was staged outside of human experience and knowledge (until it was revealed much later). It had occurred in the spiritual realm. Another part was a brief description of Job and his circumstances, a set of experiences for Job, the discussions about the cause(s) of his calamities by four guests, God's communication to Job in the presence of the others, and a brief summary. The second or major part of the text occurred on earth. Those discussions about the cause(s) of his calamities were argued based upon the perspectives of the five individuals given by name, including Job himself.

The question to ask was this. When did the information regarding the part that transpired in the spiritual realm get transferred to a human who recorded the necessary background material and related it to Job's experience? Nothing in the book of Job told us when that happened or to whom the information was given. In fact, Job stated this in Job 23:8-9, *"Behold, I go forward, but he is not there; and backward, but I cannot perceive him: On the left hand, where he doth work, but I cannot behold him: he hideth himself on the right hand, that I cannot see him."*

When God talked to Job before the four witnesses He did not explain anything about the cause of Job's calamity. But God did ask lots of questions. That prompted searching outside of the five characters who argued the cause(s) of Job's afflictions to discern who was that recipient. God could have conveyed that information to any prophet He chose. But who made a good candidate?

From multiple perspectives, in proximity in time, in location, in receiving messages from God, in personal knowledge regarding peripheral information, that person was Moses. This same Moses wrote the Pentateuch as ascribed by Hebrew scholars in Jewish antiquity across many generations up through the quotations acknowledged to be from his pen in the New Testament. Moses wrote from previous written materials that started from Adam to Noah, proceeded from Noah to Abraham, and continued from Abraham through his multiple family sections.

Part of the larger extended family of Abraham were characters that were given by name and relationship in the book of Job. Moses had lived many years in Midian with Jethro and tended his flocks over broad ranging pastures (Exodus 2:15; 3:1; 7:7). Midian was an area a little west of Uz. That made Moses intersect with those people on the eastern areas, the front side since Exodus 2:15 said the west side was the backside.

Those eastern people, including Job's descendants, in their communications with Moses probably revealed the lineage and remarkable experience of Job. These details Moses could have verified with those elders who came out of Egypt. This was distinctly possible since Job's family from Egypt had visited him in Job 42:11.

> Then came there unto him all his brethren, and all his sisters, and all they that had been of his acquaintance before, and did eat bread with him in his house: and they bemoaned him, and comforted him over all the evil that the Lord had brought upon him: every man also gave him a piece of money, and every one an earring of gold.

This visit was the most probable time period and method of getting the discussions written into text when Job carefully related the whole experience in sequential order to them (Job 19:23-24). Then when his brothers, sisters, and other acquaintances returned they took this written material back to Egypt or to their homes in other areas of Canaan. It was worth preserving since God spoke before four other witnesses to one of their relatives. God could have revealed the first part of the book of Job that transpired in the spiritual realm to Moses in their face-to-face communications (Exodus 33:11; Deuteronomy 34:10). In this manner both parts were available to Moses during the wilderness journey to assemble into the text of the book of Job.

The information laid out in the book of Genesis provided the anchor for the start of divergent family lines as shown in the lineages above. Their early lineage from both Abraham and Nahor was given (Genesis 11:29; 22:20-23; 24:15, 24-27; 29:5). The book of Genesis provided the promises to Abraham's offspring through Isaac and Jacob. Isaac's descendants through Esau were also detailed. The line of Jacob was started in Genesis and extended in the books of Exodus and Job. Recall that Genesis 15:13-16 gave a distinct time limit to their slavery experience in Egypt and provided the background to their initial entry into Egypt.

This meant that the information in the books of Genesis and Exodus was tied together. The books of Genesis and Job were interwoven by the lineages of the individuals named. Plus the books of Job and Exodus were connected together by the timing of the deaths of *"all that generation"* entering Egypt including Job, Hezron, and Hamul as well as the arrival of that pharaoh subsequent to God's question to Satan in Job 1:8. *"And the Lord said unto Satan, Hast thou considered my servant Job, that there is none like him in the earth, a perfect and an upright man, one that feareth God, and escheweth evil?"*

We can only understand the Israelite dilemma through the background information about Joseph's leadership in Egypt, the famine, and the invitation offered by the earlier pharaoh to his large extended family to dwell for a while (sojourn) in Egypt. The text from Genesis told us that the Israelites were free to come into Egypt, receive help through the famine in return for service to the pharaoh of Joseph's day (Genesis 47:4-6), and then to depart at will (Job 42:11; Genesis 50). But the brothers returned again. No text stated or implied that every last Israelite stayed in Egypt. The actions of that first pharaoh given in the book of Exodus cannot stand isolated from the necessary material in Genesis and pertinent information given in Job.

Readers of the book of Job must have the prior material in Genesis to make any sense of the lineage of the five individuals named in it or of the comparisons made. The book of Job cannot be given a proper time frame without the material in both Genesis and Exodus. The depth of the

Israelite experience given in the book of Exodus stood adrift without the prior background material from both Genesis and Job.

Here we are reminded that Moses had access to all of this information by way of the congregation of Israel in the wilderness. Not only was this true but also Moses was a recipient of the directives made upon the arrival of that pharaoh and became an instrument in the demise of that dynasty. The simplest reason Job was not given any ancestry in the book of Job was because that was already detailed by Moses near the end of Genesis.

The book of Genesis also provided the direction of dispersal for the sons of Keturah where many years later one descendant appeared before Job. Genesis also gave the necessary pieces for Abraham's brother Nahor which helped establish that one of his offspring sat before Job. Distinct information about Jacob's twin Esau, when he moved and where he dwelled with his growing family, confirmed that one of his descendants attempted to console Job.

The book of Job had named five men and three women for a total of eight individuals whose ancestry can only be determined from the core material given in Genesis. Early information given in the book of Job provided the underlying setting for that pharaoh in Exodus who arose, oppressed the Israelites, enslaved them, and sought to kill their male infants.

Because of the three-way integration of material one author intimately acquainted with all of the inter-relationships was required who in turn wrote specific, connectable, yet incomplete details in each book. But this author gave sufficient information when all three books were carefully searched and integrated together. Each of these three books required parts of two other books to bring out the whole picture. This made Genesis, Job, and Exodus an interwoven triad with carefully separated yet necessarily integrated textual material.

Only one person could thoroughly know the material and cohesively write out these three significantly different books with the necessary complementary information given in the other two books. All of this pointed to only one man, the author—Moses. Moses wrote from both personal experience and the material of others about his own family who had lived in Egypt in the early part of the book of Exodus. All three books were written during the wilderness journey [A-505-545]. Plus this information and time placement of the book of Job provided the seventh verification of the time duration of Israel in Egypt.

These intertwined connections to Moses' writings in Genesis and Exodus greatly enhanced the introductory material in the book of Job, enriched our understanding of Job's experience, firmly established the ancestry of at least four of the five men, of three named daughters, and confirmed Job's one hundred forty-year life span. The introductory material from Job explained more of the underlying setting for the events of the book of Exodus. The breadth of material presented and explained reinforced that Moses was the author of Job because the whole interrelated scenario was quite personal to him. Close examination of Scripture always revealed the vast interwoven relationship of the textual material and reinforced its inherent truthfulness.[K]

Do you remember that Aaron was born in [A-422], Hezron & Hamul (and possibly Kohath) died in [A-423], and Moses was born in [A-425]? The book of Job written by Moses carefully integrated with numerous small details that he wrote out in the books of Genesis and Exodus. When all of these texts in the triad of Genesis, Exodus, and Job were woven carefully together they gave a high level of certainty to the narrow twelve-year time range for the primary events of the book of Job, but not the exact year.

The author's best fit came from Bible numerology where the number eleven denotes disorder, disorganization, chaos. Thus seventy-seven years [7 x 11 = 77] transpired from Job's experience in [A-347] or 1604 BC until that Pharaoh arose in [A-424] or 1527 BC.

Using Job's own words

Job spoke to Bildad and said two specific things in Job 19:25-27. First he said, *"For I know that my redeemer liveth, and that he shall stand at the latter day upon the earth."* The first part of this longer statement was drawn from Jacob's words in Genesis 49:8-10 when Jacob gave a final

---

K. Harrison, C., *Bible Cross-References*. Please explore a unique visualization of these inter-connections using more than 63,000 cross references at: http://www.chrisharrison.net/index.php/Visualizations/BibleViz, accessed 6/1/2019.

blessing to his twelve sons. That specific revelation of the future given by prophecy occurred when Jacob was 147 years old in [A-307].

Job referred back to Shiloh coming to earth when Job spoke of *"my redeemer."* Job had understood, integrated, and applied Jacob's words about *"the people gathering unto him"* when Job said, *"he shall stand at the latter day upon the earth."*

Then Job added a second part, *"And though after my skin worms destroy this body, yet in my flesh shall I see God: Whom I shall see for myself, and mine eyes shall behold, and not another; though my reins be consumed within me."* Here Job was pointing back to the event of Abraham with Isaac at Mount Moriah where Isaac was given back to Abraham as if he was just killed and raised to life again. This understanding of that scenario was confirmed in Hebrews 11:17-19, *"Accounting that God was able to raise him up, even from the dead; from whence also he received him in a figure."*

Job affirmed, from prior information passed from Abraham to Isaac to Jacob and his progeny, that there was to be a resurrection of the dead, that Job would stand alive again, and then come before God the redeemer, whom Jacob had called Shiloh. The first of these specific granular details occurred when Abraham was over 115 years of age. Abraham's six sons through Keturah and both Esau's and Jacob's lineages could know about the resurrection through Isaac's experience on mount Moriah, which came years after Ishmael was sent away. Abraham's journey and return with Isaac was carefully recorded, preserved, and passed to Isaac and his successive lineage.

The Messianic detail which was spoken as a prophecy by Jacob was given in Egypt in [A-307] about 190 years later. That meant the combination of these two truths (both recorded and passed along) were only available to someone who lived after this later date and descended from Jacob. If you have been attentive you may have noticed that Job was age thirteen at entry to Egypt, at age thirty when Jacob died, and forty years later at age seventy for the book of Job.

In Job 23:12 Job had responded to Eliphaz saying, *"Neither have I gone back from the commandment of his lips; I have esteemed the words of his mouth more than my necessary food."* Job had endeavored to live out God's words from Genesis 18:19, *"For I know him, that he will command his children and his household after him, and they shall keep the way of the Lord, to do justice and judgment; that the Lord may bring upon Abraham that which he hath spoken of him."*

From the time when God gave directives to Noah both before and after the great flood, no one else was recorded as having been given commandments by which to live until Abraham. Only Abraham was spoken about in this type of context of passing on God's commandments. All of these parts, from the lineages of those who sat before Job, the comparisons of wealth, of longevity, of beauty for his daughters, the connection with the oppressing pharaoh, Job's words referring to God's revelations to his recent ancestry, and more, pointed to Job being the descendant of Abraham through Jacob.

Answering unasked questions

In paragraph three of Section II, Part 2., a simple statement was presented about how to interpret Exodus 12:40 by placing part of the text into a parenthesis and adding punctuation, *"Now the sojourning, of the children of Israel (who dwelt in Egypt), was four hundred and thirty years."* We expect that some Israelites departed from Egypt after the five remaining years of famine were ended. The brothers had spoken to pharaoh and requested to "sojourn" in Egypt only because of the famine (Genesis 47:4).

At the least, Job and his growing family, Benjamin's or Simeon's family leading to Zophar the Naamathite, and perhaps various other Israelites returned to Canaan. Job was recorded as living outside of Egypt in Job 1:1, *"There was a man in the land of Uz, whose name was Job."* This was reinforced in Job 42:16, *"After this lived Job [to] an hundred and forty years, and saw his sons, and his sons' sons, even four generations."*

This meant that Moses in Exodus 12:40 referred only to those Israelite descendants that had remained in Egypt and dwelled there. They had sojourned through Abraham, Isaac, Jacob, and their fathers in Canaan and now for 215 years in Egypt up to their departure for a total duration of *"four hundred and thirty years."* The explanatory parenthetical phrase, *"of the children of Israel who dwelt in Egypt,"* was used by Moses to carefully reinforce that most Israelites stayed in Egypt, but some did not.

That information raised another question. Did Israel in their journey away from Egypt collect those separated Israelites on the way to their inheritance in Canaan? That would have been an antecedent to our evangelism today.

Israel in their journey went past Midian (Exodus 18:1-8; Numbers 10:28-30), proceeded through Uz, stayed in the wilderness of Paran (Numbers 10:12; 12:16), went around the south side of Edom, and journeyed northward around the east side of Moab past Arnon to Heshbon (Numbers 21:4-31). At the various encampments Israel could have communicated with and invited their distant relatives to join with them and receive the benefits promised to Abraham's descendants (Genesis 15:18-21; 50:24). [See: Numbers 26:23-25] Moses personally invited and encouraged some individuals to join with Israel.

> And Moses said unto Hobab, the son of Raguel the Midianite, Moses' father in law, We are journeying unto the place of which the Lord said, I will give it you: come thou with us, and we will do thee good: for the Lord hath spoken good concerning Israel. (Numbers 10:29)

> Now Heber the Kenite, which was of the children of Hobab the father in law of Moses, had severed himself from the Kenites, and pitched his tent unto the plain of Zaanaim, which is by Kedesh. (Judges 4:11)

What we learned:

1. One person from Abraham's brother's family and three of Abraham's descendants came and sat in front of Job who was their kinsman and Abraham's great-great-grandson.

2. The narrow time period of twelve years in which Job was born.

3. Job's siblings and acquaintances freely traveled out of Egypt and returned before that Pharaoh arose.

4. The additional use of the expression, *"and all that generation."*

5. That Job only lived 140 years and not 210 years.

6. How to connect the book of Job to when the new pharaoh arose that *"knew not Joseph"* reflecting the irony of Satan's man of power defeated by way of an infant wholly entrusted to God.

7. How to use the Scripture to go beyond the obvious and make meaningful connections to other events.

SECTION II Part 4.

Make a visual tool:

Add a note to the timeline. The book of Job occurred in the period of [A-340–352]. [Author's best fit: A-347 or 1604 BC, fourteen years before Joseph died in A-361.] Job died in the period of [A-410–422] before [A-423]. [Author's best fit: A-417 or 1534 BC.] Start at Abram-75, measure 6 13/16 inches (just under 17.3 cm) to the right and label it, "Book of Job" and "Abram-347." Joseph died at just under 7 3/16 inches (18.2 cm) from Abram-75. Label it "Joseph died, 110," and "Abram-361."

Can Rahab of Jericho be the wife of Salmon?

Part 5: The children of Jacob and the intersections of their descendants.

Rahab and Rachab

The Scriptures mention Rahab in both the Old and New Testaments, and they speak of a Rachab. Some think that the verse in Matthew 1:5 meant that Salmon married Rahab of Jericho and that Boaz was conceived from that union. The texts mentioning Rahab (Ραάβ) include: Joshua 2:1-24; 6:17-25; Hebrews 11:31 and James 2:25. A Rachab (Ραχάβ) was named in the lineage of Jesus given in Matthew 1:5, "*And Salmon begat Booz of Rachab; and Booz begat Obed of Ruth; and Obed begat Jesse.*"

The word sources in Hebrew and Greek were: Strong's Hebrew number: H7343, Word: בָּחָר Pronounced: raw-khawb', Origin: the same as 7342; proud; Rachab, a Canaanitess; a harlot in Jericho: Rahab. Strong's Greek number: G4460, Word: Ραάβ (Hebrews 11:31; James 2:25); Ραχάβ (Matthew 1:5), Pronounced: hrah-ab', Rahab = "wide," a harlot of Jericho.

Various translations of Matthew 1:5 include these which emphasize Rahab.

> Salmon the father of Boaz, whose mother was Rahab, Boaz the father of Obed, whose mother was Ruth, Obed the father of Jesse. AMPC

> Salmon was the father of Bo'az (his mother was Rachav), Bo'az was the father of 'Oved (his mother was Rut), 'Oved was the

father of Yishai. CJB

Salmon, Boaz (his mother was Rahab), Obed (his mother was Ruth), Jesse. CEV

Salmon was the father of Boaz, whose mother was Rahab. Boaz was the father of Obed, whose mother was Ruth. Obed was the father of Jesse. CSB

And Salmon fathered Boaz by Rahab, and Boaz fathered Obed by Ruth, and Obed fathered Jesse. DLNT

Salmon was the father of Boaz. (Boaz's mother was Rahab.) Boaz was the father of Obed. (Obed's mother was Ruth.) Obed was the father of Jesse. EXB

Salmon the father of Boaz (by Rahab), Boaz the father of Obed (by Ruth), Obed the father of Jesse. NET

To arrive at a complete answer to the chapter title's question, "Can Rahab of Jericho be the wife of Salmon?," numerous other texts must be brought forward and applied. These texts were necessary to consider in order to understand when Salmon was born and then to determine if his life period sufficiently overlapped that of Rahab of Jericho to have married her and together produced a son named Boaz.

The lineage of Levi and Judah intersected in Aaron's marriage to Elisheba and the birth of their progeny. Numerous scriptural texts have a bearing upon Judah's lineage and the timing of individual births. These established when Salmon could have been born.

Naashon, son of Aminadab and father of Salmon, was named as the prince of Judah leading the tribe in their placement around the tabernacle in the wilderness (Numbers 2:3; 1 Chronicles 2:10). [See: Part 1, Naashon] Naashon, therefore, was born before the exodus from Egypt and was of sufficient age to be a tribal leader. He was greater than twenty years of age at the census in Exodus 28:1 and more probably at fifty to seventy years of age. Salmon could have been born any time in the wilderness, but to have his birth earlier required super-sized ages for his male descendants Boaz, Obed, and Jesse to reach unto David.

If Naashon was less than twenty at the census in Numbers 1:18-19, then he lived through the wilderness and many years past the entry to

Canaan. But how then could he be a *"prince of the children of Judah"* as a youth and not have another older male of the tribe of Judah be established as the primary leader? That was ruled out.

If Salmon had Boaz earlier in age, then Boaz, Obed, and Jesse must each have sons later in age. But that stretched ages at their sons's birth and their life spans way beyond credible. Most likely Salmon was born as late as possible, i.e. in the year before entry to Canaan or within a few months after entry.

If his mother was less than twenty years of age at the exodus from Egypt, she was less than sixty at the end of the forty-year journey and easily of age to bear a child at that time. Naashon must have died in the wilderness since all those twenty and upwards at the census (Numbers 1:1-18) were never to enter Canaan, except Caleb and Joshua (Numbers 14:30, 38; 26:64-65; 32:12). This information made great restrictions upon the time range in which Salmon could have been born. This enabled a determination of whether his life period sufficiently overlapped that of Rahab of Jericho to have her become his wife.

The time span from the year of entry into Canaan to David's birth^L [A-545 to A-911] was 366 years [366 / 4 = 91.5 years average unto the following male generation]. Two potential pathways of lineage for David were given in Scripture. The shortest route was from Salmon to Boaz, to Obed, to Jesse, and then to David. The complete examination of both required bringing together numerous passages and Biblical principles and applying each to this scenario.

The first text was that of Psalm 90:10, *"The days of our years are threescore years and ten; and if by reason of strength they be fourscore years, yet is their strength labour and sorrow; for it is soon cut off, and we fly away."* This informed us that life spans were shortening and not to expect exorbitant

---

L. David's birth year was calculated in this manner. The exodus from Egypt was in [A-505 or 1446 BC]. In 1 Kings 6:1 it stated that 479 years transpired from the exodus from Egypt to when Solomon started the temple in the beginning of the 4th year of his reign. The expression "in the 480th year" meant 479 years had gone by and the 480th year had just started. [A- 505 + 479 = A-984]. Then subtract from [A-984] the first three years of Solomon's reign, and get [A-981] when he started. Add back <1 year of co-regency for David's death in [A-982]. For David's life span note that he started to reign over Judah at age thirty. He had seven and one-half years of rule over Judah and then a thirty-three-year reign over all Israel. Subtract those years [A-982 - 70.5] to get David's birth year [A-911 or 1040 BC].

ages for Salmon, Boaz, Obed, and Jesse for the birth of their respective sons. Second, Scriptures have already laid out old age births in recent centuries and this template must be considered and applied.

Third, Sarah was ninety with the conception and birth of Isaac, and she lived to 127 years (Genesis 23:1-2). This was at 71% of her life span. Abraham's last son was Shuah through marriage to Keturah (Genesis 25). He was born when Abraham was at or just before 147 of his 175 years which was at or just less than 84% of his life span.

We must not require unnamed miracles of extreme age at the births of the sons of Salmon (Ruth 4:20; 1 Chronicles 2:11), Boaz (Ruth 4:21), Obed (Ruth 4:21), and Jesse (Ruth 4:21-22; 1 Samuel 17:12) to reach to David. Most likely Salmon was born just before entry to Canaan or within a few months afterward [~A-544-545]. In turn that implied a workable younger age for Naashon to conceive his son Salmon before his own death in the wilderness. With Salmon born about [A-545] and matching the ratio shown for Abraham, Naashon could have a late born son at ninety-six years.

Table 3. The calculated ages for begetting or birth with unusually long life spans to reach from Salmon to David, if the ratio of 0.81 was used. Here the next four generations lived much longer lives than others.

Ages required for birth of respective sons to reach to David.

0.81 Ratio	Birth year	Expected Life span	Son's Birth year	Age at son's birth	Year of death
Naashon	449	118	545	96	545
Salmon	545	118	641	96	663
Boaz	641	115	734	93	756
Obed	734	112	825	91	846
Jesse	825	110	**911**	86	935
David	**911**	70.5			982

Table 3 displayed this possibility which forced Naashon to have an expected life span of 118 years, conceive his son Salmon at age ninety-six, and then die right after Salmon's conception before entry into Canaan. [See: Part 1. footnote F] Salmon would need to have Boaz born at age 96 of 118 years. In turn Boaz at ninety-three years of a definitely longer life span of 115 years could have Obed.

Obed at ninety-one years of a definitely longer life span of 112 years could have Jesse. Then Jesse at eighty-six years of a definitely longer life span of 110 years could have David. [Add 96 + 93 + 91 + 86 to reach the 366 years to David's birth in A-911.] This potential scenario was under special conditions with each generation living out extra long lives. That scenario was displayed in Table 3 under those ideal conditions.

Do you remember part of our introductory premise? The requirement was asserted that all relevant Scripture facts must be sought, assembled, and applied to get reliable results from which to draw any conclusions with a high confidence level in the results. With that in mind, note that David took his parents to be protected by the king of Moab in 1 Samuel 22:1-4, *"And David went thence to Mizpeh of Moab: and he said unto the king of Moab, Let my father and my mother, I pray thee, come forth, and be with you, till I know what God will do for me."*

This was when David was about twenty-six or twenty-seven years of age (1 Samuel 17:12; 22:3). Start with the scenario of Jesse at age eighty-six for David's birth as shown in table 3 and add twenty-six years to reach 112 years of age. This length of life span surpassed Jesse's extra long 110 year life expectancy. (See Tables 3 and 4)

Table 4. The calculated ages for begetting or birth with unusually long life spans to reach from Salmon to David, if the ratio of 0.84 was used and each father had a son at the last possible age.

Ages required for birth of respective sons to reach to David.

0.84 Ratio	Birth year	Expected Son's Life span	Son's Birth year	Age at son's birth	Year of death
Naashon	446	118	545	99	545
Salmon	545	115	641	96	660
Boaz	641	112	735	94	753
Obed	735	108	825	90	843
Jesse	825	102	**911**	84	927
David	**911**	70.5			982

Examine both tables and then compare Table 3 to Table 4. Then note four problems: 1) the exceptional life spans, 2) the ages at their respective sons' births that these scenarios generated across multiple generations, and, 3) the immense problem with Jesse outliving his enhanced life span. This scenario in Table 4 forced Naashon to have an expected life span of 118 years, conceive his son Salmon at age ninety-nine, and then die right after Salmon's conception before Israel's entry into Canaan. That scenario also forced Jesse to live to 110 years which was eight or more years past his life span to fulfill David taking his parents to the king of Moab with Jesse dying later.

The expression "an old man"

In this time period reaching eighty years qualified for a very "*old*" or "*very aged*" man when applying 2 Samuel 19:32, "*Now Barzillai was a very aged man, even fourscore years old: and he had provided the king of sustenance while he lay at Mahanaim; for he was a very great man*" [of wealth]. Barzillai's carefully stated age established that this expression or descriptive title meant the person had reached or exceeded eighty years. The expression, "*an old man*", was used of the second Eli, Meraioth, just before he died at age ninety-eight when the text in 1 Samuel 4:15-18 stated, "*he was an old man.*" This was confirmed in the New Testament with Anna the prophetess in the text of Luke 2:36-37.

> And there was one Anna, a prophetess, the daughter of Phanuel, of the tribe of Aser: she was of a great age, and had lived with an husband seven years from her virginity; And she was a widow of about fourscore and four years, which departed not from the temple, but served God with fastings and prayers night and day.

David was also described as "very old" in 1 Kings 1:15. In David's case as a seasoned warrior in many battles it was exceptionally unlikely for him to come out unscathed. With the effects of wounds, bruises, and severe fatigue affecting the aging of his body it appears that 1 Kings 1:15 was describing him as if he was wearing out at age eighty or so. But David died about age seventy and one-half as shown earlier in Footnote[L]. The same type of expression was true of Jesse the father of David, "*Now David was the son of that Ephrathite of Bethlehem-judah, whose name was Jesse; and he had eight sons: and the man went among men for an old man in the days of Saul*" (1 Samuel 17:12).

Consider the extra comment, "*the man went among men for an old man in the days of Saul,*" a parenthetical statement about Jesse. Now Saul was unknown in Israel before his anointing, so "*the days of Saul*" referred to the period of his anointing and reign as king over Israel. That was a wide window of forty years in which *"the man [Jesse] went among men for an old man."* If this meant that Jesse was eighty years old when Saul was inaugurated as king in [A-901], then Jesse was born in the year [A-821] and age ninety at David's birth.

The scenario in Table 5 made Jesse age ninety at David's birth in [A-911] and skewed other data. That scenario was wholly unworkable because it made nonsense of the statement about David taking his parents to the king of Moab where Jesse died sometime later. Then Jesse must outlive his extra long life span by more than nine extra years [90 + ~26 = 116 + time in Moab = >116]. [See: Section V. The reign of Saul]

To use the slightly lower ratio of 0.81 for Jesse in Table 5 he must have an expected life span of 111 years and out live that by five years for David to take him to Moab. As presented in Table 5 Jesse must outlive his expected life span of 107 years by more than nine years. All four generations after Naashon still needed to live much longer lives than any others. Neither Table 3 nor Table 4 worked with ordinary life spans and birth ages for these fathers and Table 5 did not work at all.

Table 5. The results if Jesse was age eighty when Saul was anointed in [A-901]. This table showed calculated ages for begetting or birth with unusually long life spans to reach from Salmon to David. If the ratio of 0.81 was used, except for Jesse (0.84 x 107), five generations of fathers had a son at a very late age.

Ages required for birth of respective sons to reach to David.

	Birth year	Expected life span	Son's Birth year	Age at son's birth	Year of death
0.81 Ratio					
Naashon	445	118	541	96	545
Salmon	541	118	637	96	659
Boaz	637	115	730	93	752
Obed	730	112	821	91	842
0.84 ratio, Jesse	821	107	**911**	90	928
David	**911**	70.5			982

Jesse became "an old man"

Jesse became eighty years of age sometime in Saul's forty-year reign. Six possibilities existed where Jesse was directly or indirectly mentioned when he could have become eighty years of age: 1) when David was born (Ruth 4:22), 2) when David was anointed (1 Samuel 16:1), 3) when David was called to serve Saul (1 Samuel 16:15-23), 4) when David was sent to check on his brothers in the army where Goliath challenged Israel (1 Samuel 17:12-20), 5) when David took his father Jesse and his mother to Moab (1 Samuel 22:1-4), and, 6) another early year in those forty years.

If Jesse was eighty at David's birth, then that meant Jesse was 106 when he was transported to Moab for protection from Saul's rampage against David. If Jesse became eighty when going to Moab when David was about twenty-six years of age, then the time span from Salmon to Jesse was greatly increased. Some other scenario was much more probable which left these four choices: 1) when David was anointed (age 12-14), 2) when David was called to serve Saul, 3) when David was sent to check on his brothers (age 17-18), and, 4) another early year during Saul's reign.

Solutions one and two decreased the spread of time between individual son's births from Salmon to David. And if Jesse became eighty years of age later, this increased the time between these individual son's births. More pieces must be considered before an answer can be determined for Jesse's age at David's birth.

Life spans and birth ages

This brought a set of three tensions, possible life spans, age for copulation and birth, and decreasing life spans, each of which must be honestly satisfied. Note there was no statement in the Scriptures about any miracle of longevity or of extreme late in life conception from Salmon to David. Applying the ratios mentioned above became necessary to get to a balanced, consistent solution.

Table 3 applied the ratio (0.81) for a near maximum age for male sexual reproduction. While Table 3 displayed calculations with decreasing ages it had exceptionally long life spans for the period, much greater than Joshua's 110 years of age at death. As shown under those ideal conditions with extra long life spans, that scenario made Jesse age eighty in the year [A-905] when Saul was in the fifth year of his forty-year reign [A-901-941].

Rahab of Jericho

Now we must consider Rahab of Jericho who was named in Joshua 2:1-24; 6:17-25; Hebrews 11:31 and James 2:25. Rachab was named in

Matthew 1:5 in the royal lineage list of Jesus. This verse stated, "*And Salmon begat Booz of Rachab; and Booz begat Obed of Ruth; and Obed begat Jesse.*" If this Rachab was understood to be Rahab of Jericho, she was at a minimum about age eighteen or more at the time of the spies going to Jericho (Joshua 2:1).

To fulfill the request of Joshua, "*Go view the land, even Jericho,*" the two spies "*went, and came into an harlot's house, named Rahab, and lodged there.*" Rahab of Jericho was described as owning her own home and a harlot / innkeeper, therefore, not a youth. This placed her minimum age at eighteen and probably much greater (Joshua 2:1, 4; 6:22) at the entrance of Israel into Canaan. Note that her parents were alive in Joshua 2:12-13, 18 and 6:23 which implied that she lived in a separate house when considering the statement, "*thou shalt bring ..., home unto thee*" (v.18).

Start with the year of entry to Canaan and subtract eighteen years [A-545 - 18 = 527] for Rahab of Jericho's latest possible birth year. If Salmon was born about the year of the entry as discussed above, then Rahab was about eighteen years or greater in age than Salmon. When Salmon was twenty she was about thirty-eight or more years in age.

By using Salmon at age ninety-six (Table 3, above) to have Boaz and supposing Rahab of Jericho was the mother, then she was at least 114 years old to give birth [545 + 96 - 527 = 114]. Now that was a far greater miracle than Sarah at ninety of 127 years or 71 percent of her life span. With an 114-year life span that ratio calculated to eighty-one years for the birth of a child or using the same ratio it calculated to age 114 of an expected 161-year life span. This was not possible for Rahab of Jericho, especially when considering her ancestry, occupation, and potential diseases limiting her life. Salmon could not have married Rahab of Jericho and later conceived Boaz through her when he was about ninety-six years of age when she was 114 or older, if even alive.

Other scenarios and calculations

With either an earlier or later birth for Salmon unusually long life spans were required in succession for Salmon, Boaz, Obed and Jesse to reach to David. The longer potential pathway of lineage leading to David was given in Matthew 1:5, "*And Salmon begat Booz of Rachab; and Booz begat Obed of Ruth; and Obed begat Jesse.*" This inserted one more person not given in the male lineage of 1 Samuel 17:12, Ruth 4:20-22, and 1 Chronicles 2:1-15. We have explained above that Rahab of Jericho was not able to birth Boaz around 114 years of age.

Because Rachab was given in the lineage and when taken into the context of the information explained and detailed in Tables 3, 4 and 5 (above) the integrated information highly suggested that Rachab was a daughter of Salmon. That meant Boaz was her son and Salmon's grandson. In Genesis 31:22-28 about 370 years earlier Laban used the expression "sons" when referring to his grandsons and "daughters" when referring to his two natural daughters and to Dinah his granddaughter.

This meant the term "son" when used generically was referring to the next male descendant, the same as the "sons of Jacob" used in 1 Kings 18:31, Psalm 77:15, and Malachi 3:6. The term "son" in Luke 3:23-38 was also used that way in verse 23, *"being (as was supposed) the son of Joseph,"* and verse 32, *"Booz, which was the son of Salmon."* This was also true of the expression, "begat," used in Matthew 1:1-16 when three generations were excluded.

Now consider that the text of lineage in Matthew 1:8 had left out three successive generations given in the Old Testament scriptures: Jehoram (Joram) begat Ahaziah who begat Joash who begat Amaziah (2 Kings 8:25; 13:1–15:38; 2 Chronicles 22–25) who begat Ozias (aka: Uzziah and Azariah). But Matthew 1:8 said, *"And Asa begat Josaphat; and Josaphat begat Joram; and Joram begat Ozias."* These three middle generations between Joram and Ozias were sons that by parental marriage had a greater percentage of Omri's bloodline in the children than that of Judah. They were left out of the royal lineage for that reason. So if leaving out some unfit generations in the royal lineage was right or appropriate, then telling of a female generation that was left out was also right or proper in the text of Matthew 1:5.

Contemplate a tentative scenario. If Salmon married Rahab of Jericho, then their child was 50% Israelite and 50% foreigner. In turn, if that child married a foreigner, the next generation was 33% Israelite and 67% foreigner. That generation needed to marry an Israelite so their children were 50% Israelite and 50% foreigner. This tentative scenario required some intermediary generations until dominant Israelite lineage was

Can Rahab of Jericho be the wife of Salmon?

restored. A group of missing descendants could not be applied to Salmon and skipped over in the royal lineage given by Matthew without another passage in Scripture naming those individuals.

What happened when Rachab of Matthew 1:5 was being described as a daughter of Salmon and the mother of Boaz? Using that information made for workable ages for each generation from Salmon to David. When the same set of three tensions, possible life spans, age for birth, and decreasing life spans, with each honestly satisfied, were applied to Salmon through Jesse different results occurred. Table 6 was the result of when the five generations after Naashon have their children at 70% of their much more appropriate life expectancy. This did not require the necessity of greatly extended life spans and applying the 81% ratio for each generation as shown in Table 3.

Table 6. The life spans and birth ages to reach from Salmon to David with Rachab as Salmon's daughter, when the ratio of 0.70 was used except for Naashon.

Ages required for birth of offspring to reach to David with Salmon having a daughter Rachab.

0.70 Ratio	Birth year	Expected Life span	Son's Birth year	Age at son's birth	Year of death
Naashon	455	110	545	90	545
(0.82 ratio)					
Salmon	545	110	622	77	655
Rachab	622	107	696	74	729
(Matthew 1:5)					
Boaz	696	106	770	74	802
Obed	770	104	841	71	874
Jesse	841	98	**911**	70	939
David	**911**	70.5			982

Table 6 showed the benefits of God's care over those in the wilderness with a later age conception and subsequent birth just for Naashon's son. Then with Salmon at about seventy-seven years daughter Rachab was born [~A-622], she at about seventy-four years had a son when Boaz was born [~A-696] (Matthew 1:5), at about seventy-four years Obed was born of Ruth [~A-770], at about seventy-one years Jesse was born [~A-841], and at about seventy years David was born [A-911]. [77 + 74 + 74 + 71 + 70 = 366] A small amount of variation remained, but this placement was scripturally consistent with life spans and ratios for later age births to life spans.

The idea that Rachab was another generation can appear to be suspect. But this was not the only lineage list in the New Testament that added another person into the ancestral lineage of Jesus. Take a look at the list written by Luke who is known as an impeccable historian. Everything that was possible to be physically verified from his writings was examined by archaeologists and scholars and he passed careful scrutiny. Here is that text from Luke 3:35-36.

> Which was the son of Saruch (Serug), which was the son of Ragau (Reu), which was the son of Phalec (Peleg), which was the son of Heber (Eber), which was the son of Sala (Salah), Which was the son of Cainan, which was the son of Arphaxad, which was the son of Sem (Shem), which was the son of Noe (Noah), which was the son of Lamech.

This text gave an additional person, Cainan, between Arphaxad and Salah from Genesis 11:10-13. There were several possible ways to decipher it. The simplest and most straight forward method usually became the best solution. If Arphaxad had an early birth of a son named Cainan and likewise Cainan had an early birth of his son Salah, then this could occur across the thirty-five years given for Arphaxad at the birth of Salah. The simplest reason that Cainan was not given in the Genesis lineage list was that Cainan died early, perhaps before Salah's birth or long before Salah had grown and became an adult.

Then Arphaxad took his grandson Salah into his household, much like adoption, finished rearing him, and passed the family heritage and blessing on to Salah This not only give Salah the right to be counted as the next generation and heir in Genesis 11 but also did not contradict the ancestral detail given in Luke 3:35-36 (That scenario was very plausible if Cainan was truly in the original text or autograph.). If so, then both scripture texts in Matthew 1:5 and Luke 3:35-36 gave us missing pieces.

If Matthew 1:5 was discounted as accurately giving a generation for Rachab as a daughter of Salmon, then Boaz, Obed, and Jesse were born much later in age as shown above in Table 3. But the obvious conclusion was reasonable that Salmon named his daughter after Rahab of Jericho, since she was a notable contemporary person.^M

The general length of life at this time was decreasing from 110 years with Joshua, to about ninety-eight years for David's father Jesse, and down toward eighty plus for Barzilla [age 80 at A-968]. Barzilla stated that he expected to die relatively soon in 2 Samuel 19:33-37. In this same time period only Eli was reported to live to ninety-eight years. And his son's lives were cut short due to Eli's failure to restrain his corrupt sons in their Levitical service as priests (1 Samuel 2:12-36).

With Rachab providing another generation as shown in Table 6, the decreasing ages from seventy-seven years given for Salmon to beget Rachab, Rachab to birth Boaz, Boaz to beget Obed, and Obed to beget Jesse were thoroughly realistic and credible. This was true when considering, 1) that most healthy men can successfully copulate to a later age than women can conceive and gestate to birth, and 2) that their life spans were decreasing as stated in Psalm 90:10. But the scenario in Table 3 required exceptional hereditary factors or a long series of unnamed miracles to have four successive generations of fathers with extra long lives generate offspring when they were at about 81% instead of about 70% of their life spans.

These birth ages and generations when including Rachab spanned this time period without unnamed miracles and showed that there was little room to adjust their estimated birth times. Then only Naashon who was born in Egypt had the late aged birth and not any others (Nehemiah 9:19-21).

As shown in Table 6, divide age seventy-seven by 110 year life span. Compare this percentage to an eighty year life span to get male copulation with subsequent birth or female conception, gestation, and birth to about fifty-five to fifty-six years of age, which was truly realistic and credible. Two similar late aged female conceptions, gestations, and births occurred in Great Britain in the last sixty years and another similar birth occurred in early 2019 in India, all publicly reported in the news media. These support the reasoning presented about Salmon's daughter

---

M. If Rahab of Jericho was born on or before [A-527], as suggested, then she was about age ninety-five [A-527 + 95 = 622] and probably had recently died when this scenario occurred for the birth of Salmon's daughter [A-545 + 77 = 622]. This daughter was named to honor the faith of Rahab of Jericho.

having a son at a later age and fitting into David's ancestry.

Perhaps another son . . .

But there were more pieces from the Scripture to consider. If Naashon had another son born earlier than Salmon, he could have been twenty or more years old at the crossing of Jordan into Canaan. This older brother to Salmon could have married Rahab of Jericho. According to Mosaic Law stated in Deuteronomy 25:5-6 if a man died childless, then his brother (or next in lineage) could be required to raise up seed on behalf of the dead brother (see also Matthew 22:24; Mark 12:9; Luke 20:28).

> If brethren dwell together, and one of them die, and have no child, the wife of the dead shall not marry without unto a stranger: her husband's brother shall go in unto her, and take her to him to wife, and perform the duty of an husband's brother unto her. And it shall be, that the firstborn which she beareth shall succeed in the name of his brother which is dead, that his name be not put out of Israel. (Deuteronomy 25:5-6)

In this circumstance Salmon could have been required to take up the duty of marriage on behalf of a dead brother. This assumed that Rahab of Jericho was only eighteen to twenty years old at the destruction of her city. If Boaz was born through this scenario, he was born earlier when Rahab of Jericho was young enough to conceive and birth a child, most likely no later than age seventy at about [A-597]. But this circumstance, with Salmon at age fifty-two, forced Boaz, Obed, and Jesse to each have fourteen to fifteen greater years of age (641 - 597 = 44) at the births of their respective sons which was unrealistic and wholly unworkable as shown in Tables 3, 4, and 5.

Applying Mosaic law to the unique scenario of Ruth

The scenario from Deuteronomy 25:5-6 would not apply to Salmon who had a daughter. *"If brethren dwell together, and one of them die, and have no child, the wife of the dead shall not marry without unto a stranger: her husband's brother shall go in unto her, and take her to him to wife, and perform the duty of an husband's brother unto her. And it shall be, that the firstborn which she beareth shall succeed in the name of his brother which is dead, that his name be not put out of Israel."* But the scenario of Numbers 27:1-10 became applicable.

> Then came the daughters of Zelophehad, the son of Hepher, the son of Gilead, the son of Machir, the son of Manasseh, of the families of Manasseh the son of Joseph: and these are the names of his daughters; Mahlah, Noah, and Hoglah, and Milcah, and Tirzah. And they stood before Moses, and before Eleazar the priest, and before the princes and all the congregation, by the door of the tabernacle of the congregation, saying, Our father died in the wilderness, and he was not in the company of them that gathered themselves together against the Lord in the company of Korah; but died in his own sin, and had no sons. Why should the name of our father be done away from among his family, because he hath no son? Give unto us therefore a possession among the brethren of our father. And Moses brought their cause before the Lord. And the Lord spake unto Moses, saying, The daughters of Zelophehad speak right: thou shalt surely give them a possession of an inheritance among their father's brethren; and thou shalt cause the inheritance of their father to pass unto them. And thou shalt speak unto the children of Israel, saying, If a man die, and have no son, then ye shall cause his inheritance to pass unto his daughter. And if he have no daughter, then ye shall give his inheritance unto his brethren. And if he have no brethren, then ye shall give his inheritance unto his father's brethren.

The three texts of Numbers 27:1-11, Numbers 36, and Joshua 17:3-6 discussed this very scenario at length, and the Lord gave command by Moses. *"And every daughter, that possesseth an inheritance in any tribe of the children of Israel, shall be wife unto one of the family of the tribe of her father, that the children of Israel may enjoy every man the inheritance of his fathers."* (Numbers 36:8) To preserve the family line and their land inheritance the first male child from Salmon's daughter became the inheritor of the lineage and land for the line of Salmon.

That first son was named Elimelech in Ruth 1:2. A second son was the unnamed near kinsman of Ruth 3:12 and the next or third son was Boaz.

According to Numbers 27:1-11, chapter 36, and Joshua 17:3-6 the first son born to Rachab was assigned as the descendant of Salmon to carry on his lineage and inheritance (Deuteronomy 25:5-6). The second son was assigned as the first son for Rachab's husband and in turn became the default first son by which to pass on his own family lineage and land inheritance.

Any successive sons would inherit in a normal manner from their father's ancestry. Without this method the man who had only daughters would have no son as a successor, his family line would expire, plus no land rights passed to any successive male progeny. Without this transfer of lineage and thus of land rights various pieces of land would become unowned, vacant, and without legitimate right for usage and additionally unable to be returned in the year of release to its proper landowner.

Elimelech with Naomi had two sons, Mahlon (married Ruth, Ruth 4:10) and Chilion (married Orphah). Elimelech died first, then Mahlon and Chilion died (Ruth 1:3-5). This ended the lineage of Salmon through Rachab, through Elimelech and his two sons without a rescue from a near kinsman, also known as a kinsman–redeemer.

When Naomi discharged her daughters-in-law she firmly stated she was too old to have any further sons (Ruth 1:12) and thus recognized her futility to have a kinsman to marry her to raise up a son for Elimelech according to Deuteronomy 25:5-6. Therefore, she lamented (Ruth 1:20). Much of the book of Ruth entailed how God rescued the line of Judah descending from Salmon.

Boaz agreed to help Ruth with her claim (Ruth 3:13) and proceeded the next day in chapter four. But there was a twist. The nearest of kin, the middle brother, was unwilling and clearly stated, *"I cannot redeem it for myself, lest I mar mine own inheritance: redeem thou my right to thyself; for I cannot redeem it."* (Ruth 4:6) *"I cannot redeem it"* and it would *"mar mine own inheritance,"* what did those two distinct and different things mean?

Let's step back and review a little before proceeding. Salmon had only one daughter who married and with her husband had three sons: Elimelech, the unnamed son, and Boaz (Ruth 4:3-4). Elimelech as the first son of Rachab was assigned to represent the line of Salmon (Numbers 36:8; Deuteronomy 25:6). He married and had two sons with Naomi but both died already.

Thus there were two intertwined scenarios. The first was the problem of a man having only daughter(s). And the second problem was son Elimelech had a termination of lineage by his own two sons' deaths unless a kinsman–redeemer could raise up a son for Elimelech's family line.

The statement *"I cannot,"* by the unnamed second son of Rachab in Ruth 4:6 meant that he was already too old to conceive a child to raise up offspring, especially if he was a much older brother. The expression *"lest I mar mine own inheritance"* meant that he did not have a son to carry on his assigned inheritance from the three brothers' natural father, the husband of Rachab. This middle brother suggested, even asserted, by his statement that he had one or more daughters by which to manage recovery of their father's lineage and inheritance.

This type of event with only daughters had occurred earlier as recorded in 1 Chronicles 23:21-22 and with Zelophehad. This revealed that there were three intertwined scenarios detailed in the book of Ruth. Two successive family generations had only daughter(s) and one family generation had no surviving son.

The ownership of the land parcel of Elimelech was essentially vacated by two methods: Elimelech voluntarily moving to Moab to seek his well-being outside of God's covenant promise and by the death of his sons as inheritors while in Moab. Because Elimelech's sons had married [i.e. reached the age of personal responsibility physically, morally, and spiritually], willingly remained outside of Israel, and died in Moab the right of inheritance through Elimelech was already vacated by the two sons. Thus the recovery of both family lineage and land rights fell to the nearest kinsman, i.e. the next younger brother to Elimelech (Ruth 4:3-4; Numbers 27:8-10).

If the unnamed second son married Ruth, the first and prospectively only son would be assigned to Salmon's lineage and he would lose his position to carry on his natural father's lineage. [That would in turn fall to Boaz.] There was no certainty or even a possibility to have a son by this marriage because the unnamed second son was probably much older than Boaz, while Boaz was himself an older man.

Therefore, the unnamed second son, the kinsman nearest in line to

Elimelech, declined, took off his sandal, and gave it to Boaz as a certification of passing this duty/privilege/assignment unto his next younger brother to marry Ruth (Ruth 4:7-10). Boaz was thereby urged to carry on the lineage and land rights of Salmon passing through their mother Rachab in accordance with Numbers 27:8, *"If a man die, and have no son, then ye shall cause his inheritance to pass unto his daughter."* This was expanded in Numbers 36:8, *"And every daughter, that possesseth an inheritance in any tribe of the children of Israel, shall be wife unto one of the family of the tribe of her father, that the children of Israel may enjoy every man the inheritance of his fathers."* This was even more carefully stated in Deuteronomy 26:5-6 which was quoted at the subheading above.

When Naomi returned to Bethlehem (Ruth 1:6-19) she reaffirmed her heartfelt position as a descendant of Israel in covenant relationship with God. This restored her to all rights and privileges her husband had lead her away from by departing from God's promises to seek his family's welfare in Moab (Ruth 1:1). Naomi was the specific individual living under the Mosiac law who had the right to make a claim for a kinsman–redeemer.

Naomi had already emphasized that she was too old to have offspring (Ruth 1:12) and realized that Ruth could not make a direct and valid claim on behalf of Mahlon (Ruth 2:19-22; 3:1), as detailed above. When Naomi directed Ruth to go before Boaz that night upon the threshing floor Naomi was emphasizing that Ruth was a substitute for herself (Ruth 3 chpt.). Ruth, as Naomi's delegated substitute, carried out Naomi's rightful claim to have a near kinsman marry her and raise up seed for Salmon, Rachab, and Elimelech in family succession.

This concept of substitution was common and well understood in Israel because they offered specific animal sacrifices as substitutes for themselves, another person could pay the fine or cost of restoration on behalf of a guilty party, pay on behalf of someone in debt to redeem them, substitute an adopted son for a natural born son, etc. Naomi simply substituted Ruth to fulfill her right of invoking the near kinsman's duty/privilege/assignment to raise up seed for a childless brother.

The women of Bethlehem clearly understood this substitution of Ruth on Naomi's behalf when they declared *"There is a son born to Naomi."*

Can Rahab of Jericho be the wife of Salmon?

> Blessed be the Lord, which hath not left thee this day without a kinsman, that his name may be famous in Israel. And he shall be unto thee a restorer of thy life, and a nourisher of thine old age: for thy daughter in law, which loveth thee, which is better to thee than seven sons, hath born him. ... And the women her neighbours gave it a name, saying, There is a son born to Naomi; and they called his name Obed: he is the father of Jesse, the father of David. (Ruth 4:14-15, 17)

Naomi probably did not know that the middle brother would not be able to carry on the lineage of Rachab from Salmon and that it would fall to Boaz. [If this middle brother had a son, he had already died, too.] Elimelech's assigned place as the first son was vacated. This position was declined by the middle brother (both for his inability to propagate any offspring due to his age and for the disruption to his assigned "firstborn" inheritance from the three sons' natural father since he only had one or more daughters) and was fulfilled by Boaz.

Ruth did not marry a younger man who was remote kin to Mahlon, i.e. in the same family of the same tribe in conformity to the Mosaic law. She had reached backward up the chain of lineage to marry Mahlon's uncle, Boaz. Ordinarily this lineage would be described from Salmon through Rachab, through Elimelech, through Mahlon, and then through Ruth's and her Israelite family's kinsman/husband's first son. [Salmon, *Rachab*, Elimelech, Mahlon, and then the first son of the substitute husband for Mahlon.]

But Boaz himself on that day in chapter four, as described, had become the assigned son to restore the line of Salmon. Note here that the scenario in Numbers 27 superceded that in Deuteronomy 25 because it occurred first. Therefore, the correct lineage of descent was given as Salmon though Rachab, through Boaz (no matter who Boaz had married), and then to Obed (Ruth 4:21; Matthew 1:8).

Boaz had willingly accepted and fulfilled the Mosaic law's duty/privilege/assignment and restored the lineage and land rights of inheritance for his grandfather Salmon which had passed through his daughter Rachab. At the same time Boaz was raising up a son for Elimelech and Naomi by way of the substitution of Ruth but the lineage of Salmon took precedence.

Boaz was described as *"a mighty man of wealth"* (Ruth 2:1) and blessed Ruth saying, *"Blessed be thou of the Lord, my daughter: for thou hast shewed more kindness in the latter end than at the beginning, inasmuch as thou followedst not young men, whether poor or rich."* (Ruth 3:10) He commended Ruth by saying, *"all the city of my people doth know that thou art a virtuous woman"* (Ruth 3:11). Boaz had accepted three tasks: provide support for the widow Naomi who was his sister-in-law (Ruth 4:15), marry and maintain support for Ruth as a near kinsman, and raise up offspring on behalf of his grandfather Salmon to restore the progression of the male lineage and secure the transmittal of land rights from Salmon.

The words of Matthew 1:5 were given this way, *"And Salmon begat Booz of Rachab,"* consistent with Deuteronomy 25:5-6, Numbers 27:1-11, Numbers 36, Joshua 17:3-6, and the very intertwined scenario of Ruth. This put both Naomi and Boaz in a unique position. Naomi, as sister-in-law to Boaz, was an aunt to Obed plus she was a grandmother to Obed as Ruth's mother-in-law. Boaz was both Obed's father and his great-uncle since Ruth was his nephew's wife.

New Testament validation

When Jesus was having an interchange with the pharisees in Matthew 21:23–22:46 he finished that episode with a very specific set of questions that used or referred to the scenario of the book of Ruth. He asked them this, *"What think ye of Christ? Whose son is he?"* The pharisees and those with them replied, *"The son of David."*

Then Jesus used that Old Testament preview which the pharisees, as self-professed expounders of the law, should have clearly understood by asking them this question. *"How then doth David in spirit call him Lord, saying, The Lord said unto my Lord, Sit thou on my right hand, till I make thine enemies thy foot stool? If David then call him Lord, how is he his Son?"* (Matthew 22:41-46)

The answer was the same as for Salmon. Boaz did not directly come from Salmon but indirectly through the seed of a woman, namely Salmon's daughter. Jesus had entered into this world not as a direct son of Joseph who had descended from David (Matthew 1:1, 16; Luke 3:23) and, therefore, under the sin of Adam but indirectly as the seed of the woman Mary (Matthew 1:18-20; Genesis 3:15; Galatians 3:16; 4:4, 27-31). Jesus entered this world by becoming the "seed" or offspring of the antitypical woman to Eve, a mature Mary[16] (Genesis 3:15; 1 Timothy 5:8-11; John 19:25-27). [Mary was at or greater than age sixty to be included in the public care of the disciple(s), minus about thirty-three and one half years of Jesus' life and ministry, minus nine months of gestation, equals at least twenty-five and three-quarters years of age for Mary at the incarnation.]

Jesus, therefore, was without inherited Adamic sin. And without personal sin (Hebrews 4:15; 7:26; 2 Corinthians 5:21) He had offered himself as payment for sin (1 Peter 3:18) to reconcile mankind to God. Christ Jesus restores to "whosoever will" of humanity (Revelation 22:17; Romans 5:10; 11:15; 2 Corinthians 5:18; Colossians 1:20; Hebrews 2:17) all that was lost by Adam as the original human steward/landholder of earth. And Christ Jesus reinstates those who believe and accept God's offer of reconciliation into the untarnished lineage of descent as sons of God (John 1:12; Galatians 4:6; Philippians 2:5; 1 John 3:1-2).

This inheritance situation in the book of Ruth was a subtle display of the problem with humanity who were certainly dying because of sin, with no real successor, and unable to pass on any rightful claim to earth. The first son, Elimelech, was reminiscent of Cain who wandered away as a vagabond from God's people. The second son, the unnamed son, was reminiscent of Noah who could carry on the lineage of Adam his father in the new post-flood world only by way of his children's marriages and their subsequent offspring. The third and much later son Boaz, was a veiled preview of the ultimate Son who would be able to fully rescue the lineage and land inheritance for his great Father while being a kinsman–redeemer. Both Genesis 3:15 and Numbers 27:8 affirmed that the woman's seed would bring a resolution.

By carefully noting the details and applying the appropriate Scripture texts to the whole scenario the book of Ruth was shown to fully reinforce that Rachab was intended by Matthew to fill a generation. The scenario with Boaz born to Salmon's daughter Rachab was explained, supported, and displayed. Table 6 covered the five generations immediately preceding David and gave the best fit for the parental age range for the birth of each successive offspring. Only that scenario met all related

Scripture criteria without forcing any miracles.

The abundant evidence for Rachab as Salmon's daughter also showed how to resolve Matthew's list of genealogy for Jesus Christ. Matthew stated in chapter 1:17 there were three sets of fourteen generations, *"So all the generations from Abraham to David are fourteen generations; and from David until the carrying away into Babylon are fourteen generations; and from the carrying away into Babylon unto Christ are fourteen generations."* Traditionally one generation was considered missing but not if Matthew 1:5 was used correctly as intended by him.

Matthew gave three women in that list with only two directly named as wives in the Scriptures (Bathesheba wife of David in 2 Samuel 12:24 and Ruth wife of Boaz in Ruth 4:10, 13). That meant that Rachab filled a generation between Salmon and Boaz. These details affirmed as true Matthew's statement that *"from Abraham* [up] *to David are fourteen generations."* The corrected layouts of these three sets of fourteen generations are displayed on the next page.

Narrowing Jesse's age

Jesse's age at the birth of David can now be considered more fully. If Jesse was 66 at David's birth, the extra or parenthetical comment about Jesse given in 1 Samuel 17:12, *"and the man went among men for an old man in the days of Saul,"* could be applied when David was fourteen years of age. This was after the time of the special sacrifice with Samuel and Jesse's sons when they were called to the feast and when David was anointed (1 Samuel 16:1-13). This fit with 1 Samuel 16:22 when David served Saul by playing music. [See above: The expression "an old man"]

But if Jesse was age seventy (7 x 10) at David's birth as suggested in Table 6, then he was 84 (7 x 12) when David was 14, already anointed, and served before Saul as musician. Jesse was then at age ninety-one (7 x 13) when David fled Saul, the ark was captured, and Eli died at ninety-eight years. He was about 96 [70 + ~26] when taken to Moab and near the end of his life. Most likely Jesse also died at about ninety-eight (7 x 14) years. This was the time frame when Samuel died (1 Samuel 25:1, [A-939]) when David was staying hidden from Saul.

Note too that the Scriptures gave no mention of David mourning for his parents' deaths, just the deaths of others. This fit well with option six above, another early year in those forty years. The best fit for Jesse was [A-841-~939], he became an *"old man,"* reaching age eighty midway in [A-921] in Saul's reign [A-901-941].

The three sets of fourteen generations from Matthew 1:17 are presented.

1 Abraham *born in Chaldea, entered Canaan, father of faith*	15 David *born in Judea, conquered Canaan, king of Israel*	29 Jeconiah *born in Judea, exiled to Babylon, unfaithful to God*
2 Isaac *dug wells, peacemaker*	16 Solomon *temple builder, peaceful ruler*	30 Shealtiel *temple sponsor, lived during peace*
3 Jacob *sought God's blessing*	17 Rehoboam *forsook wise counsel*	31 Zerubbabel *temple rebuilder with God's blessing*
4 Judah	18 Abijah	32 Abiud
5 Perez	19 Asa	33 Eliakim
6 Hezron	20 Jehoshaphat	34 Azor
7 (A)Ram	21 Jehoram	35 Zadok
8 Amminadab	22 Uzziah	36 Akim
9 Nahshon	23 Jotham	37 Eliud
10 Salmon	24 Ahaz	38 Eleazar
11 Rachab (f.)	25 Hezekiah	39 Mattan
12 Boaz	26 Mannasseh	40 Jacob
13 Obed	27 Amon	41 Joseph
14 Jesse	28 Josiah	42 Jesus the Christ

Unnamed Lineage

Noting that longer life spans and later age paternal sexual reproduction of a child was neither realistic nor implied, like that displayed in Table 3, some scholars and Bible students have accepted or suggested the idea that the lineage up to David was incomplete. They proposed that there were unnamed progeny and, therefore, additional individuals in the generational lists given in Ruth 4:18-22, 1 Chronicles 2:1-15, Matthew 1:1-16 and in Luke 3:23-38 and that these lists just gave the highlights.

However, some reasoning ought to be applied here. If the Scriptures gave a list of generations in one place and another list in another place and these can be interwoven, then the Scriptures did give a complete set of information. This occurred in the numerous partial lineages of the high priests from Aaron through Ezra (Ezra 7:1-5; 1 Chronicles 6:14; Nehemiah 12:10-11, 26) and with Matthew 1:1-16 shown above.

If the assumption that lineage was missing (i.e. that was not given anywhere else in the Scripture) was correct, then it logically followed that any list of lineage in the Scriptures was also suspect. Then the Scripture was broken and untrue. Therefore, to use any list or abbreviated list we must require Scripture to be true. Only when all of the pertinent lineage lists are sought, accessed, and collated can true and complete information be obtained and used with certainty.

Consider this. If unnamed progeny were accepted in any list, except for those that were shown to be abbreviated by another Scripture list or other verses giving pertinent information, then unnamed progeny can be inserted elsewhere and those lists no longer have any valid meaning. In that scenario words can be added to the Scriptures. If Matthew 1:5 and the intertwined scenario of the book of Ruth was not fully used, then words can be taken away from the Scriptures.

> For I testify unto every man that heareth the words of the prophecy of this book, If any man shall add unto these things, God shall add unto him the plagues that are written in this book: And if any man shall take away from the words of the book of this prophecy, God shall take away his part out of the book of life, and out of the holy city, and from the things which are written in this book. (Revelation 22:18-19)

Here each reader is faced with two serious questions: Did God's word give information sufficient to establish the lineage of David and, therefore, of Jesus Christ? Did God's word leave out anyone in the list of generations for David and thus for Jesus Christ? After accessing, collating, and interweaving all pertinent lineage lists in Ruth 4:18-22, 1 Chronicles 2:1-15, Matthew 1:1-16, Luke 3:23-38 and incorporating peripheral details from the book of Ruth, nothing was missing. Matthew

1:5 named Rachab in the standard male lineage list, without attaching her to a husband like Ruth and Bathsheba were in the scriptures, and that told us, albeit somewhat indirectly, that Rachab (a daughter of Salmon) filled a generation, *"And Salmon begat Booz of Rachab ... ."*

Logical results

The first scenario given in Table 3 without the generation of Salmon's daughter was highly suspect and unrealistic. It required excessive life spans with late age births of sons across multiple generations. This provided for only one functional or even rational conclusion.

If Salmon's daughter Rachab was not considered in the lineage, as given in Matthew 1:5, consistent with Numbers 27:1-10, and detailed in the book of Ruth, then Salmon's son was born about nineteen years later, likewise for Boaz eighteen years later, Obed nineteen years, and Jesse sixteen years later. In every scenario, Rahab of Jericho was at least eighteen or more years older than Salmon–an unlikely marriage. The only solution that met the words of Scripture without forcing miracles and without two separate individuals named Rahab in the lineage was when Rachab from Matthew 1:5 was recognized and placed as Salmon's daughter. Because no hint of a miracle was given for David's ancestors and no prophecy was spoken regarding Jesse until prophet Isaiah came upon the scene, the scenario brought before Moses by the daughters of Zelophehad became the only possible solution fitting all facts.[N]

The information that Rachab was Salmon's daughter was not written

---

N. The lineage of Judah to David had eleven generations from Judah [A-247] to David [A-911] for an average of 60.4 years per generation. Since the distance from Judah to Hezron was forty-three years other descendants needed older ages to reach that average.

23rd: Judah
24th: Pharez (Phares)
25th: Hezron (Esrom)
26th: Aram (Ram)
27th: Aminadab (Amminadab)
28th: Naasson (Naashon, Nahshon)
29th: Salmon
30th: Rachab (mother of Boaz, Matthew 1:5)
31st: Boaz (Booz)
32nd: Obed
33rd: Jesse
34th: David.

in the text in Ruth 4:21-22 which only followed the male descendants, like almost every other lineage list in Scripture. But it was quietly and effectively detailed in the book of Ruth. Orally transmitted information was remarkably prevalent and David's ancestral lineage was probably common knowledge with David capturing Israel's hearts and rise to become king.

Though translations into English of the written Greek text in Matthew 1:5 were correct that Salmon begat or was the ancestor of Boaz, it is functionally weird in our era to translate that a person was a father to another generation through their daughter since it falsely hints at incest. What then was the best form of translation of Matthew 1:5 into English? That was one that took into account all of the pertinent Scriptures, that noted that Salmon was the grandfather, and that Rachab took up another generation and was the daughter of Salmon.

Now you know with certainty that Salmon did not marry Rahab of Jericho and beget Boaz through her. The information, as presented and discussed, established with quite reasonable certainty that Salmon's daughter was named after a contemporary and notable person of faith toward God, i.e. Rahab of Jericho, and that Boaz was born as a grandson to Salmon through the marriage of his daughter Rachab.

What we learned:
1. Rahab was at least eighteen or more years older than Salmon.
2. Rahab of Jericho was too old to birth Boaz from Salmon.
3. Rachab of Matthew 1:5 was being described as a daughter of Salmon.
4. The book of Ruth affirmed the daughter of Salmon through its intertwined scenario resolving the inheritance from Salmon validated by the declared lineage.
5. That Boaz rescued the lineage and land inheritance for Salmon while being a kinsman-redeemer.
6. The most probable age of Jesse at the birth of David was 70.
7. God's word from Matthew and Luke gave sufficient information to establish the unabridged ancestral lineage up to David and, therefore, of Christ Jesus.

Can Rahab of Jericho be the wife of Salmon?

Make a visual tool:

Add more to the timeline constructed earlier. Draw a second horizontal line about 5 inches (12.7 cm) from the top of the sheet. Draw it like the first line from the left side to the right side with a very small margin (1/8 inch or 3 mm) to the end of the paper on each side. Then draw a vertical line about 1/2 inch (1.2 cm) high at both ends of the horizontal line and likewise draw below about 1/4 inch (6.4 mm). At the far right side (in small print) label it "Abram-984" and "Solomon's temple," on the far left side label it "Abram-505" and "Exodus" from Egypt or "depart-Egypt." [The same scale will be used for the most part. Measurements will be made from either end to keep the scale, except the middle part will end up compacted or visually out of scale, 48 years will be missing so it fits the paper.]

Measure and draw a vertical line 1 inch (2.5 cm) from the left end of the line, label it "Entry" and "Abram-545" for when the Israelites crossed Jordan into Canaan. Salmon was born just before entry to Canaan, label "Salmon" at the "Entry" position. Rahab of Jericho was born at least eighteen years earlier at [A-527] which measured from "Exodus" just over 5/8 inch (1.7 cm) to the right before "Entry," label it "?Rahab-born" and "?Abram-527." The land division was measured 1 3/16 inch (3 cm) from the "Exodus," label it "Division" and "Abram-552."

When did the book of Ruth occur?

Part 6: The children of Jacob and the intersections of their descendants.

[*Author's note: Before examining Part 6 please be sure to review part 5, "Can Rahab of Jericho be the wife of Salmon?" The information repeated here in Table 3 and Table 6 displayed the year of Obed's birth obtained under two carefully framed but different scenarios discussed above.*]

As explored in Part 5, Table 3 presented Salmon born about the year of entry to Canaan. That showed the results when sons were born to Salmon, Boaz, Obed, and Jesse at 81% of their extra long life spans. This made each of them quite late aged at the birth of their respective sons. Table 3 is redisplayed below for convenience.

When the book of Ruth occurred appeared to be simple to resolve. It fit best with either the first scenario from Table 3 or the second scenario from Table 6. Remember that the year of the exodus from Egypt was [A-505] and forty years later (after the wilderness journey and crossing the river Jordan) was the Israelite entry into Canaan [A-545]. Obed's birth in scenario one occurred 189 years after entry to the land. His birth in scenario two occurred 225 years after entry, a difference of thirty-six years from [A-734 to A-770].

If Boaz was at age 93 in the first scenario, then his son Obed was born in the year [A-734]. If Boaz was at age 74 under the second scenario, then his son Obed was born in [A-770]. Table 6 is redisplayed below for convenience.

SECTION II. Part 6.

Table 3 redisplayed. The calculated ages for begetting or birth with unusually long life spans to reach from Salmon to David, if the ratio of 0.81 was used. Here the next four generations lived much longer lives than others.

Ages required for birth of respective sons to reach to David.

0.81 Ratio	Birth year	Expected Life span	Son's Birth year	Age at son's birth	Year of death
Naashon	449	118	545	96	545
Salmon	545	118	641	96	663
Boaz	641	115	734	93	756
Obed	734	112	825	91	846
Jesse	825	110	911	86	935
David	911	70.5			982

Table 6 redisplayed. The life spans and birth ages to reach from Salmon to David with Rachab as Salmon's daughter, when the ratio of 0.70 was used except for Naashon.

Ages required for birth of offspring to reach to David with Salmon having a daughter Rachab.

0.70 Ratio	Birth year	Expected Life span	Son's Birth year	Age at son's birth	Year of death
Naashon (0.82 ratio)	455	110	545	90	545
Salmon	545	110	622	77	655
Rachab (Matthew 1:5)	622	107	696	74	729
Boaz	696	106	770	74	802
Obed	770	104	841	71	874
Jesse	841	98	911	70	939
David	911	70.5			982

The book of Ruth also required alignment of its text within the oppressions and rescues by Israel's judges. Depending upon the placement of these oppressions and each judges' period of service the ten years of the book of Ruth will be aligned with one period or overlap part of both the oppression and the judge. Therefore, placing the book of Ruth has been difficult and subjective because of the uncertainty of the early period of the book of Judges and when successive judges served. Though some have been admirably close to or within this time period between the scenarios from Table 3 and Table 6.

Begin with Joshua 24:31 and Judges 2:7. In Judges 2:7 Samuel

When did the book of Ruth occur?

repeated an earlier verse to connect the later book of Judges to the prior text of Joshua, "*And the people served the Lord all the days of Joshua, and all the days of the elders that outlived Joshua, who had seen all the great works of the Lord, that he did for Israel.*" Exactly how many years transpired during these two verses will be shown later in Sections III through V. Likewise, how many years elapsed for Judges 1:1–3:7 or Judges 2:10-13 will be explored there. Those results are used below.

> And also all that generation were gathered unto their fathers: and there arose another generation after them, which knew not the Lord, nor yet the works which he had done for Israel. And the children of Israel did evil in the sight of the Lord, and served Baalim: And they forsook the Lord God of their fathers, which brought them out of the land of Egypt, and followed other gods, of the gods of the people that were round about them, and bowed themselves unto them, and provoked the Lord to anger. And they forsook the Lord, and served Baal and Ashtaroth. (Judges 2:10-13)

After this the first oppression in Judges 3:8 began under Chushan-rishathaim, king of Mesopotamia, for eight years. "*Therefore the anger of the Lord was hot against Israel, and he sold them into the hand of Chushanrishathaim king of Mesopotamia: and the children of Israel served Chushanrishathaim eight years.*" This first deliverance under judge Othniel began a period of many years under judges interspersed between oppressions for Israel's waywardness. Othniel's possible age at death of about 110 [A-639] made his birth [~A-529] about sixteen years before entry to Canaan.

Othniel was about twenty-four years old when he smote Kirjathsepher (Joshua 15:16-18; Judges 1:13). This was because the Israelite tribes had dispersed in the seventh year to dwell upon their own portions of land and then began to take control of them [A-545 + 7 + 1 = 553; 553 - ~529 = ~24]. This was functional for Othniel's birth and death years and for his father Kenaz [~A-<=447- 544] to beget Othniel in the wilderness when using the template from Abraham.

Othniel provided the first deliverance of the judges in Judges 3:9-11 with a period of rest for forty years [A-599-639]. The expression that the land had rest meant that the effect of his deliverance and leadership remained until forty years had transpired, but then it faded into another punishment. The same was true regarding judge Ehud whose period of rest spanned eighty years [A-657-737].

Only if judge Ehud was from twenty to thirty years old when he served, and then died eighty years later about age 100-110, was he alive at the end of this eighty-year period. Otherwise the effect lasted beyond his life time. Gideon served Israel and destroyed the Midianites in [A-804], but the effect lasted forty years [A-804-844].

If Judges 8:32 meant that Gideon was eighty years of age at his death when it used the expression, *"Gideon the son of Joash died in a good old age,"* then he was at age forty when he began to serve as judge (Judges 8:28). That age was consistent with the material shown earlier concerning the descriptive title, "an aged man." Othniel, Ehud, and Gideon lived through all of those years when the land had rest consistent with Judges 2:18-19 and 3:11. [The time period for the placement of these three judges was based upon the body of evidence presented later in Sections III through V.]

The time for Ruth

This was a fascinating question to many Bible students and scholars: When did the book of Ruth occur? Would you be surprised to learn that the book of Ruth answered this question before it was ever asked? This was discerned by rethinking how to interpret the textual information presented in the book itself. For so many generations the book of Judges was correctly understood to be about God's work to fulfill his promises to Abraham from Genesis 12:1-3 that some expressions were always viewed within a certain perspective.

The process of rethinking the period of the judges required a shift in perceiving and understanding how writers in their era laid out information. That essential time related clue was neither given in any unique or eclectic way nor was it hidden. It was in plain sight. But to understand the expression, first it must be recognized, and then the scriptural meaning can be discerned. After this, the meaning must be applied to get a solution.

The book of Ruth opened with, *"Now it came to pass in the days when*

When did the book of Ruth occur?

the judges ruled, that there was a famine in the land. And a certain man of Bethlehemjudah went to sojourn in the country of Moab, he, and his wife, and his two sons." Almost every person would translate the expression, "*when the judges ruled,*" to apply during the time period of the judges from Othniel (Judges 3:7-11) through Abdon (Judges 12:13-15). Exceedingly few would expect this phrase to apply to the extended use of the term judges since the Scriptures also used this term for high priests and elders of the tribes of Israel.

If the expression, "*when the judges ruled,*" applied generically during the entire period of the judges, then there was a long window of time which gave no precision for application. But if the phrase, "*when the judges ruled,*" applied to two judges ruling or serving at the same time, then a careful survey of facts must ensue.

The high priests were named judges as Israel's highest judge (Deuteronomy 17:9; 19:17). They were present in Israel from Aaron up to Israel's dispersion to Babylon (one unusual exception is shown later in Section V.). Across the period of the book of the Judges successive high priests overlapped other judges and made two concurrent judges many times.

When the judge named Samuel served Israel he was concurrent with the high priests and other judges until his years of service ended. Judge Samson's twenty-year period was understood to overlap another oppression. None of those high priests were named at a specific event, nor placed in time, nor given a time period that fit with or gave precision to place David's early ancestry, i.e. Boaz or Obed. Both Eli and Samuel were named as judges, but then only in the book of 1 Samuel. [See Section IV. The meaning of "judge," and, Judges as deliverers]

That left one other possibility. The word "*judges*" linked or referred back to individuals in the immediately prior book with respect to chronological time. The expression, "*when the judges ruled,*" from Ruth 1:1 applied specifically to the term "judge" as used during the period addressed in the book of Judges, placed before the book of Ruth in the contemporary Old Testament. In the book of Judges, the term "judge" was only applied to those who delivered Israel or a portion of Israel from oppression. Amongst those named a "judge" two or possibly three of these judges or deliverers served at the same time. [See Section V.

SECTION II. Part 6.

Simultaneous judges]

Judge Shamgar the son of Anath, judge Deborah, and judge Barak the son of Abinoam of Kedesh-naphtali briefly served together during the same period (Judges 3:31; 4:4-24; 5:6, 31). More precisely judge Deborah and judge Barak served together against Sisera, captain of the army of Jabin king of Canaan (Judges 4:4-24). This was what the author of the book of Ruth conveyed by the expression, *"when the judges ruled,"* it meant that two or even three of these delivering judges served or ruled at the same time.

As presented above with Tables 3 and 6 there were two distinct possibilities for the placement of the birth of Boaz and then of Obed, and Jesse to follow. Table 3 gave the shorter, male only, lineage with resultant time placements that closely followed Abraham's pattern of late age to life expectancy for the birth of his last son, Shuah. Table 6 showed the application of Matthew 1:5 and the subsequent time placements that followed the ratio of Sarah's late age to life expectancy to birth a child.

Table 3 placed Obed's birth before the period of judge Deborah and judge Barak while Table 6 placed his birth inside of the two or three judge period. Either the book of Ruth had occurred around [~A-724-734], for the ten-year period of Ruth 1:4, during the period of judge Ehud or it occurred after the oppression of king Jabin around [~A-760-770]. As explained below in Section IV and Section V, the period of service for Deborah and Barak started in [A-757] and ended after forty years in [A-797]. The years of [A-760-770] were after judges Deborah and Barak defeated Sisera and then truly *"ruled"* in their leadership to Israel.

The book of Ruth occurred in the middle period of the various judges and connected Salmon to David. This location for the book of Ruth might vary just slightly within possible limited variations in the individual birth years from that presented in Table 6. However, only this time placement established Obed's birth year in [A-770] exactly halfway between the start of judge Othniel [A-599] through the death of judge Abdon [A-941]. The years of [A-760-770] for the book of Ruth fit so remarkably well inside of the early period of judges Deborah and Barak that this placement affirmed the reasoning and lineage that derived Table 6. [See: Part 5. Can Rahab be the wife of Salmon?, Section IV and

Section V]

What we learned:
1. When the book of Ruth occurred and why it fit with this period of service for judge Deborah and judge Barak.
2. That this time placement for the book of Ruth affirmed the daughter of Salmon as mother to Boaz.

Make a visual tool:
Place more into the timeline. Obed's birth year from Table 6 was in [A-770], measure that 6 5/8 inches (16.8 cm) from "Exodus," mark, and label it "Obed-born." This placed the book of Ruth very near [A-760-770]. Judges Deborah and Barak served together from [A-757-797], measure almost 6 3/8 inches (16 cm) from "Exodus," mark it, label it "Deborah-Barak," and below write "Abram-757." Draw an angled vertical line above and below 6 3/8 inches (16.2 cm) from "Exodus" and label it "Book-Ruth" and "~A-760-770." Then measure just over 7 1/4 inches (18.5 cm) from "Exodus", mark it, label that "End-Deborah-Barak," and below write "Abram-797." They gave the land rest for forty years, label that span "40 yrs," if desired.

The real difference between the "End-Deborah-Barak" and the birth of Eli was 15/16 inch (23.5 mm). The 8" x 11" (21.7 cm x 28 cm) sheet of paper was not long enough for a true scale.

SECTION III

Connecting Joshua and Judges

Background

The book of Judges connected with the record started by Joshua by repeating a significant statement in its introduction. That repeated text was about the time duration of *"all the days of the elders that outlived Joshua."* This expression was given twice with the first in Joshua 24:31 and repeated in Judges 2:7. That duplication meant for us to connect the starting time of the book of Judges with the earlier statement given in Joshua 24:31. The book of Judges started marking time from that text in Joshua and then proceeded through successive events until it applied the same technique again by repeating a previous text.

This repetition became a most puzzling piece of information in relation to the length of time that it covered. The original statement from Joshua 24:31 was this. *"And Israel served the Lord all the days of Joshua, and all the days of the elders that overlived Joshua, and which had known all the works of the Lord, that he had done for Israel."*

The repeated statement was written in Judges 2:7, *"And the people served the Lord all the days of Joshua, and all the days of the elders that outlived Joshua, who had seen all the great works of the Lord, that he did for Israel."* This method asserted both the significant importance of replication and the time connection between twice stated material. [Hint: Twice stated material solved the placement of Samson's life and period as judge. As presented earlier, Christ Jesus used the same technique when upon the cross. He began to recite Psalm 22, so that his observers would connect what was occurring to him with what was foretold and written in that psalm.]

Before this in Joshua 24:29 the text stated, *"And it came to pass after these things, that Joshua the son of Nun, the servant of the Lord, died, being an hundred and ten years old."* This was repeated in Judges 2:8, *"And Joshua the son of Nun, the servant of the Lord, died, being an hundred and ten years old."* To some degree, *"Israel served the Lord all the days of Joshua."* Their obedience toward God generally remained after Joshua charged the Israelites (along with their elders, heads, and judges) to commit themselves to serve God in Joshua 24:1-29 and recorded their pledge. Israel refrained, to some degree, from profound waywardness *"all the days of the elders that overlived Joshua."*

Here, some questions arose. When did Joshua die? How long past Joshua's death at 110 years did Israel serve God? How long did those elders live? How long did Israel's waning obedience last before their first oppression came under the king of Mesopotamia, Chushanrishathaim?

Joshua's estimated age

Joshua was mentioned each time that Caleb's age was given. That Joshua's age matched that of Caleb was reasonable to infer, except his age was not expressly given. If their age was the same, then Joshua's age can be derived by using the information given in these blocks of text: Joshua 24:29, birth; Numbers 13:6-8, lineage || Joshua 14:7-9, age thirty-eight at their exodus || Exodus 33:11; Numbers 11:28; (Joshua 1:1), about age thirty-eight before the tabernacle as Moses' servant || Numbers 13:1–14:10, 24; Joshua 14:7-9, age forty sent to spy out Canaan || Numbers 26:64-65; Joshua 1:1, age seventy-eight at end of the wilderness journey and crossing Jordan river || Numbers 34:17; Joshua 13–19 chpts.; Acts 13:19, age seventy-eight to eighty-four conquering Canaan || Joshua 14:7-11, age eighty-five, division of the land [A-552], Caleb at eighty-five years was born in [A-467] || Joshua 24:29; Judges 2:8, died at 110 years of age.

If this inference was true, then the very latest date that Joshua had died [A-577] was twenty-five years after the land division. However the Scripture records God's words to him in Joshua 13:1, *"Now Joshua was old and stricken in years; and the Lord said unto him, Thou art old and stricken in years, and there remaineth yet very much land to be possessed."* When we go to Abraham's time period, Genesis 18:11 applied *"old and well stricken in age"* first to both Abraham and Sarah together, *"Now Abraham and Sarah were old and well stricken in age; and it ceased to be with Sarah after the manner of women."* This was when Abraham was ninety-nine and Sarah was eighty-nine years in age and God announced the conception and birth of Isaac (Genesis 21:1-5).

The second use was in Genesis 24:1 when Abraham was age 137, Isaac was thirty-seven years old, and Sarah had died at 127 years, *"And Abraham was old, and well stricken in age: and the Lord had blessed Abraham in all things."* Then that expression was used with Joshua three times: first in Joshua 13:1 (shown above) and twice more in Joshua 23:1-3.

> And it came to pass a long time after that the Lord had given rest unto Israel from all their enemies round about, that Joshua waxed old and stricken in age. And Joshua called for all Israel, and for their elders, and for their heads, and for their judges, and for their officers, and said unto them, I am old and stricken in age: And ye have seen all that the Lord your God hath done unto all these nations because of you; for the Lord your God is he that hath fought for you.

This expression, *"stricken in age,"* or a very similar one was used later in the Bible for three additional times. The sixth use was when king David was nearing the end of his life span of seventy to seventy and one-half years. Less than two years remained until David died when 1 Kings 1:1 was recorded, *"Now king David was old and stricken in years; and they covered him with clothes, but he gat no heat."*

The seventh was in Luke 1:7 which described both Zacharias and Elisabeth, *"they both were now well stricken in years,"* implying similar ages for both. The eighth and final place was by the priest Zacharias who was the father of John the Baptist. In Luke 1:18 he described himself, *"And Zacharias said unto the angel, Whereby shall I know this? for I am an old man, and my wife well stricken in years."* In this account Zacharias was at fifty years of age and was finishing his formal Levitical service as a priest at the temple in Jerusalem (Numbers 8:23-26; 4:3, 23, 30, 35, 47).

In the progression through these individuals incrementally younger ages were considered *"stricken in years."* The scriptural use of *"old and stricken in years"* was consistent with decreasing life spans and implied decreased physical capacity from aging. This suggested at least eighty-five to ninety years of age for Joshua, if using the ratio of Abraham who was at 137 of 175 years. A simple calculation [(137 / 175) x 110 = 86] offered about eighty-six years for Joshua. But Joshua's age remained uncertain; therefore, these eight uses in Scripture did not establish his birth year.

If Joshua was the same age as Caleb, then the sets of verses (separated into blocks as shown above) gave time identification by which to frame Joshua's birth [?A-467] and death [?A-577]. When Moses returned to Egypt and the plagues were begun by God they were at or almost at thirty-eight years of age. After forty years in the wilderness they were at age seventy-eight. From the time of Exodus 33:11 and Numbers 11:28 through defeating seven nations in the land and dividing the land in the seventh year Joshua and Caleb would have been seventy-eight to eighty-five years of age.

This made twenty-five more years transpire before Joshua died at 110 years of age. Otherwise, the sets of verses about Caleb's age simply showed the progression of time to these two men, but only gave Caleb's age. Notably Jewish rabbinical history gave Joshua twenty-eight years in Canaan or four years less.[O]

What was Joshua's real age?

Joshua was a descendant of Joseph's son Ephraim who was born in Egypt during the seven years of plenty (Exodus 41:50-52). His lineage was from Ephraim to Beriah, to Rephah, to Resheph, to Telah, to Tahan, to Laadan, to Ammihud, to Elishama, to Nun (Non), to Oshea (aka Joshua, Jehoshuah, 1 Chronicles 7:22-27, Numbers 13:8, 16). If Ephraim was born the last year of the seven years of plenty in [A-288], that was two years before Israel entered Egypt in [A-290]. With Joshua's latest

---

O. Jewish chronology stated that Joshua led Israel for twenty-eight years [A-545 + 28 = A-573] or dying four years earlier than [A-577]. Seder Olam (Heinrich Guggenheimer, trans. & ed. NY:Rowman & Littlefield Pub. 2005) p. 120.

possible year of birth in [A-467] there was 179 years across nine generations for an average of 19.9 years for each generation. For rabbinical time, born four years earlier, the average was 19.4 years.

Ephraim could not have been born sooner because of Genesis 48:16 where Jacob called both of Joseph's sons *"lads."* That meant they were less than 20 years of age when given their blessing from Israel at age 146 in [A-306]. This revealed that Manasseh was born in [A-287] and Ephraim was born in [A-288], the last year of plenty in Egypt.

Exodus 33:11 occurred at mount Sinai before the law was given in chapter 34 and prior to when the formal tabernacle was made. There Moses' helper was mentioned, *"servant Joshua, the son of Nun, a young man,"* and Numbers 11:28 also described him saying, *"Joshua the son of Nun, the servant of Moses, one of his young men."* With Joshua's latest possible death in [A-577] he would have been thirty-eight years old at the exodus from Egypt in [A-505] and still less than forty years old when described in these two texts. If Jewish rabbinical time was applied, he would have been four years older.

If Exodus 33:11 was a time marker for Joshua, what did the phrase mean when Moses described Joshua at Mount Sinai as *"a young man?"* The whole verse read this way. *"And the Lord spake unto Moses face to face, as a man speaketh unto his friend. And he turned again into the camp: but his servant Joshua, the son of Nun, a young man, departed not out of the tabernacle."*

This *"young man"* expression contrasted with the expression, an *"old man"* or *"a very aged man"* used in other Biblical texts. To understand these terms better, use Barzillai's age to establish that the expressions (more honorably a descriptive title), an *"old man"* or *"a very aged man,"* meant the person had reached eighty or more years. Since a male who attained eighty years of age was described as an *"old man,"* then *"a young man"* would reasonably be half that age.

That same forty-year age was when Moses changed course and aligned himself with his birth family heritage and the Israelite people (Acts 7:23-27). This descriptive expression was one half of Moses' stated age. *"Moses was fourscore years old, and Aaron fourscore and three years old, when they spake unto Pharaoh"* (Exodus 7:7). Forty years was the age of leadership and responsibility having been proven in character, skills, and capacity in full view of others. This age will surface again.

When Joshua at Mount Sinai [A-505] was assigned at forty years of age then his death was seventy years later [A-575]. That year was half way between the Rabbi's position [A-573] and the latest possible year of death [A-577]. These three separate methods gave Joshua a very narrow birth and death period. If this last application of Scripture was correct, then Joshua was forty years of age at Exodus 33:11 and two years older than Caleb. Placing Joshua's birth year in [A-465] best fit the descriptive title, *"a young man,"* in Exodus 33:11.

The elders that outlived Joshua

But this perplexing verse from Joshua 24:31 repeated in Judges 2:7 remained, *"the people served the Lord all the days of Joshua, and all the days of the elders that outlived Joshua."* Joshua had completed his 109th year and reached well into his 110th year or even filled 110 years before he died (Joshua 24:29-30). All of these younger elders were born less than twenty years before the numbering of Israel (Numbers 1:1-18).

This census was taken in Numbers 1:1, *"on the first day of the second month, in the second year after they were come out of the land of Egypt."* They lived less than nineteen years in Egypt, one year after the exodus from Egypt to the numbering, through thirty-nine more wilderness years, and during the seven years conquering and dividing the land. Add these years together [<19 + 1 + 39 + 7 = <66]. These elders were all less than sixty-six years old after dividing the land of Canaan and had many years to live past Joshua's death. And all of those older at the census died in the wilderness, as shown below.

> And they assembled all the congregation together on the first day of the second month, [i.e. one year after the exodus from Egypt] and they declared their pedigrees after their families, by the house of their fathers, according to the number of the names, from twenty years old and upward, by their polls. (Numbers 1:18)
>
> Your carcases shall fall in this wilderness; and all that were numbered of you, according to your whole number, from twenty years old and upward which have murmured against me.

Doubtless ye shall not come into the land, concerning which I sware to make you dwell therein, save Caleb the son of Jephunneh, and Joshua the son of Nun. But your little ones, which ye said should be a prey, them will I bring in, and they shall know the land which ye have despised. (Numbers 14:29-31)

After the number of the days in which ye searched the land, even forty days, each day for a year, shall ye bear your iniquities, even forty years, and ye shall know my breach of promise. I the Lord have said, I will surely do it unto all this evil congregation, that are gathered together against me: in this wilderness they shall be consumed, and there they shall die. (Numbers 14:34-36)

Take the sum of the people, from twenty years old and upward; as the Lord commanded Moses and the children of Israel, which went forth out of the land of Egypt. (Numbers 26:4)

These are they that were numbered by Moses and Eleazar the priest, who numbered the children of Israel in the plains of Moab by Jordan near Jericho. But among these there was not a man of them whom Moses and Aaron the priest numbered, when they numbered the children of Israel in the wilderness of Sinai. For the Lord had said of them, They shall surely die in the wilderness. And there was not left a man of them [i.e. age twenty years or greater at the first census], save Caleb the son of Jephunneh, and Joshua the son of Nun. (Numbers 26:63-65)

Surely none of the men that came up out of Egypt, from twenty years old and upward, shall see the land which I sware unto Abraham, unto Isaac, and unto Jacob; because they have not wholly followed me: Save Caleb the son of Jephunneh the Kenezite, and Joshua the son of Nun: for they have wholly followed the Lord. (Numbers 32:11-12)

And this is the cause why Joshua did circumcise: All the people that came out of Egypt, that were males, even all the men of war, died in the wilderness by the way, after they came out of Egypt. (Joshua 5:4-6)

What then was the expected or common life span by which to

measure these elders? That person was most likely not Joshua. He was specially sustained by manna for forty years (Nehemiah 9:19-21), had the spirit of God upon him (Numbers 27:18; Deuteronomy 34:9), actively sought and received God's guidance, had the angel of His Presence talk with him (Joshua 5:13-15; 6:2), and obeyed the Lord's commandments. This was the only age at death directly given in the books of Joshua and Judges.

Apostle Paul explained in Romans 10:5 that a person who obeyed the law and commandments of the Lord completely (i.e. perfect conduct toward God and man) would sustain his life by doing them, *"For Moses describeth the righteousness which is of the law, That the man which doeth those things shall live by [continuing to do] them."* Paul's words implied that Joshua had a longer life than many other Israelites as a result of his obedience to God under the Mosaic covenant (Ezekiel 20:13, 21).

In strong contrast to Joshua's spirit of obedience and life-long faithfulness, the Scriptures often recorded men's weakness and reported the same kind of disposition that caused the death of those in the last thirty-eight years of the wilderness journey. This was recorded in Judges 2:10-13.

> [A]nd there arose another generation after them, which knew not the Lord, nor yet the works which he had done for Israel. And the children of Israel did evil in the sight of the Lord, and served Baalim: And they forsook the Lord God of their fathers, which brought them out of the land of Egypt, and followed other gods, of the gods of the people that were round about them, and bowed themselves unto them, and provoked the Lord to anger. And they forsook the Lord, and served Baal and Ashtaroth.

And the text in Judges 3:5-7 explained how that came about.

> And the children of Israel dwelt among the Canaanites, Hittites, and Amorites, and Perizzites, and Hivites, and Jebusites: And they took their daughters to be their wives, and gave their daughters to their sons, and served their gods. And the children of Israel did evil in the sight of the Lord, and forgat the Lord their God, and served Baalim and the groves.

Connecting Joshua and Judges

The expression, *"another generation,"* did not have to mean after all of the elders had died. This propensity to be wayward started when the tribes were allotted their portions and separated throughout the land. They were running their lives in their own way (Deuteronomy 12:8; Judges 17:6; 21:25) and not transmitting the knowledge from father to son (Deuteronomy 4:9; 11:19; Psalm 78:4-7).

The Israelites neglected the valuable knowledge of God, of the Mosaic law, and all of the benefits God promised to those who obey Him. The results of this serious neglect was recorded in the tribal accounts of Dan and Benjamin in the book of Judges chapters 17–21. Both their idolatry and reprehensible behavior occurred before their first oppression under Chushanrishathaim and became the basis for God's eight year punishment upon them. [This period will be examined more fully later.]

The rearing of a disobedient generation transpired while the elders yet lived. Then the compromising and giving of their children in marriage to foreigners began as various elders died. Those parents were the ones who knew about God, quickly *"forgat the Lord their God, and served Baalim and the groves,"* (Judges 3:7), and taught this sin to their children. This later generation, the grand-children who were not taught about God's miracles and covenants were *"another generation after them, which knew not the Lord"* (Judges 2:10).

If Joshua was the same age as Caleb, he died in [A-577] twenty-five years into the thirty-nine-year period after the division of the land up to the first oppression by Chushanrishathaim, king of Mesopotamia. That gave only fourteen years for the next generation which was possible considering that both Judah and his son Pharez had such early births of their children. If the Jewish Rabbi's were correct that Joshua died four years earlier in [A-573], then eighteen years transpired after Joshua had died which matched Ishmael's and Shuah's age when they were mature enough to send out. When Joshua's year of birth was placed at [A-465] and death at [A-575] it meant that sixteen years remained after his death. Each period of fourteen, sixteen, or eighteen years met Scripture criteria for another generation to arrive, grow up, and become *"another generation after them, which knew not the Lord"* (Judges 2:10).

The statement, *"a long time after that,"* in Joshua 23:1 was twenty years after the land division. It would fit well for Joshua at 107 years old in

[A-572] when starting at [A-465]. That event was his last formal work before Israel. *"And it came to pass a long time after that the Lord had given rest unto Israel from all their enemies round about, that Joshua waxed old and stricken in age."* That year Joshua was about three years short of his death.

The elders were less than sixty-six at the start of the land division. All of them would have been at or less than eighty-nine years of age when Joshua died in [A-575]. Then, if those elders died at or less than 105 years of age they lived less than forty whole years in their allotted possession [A-552–591] in the promised land of Canaan. There was sixteen years of time remaining from Joshua's death for the next generation to appear before the first oppression in [A-591, 591 - 575 = 16]. This scenario fulfilled all texts as discussed, set the latest possible date of Joshua's death in [A-577], and made the best fit for his death in [A-575].

After all that was done for the Israelites in Egypt, experienced in the wilderness, witnessed in the recent crossing of the Jordan river, and reviewed with Joshua's rehearsal of God's miracles (Joshua 23–24 chpts.), *"they forsook the Lord God of their fathers"* (Judges 2:12). Israel quickly *"forgat the Lord their God, and served Baalim and the groves,"* and taught this sin to their children. This brought the necessity of the period of the judges.

What we learned:
1. That Joshua was at least as old as Caleb and died no later than [A-577] with a best fit at [A-575].
2. Enough time remained after Joshua's death to fulfill the other Scripture statements for another generation.

Make a visual tool:
Take the timeline constructed earlier. Draw a third horizontal line about 7.5 inches (19 cm) from the top of the sheet. Draw it like the first and second line from the left side to the right side with a very small margin (1/8 inch or 3 mm) to the end of the paper on each side. Then draw a vertical line about 1/2 inch (1.2 cm) high at both ends of the horizontal line and likewise draw below about 1/4 inch (6 mm). At the far right side (in small print) label it "Abram-984" or "A-984" for a shorter label, if preferred, and "Solomon's temple," on the far left side

Connecting Joshua and Judges

label it "A-552" and "Division" for when the land was divided.

[*On this third line measurements will be made from the left side and from the right side. Some visual distortion occurred between the second and the third lines because this common sized paper was not long enough. Some placements in the middle of the second and third timelines appear to overlap since forty-eight years are removed from the second timeline. Be attentive to the time markers placed underneath each event to bring clarity.*]

Then about 5/8 inch (1.6 cm) to the right of "Division" draw another vertical line and label it "Joshua-died" for the best fit year of his death. Underneath write "?A-575" for a shorter label. Label the twenty-three years between with "?23 yrs" for the time up to Joshua died. Between the "Division" and Judges 3:8 there was thirty-nine years. Draw another vertical line just short of 1 inch (2.4 cm) to the right of "Division," mark, and label it "Jdg 3:8" and below write "A-591." Label that period "39 yrs."

The first oppression lasted eight years and ended less than 1/4 inch (5 mm) from its start or 1 3/16 inches (3 cm) from "Division," label it "End-Jdg 3:8" and below "A-599." From there the 342 year period of the judges began. Obed was born in A-770, measure to the right from A-552 just under 5 1/2 inches (exactly 14 cm), make a vertical line, and label it "Obed-born" and below "A-770."

Then go to the far right side of the horizontal line and measure from the vertical line marked "Solomon's temple" about 1/8 inch (3 mm) to the left to get the beginning of Solomon's reign. Label that line "Solomon-king" and below "A-981" for when Solomon began as king. Label the space between them "~3 yrs." Then measure 1 1/16 inch (2.7 cm) to the left of "Solomon's temple," make another vertical line, label it "David-king," and below write "A-941" for when David began his 40+ year reign as king. Label the space between "David-king" and "Solomon-king" as "39 yrs." Solomon was crowned in the fall (Tishri) before David died in the spring (around Passover) so there was less than one year co-regency.

Subtraction will give you the space that remained between the "Jdg 3:8" and "David-king." According to 1 Kings 6:1 there was 479 years between the exodus from Egypt and the start of king Solomon's temple. This was only the beginning of the second month in the 480th year so just

479 whole years had gone by. Take 479 and subtract the time markers that were written in the timeline [479 - 40 years in wilderness - 7 years to conquer and divide the land - 39 years to the first oppression - just over 40 years of David as king - just under 3 years for Solomon = 350 years that remained].

That was the duration of time from the beginning of "Jdg 3:8" [A-591] unto "David-king" [A-941]. Subtract eight years of oppression under Chushanrishathaim, king of Mesopotamia (Judges 3:8) [ended A-599] and 342 years remain for the entire period that the judges served, from Othniel [A-599] through the death of Abdon [A-941], as shown above. [From "End-Jdg 3:8" to "David-king" will be 8 9/16 inches (21.75 cm). See Section IV. Judges as deliverers]

SECTION IV

Overview of Judges, Ruth and 1 Samuel

Setting

Events in the book of Judges must connect in time with events or people that precede, succeed, or overlap with it. The book of Judges recorded God's work to fulfill His promise to Abram in Genesis 12:1-3.

> Now the Lord had said unto Abram, Get thee out of thy country, and from thy kindred, and from thy father's house, unto a land that I will shew thee: And I will make of thee a great nation, and I will bless thee, and make thy name great; and thou shalt be a blessing: And I will bless them that bless thee, and curse him that curseth thee: and in thee shall all families of the earth be blessed.

This book followed after the sojourn of the fathers in Canaan, protection and slavery in Egypt, the wilderness journey, entry and conquer of Canaan, and the distribution of the land to the twelve tribes. Judges was connected to the book of Joshua by the specific repetition of a sentence, as shown earlier, and then carried on sequentially. The book of Judges significantly overlaid into the time period portrayed in the book of 1 Samuel because the time span across the period from the exodus from Egypt to the beginning of the temple construction was 479 years and the 480th year as given in 1 Kings 6:1 just began.

The sum of the periods of oppressions and judge deliverers was 350 years without counting Samson. They started with Judges 3:8 when Israel was oppressed, afflicted and served under Chushan-rishathaim king of Mesopotamia for eight years. That 350-year period proceeded all the way through Judges 12:13-15 to when Judge Abdon the son of Hillel had served for eight years.

From the exodus out of Egypt to the beginning of Solomon's reign (1 Kings 6:1) was about 476 years [479 - 3 = 476]. David reigned almost forty and one-half years (see SECTION II, Part 5, footnote L), so the time in years unto when David began as king was about 436 years [476 - ~40 = ~436]. Then take away from 436 the forty years in the wilderness, subtract the seven years through the conquering and land division, and subtract thirty-nine years for Judges 2:7 and arrive at 350 years for the period of the sequential judges and oppressions.

By this simple subtraction process we properly infer that the period of the judges preceded and ended with the start of the reign of David. King David was a descendant of Abraham, a descendant of Judah, a son of Jesse, a victor in every battle, a prophet of God, a king over Judah and Israel, the sweet singer of Israel, and ancestor to Christ Jesus. David was a type of Christ in both his sufferings and kingdom. For these reasons David and the other named individuals must be connected not only by a lineage list given in Scripture but also by other related information that join together or align the individuals in time. These will affirm the span of time given from Abraham to David.

Comprehensive solution

Because this time period of the judges was troublesome to resolve, a good solution to this long standing Biblical puzzle must incorporate and be consistent with many other biblical statements. The solution must explain more than the original problem of the sum of years, interconnect with other known or easily resolved pieces, and be consistent with the various pieces most have not included. To validate the solution to the puzzle of the period of the judges these details must be resolved.

The priest Ahiah named in 1 Samuel 14:3, 18-19, 36-42 must fit with the lineage of Meraioth (Eli, 1 Chronicles 6:6, 52) and their Levitical periods of service. The two sons of Eli, Hophni and Phinehas (Amariah), must fit into God's condemnation against Eli and his progeny in 1

Samuel 2:31, *"Behold, the days come, that I will cut off thine arm, and the arm of thy father's house, that there shall not be an old man in thine house."* Eli must be born neither too soon nor to late since Solomon removed his great-great-grandson Abiathar (1 Samuel 14:3; 22:9, 20) and installed his great-grandson Zadok as high priest (1 Kings 2:26-27; 4:4) before Zadok died under the family penalty of 1 Samuel 2:31.

Any solution to the puzzle of the period of the judges must take into account the fulfilled prophecies of 1 Samuel 2:12-17, 27-36; 3:11-14 with the death of Eli's sons Hophni and Phinehas, grandsons Ahitub and Ahiah, great-grandson Ahimelech, and many others at Nob. The start of priest training at age twenty-five with full service from thirty to fifty years of age must be applied (Numbers 8:23-25; Numbers 4; 1 Chronicles 23:3, 24-27). Expressions about girded with *"a linen ephod,"* in 1 Samuel 2:18, 28; 14:3; 22:18; 23:6, must fit the account for each named person before and after David became king. The periods of Levitical service for Eli's descendants, who were named up through the reign of Solomon must fit the details given in each account.

Saul's age at his death must fit all descriptions about him, likewise for Jesse. Both Jonathan's and David's absence when the ark was captured from Saul must be adequately explained. And where was Samson when the ark was captured? Moreover a good solution to the difficult puzzle of placement for the beginning of oppressions (Judges 3:8) until the end of the period of the judges (through Judges 12:13-15, a period of 350 years) must interconnect one or more of the last judges with the life spans of Eli (98 years), Samuel (89-90 years), and/or Saul (<80 years), and then with his successors Ishbosheth and David.

This comprehensive solution to the puzzle of the period of the judges with its step-by-step explanation must incorporate all of the commonly used core text plus every applicable peripheral verse into a cohesive, defendable placement in time. A good resolution must neither distort plain Scripture texts nor use multiple miracles for birth ages for either Judah's or Levi's lineages but it may apply unexpected solutions. Why events align and time periods overlap must be shown. Those requirements mentioned above plus other statements must be taken into account. Rethinking the period of the judges used the stated lineages of Judah and Levi, applied other Biblical information, and integrated these into one much larger unified solution.

Using Scriptures carefully

Many birth, death, or event years could not be resolved without knowing when an ancestor was born. Figuring out the birth ranges of people in the period of the book of Ruth and 1 Samuel required extensive use of the text of Genesis plus some pieces from the texts of Exodus, Leviticus, Numbers or Deuteronomy. Almost every solution went back in some manner to Abraham, his sons, grandsons, and great-grandsons. We will use these lineages and build the varied event times for individuals as each problem demands, sometimes repeating or accessing the same core information with emphasis focused upon a different descendant and their progeny.

Because Scripture defines its own terms, various expressions must be recognized, the scriptural meaning discerned, and applied to this lengthy word story problem. This enforced the use of the Biblical principle of substitution when meanings of terms or word phrases were integrated and substituted into the text. Those colloquial terms and their applications in the period of the judges were generally familiar to the Israelites from Joshua up to the Babylonian captivity and probably retained up through Malachi. But they were not familiar to us thirty centuries later.

The text's author(s), by using those colloquial terms, assumed a reader had a comprehensive knowledge of the Mosaic writings, especially the Levitical requirements. This was a proper expectation since Israel was directed to fulfill the law. They were to obey the requirements of the law and pass the knowledge of God from parent to child from generation to generation (Deuteronomy 4:9; 11:19; 17:10-11; Psalm 78:4-7).

Introduction to Samuel

Samuel was in a unique position to learn about, collect, collate, and record in an orderly form the material contained in the book of Judges. His work at the tabernacle from childhood through the term of formal Levitical service brought him in contact with innumerable people. His deep interest in the work of God among His covenant people, his service as a circulating judge, his calling as a prophet of God to be involved with the people of Israel, the elders, Saul, and David prepared Samuel for dialogue with numerous individuals. He met and spoke with young to old individuals as they came before the tabernacle to bring their offerings throughout his years of service.

Samuel served with a willing heart, as he declared in 1 Samuel 3:4-14, *"Here am I." "And he worshipped the Lord there."* (1 Samuel 1:28b) *"And all Israel from Dan even to Beersheba knew that Samuel was established to be a prophet of the Lord."* (1 Samuel 3:20)

The historical conviction was that Samuel wrote the books of Judges, Ruth, and the primary part of 1 Samuel with the end added after his death (1 Chronicles 29:29). Of course, nothing that occurred after Samuel died was written by him. Samuel, by virtue of his national recognition and integrity of character, could have obtained written materials from various tribal and family records, collated the material, and made one cohesive account under God's guidance. Then he could have this combined material validated by the contemporary elders of Israel (1 Samuel 8:4; 12:3) and men from the school of the prophets. This made more sense of the fine-grained details, expressions, and conversations used in the text.

But there was also the possibility that either Nathan or Gad continued Samuel's preparatory work and finished writing Judges, Ruth, and 1 Samuel under David's purview. This must be considered since the last sequential judge in the book of Judges finished his service after Samuel died, as detailed later. Recall that the book of Ruth was David's family history and that much of 1 Samuel was about David, his words, actions, and movements. A third, yet quite remote possibility, was that Solomon in his great wisdom took the prior notes and writings of both Samuel and David, sorted out the placement of these details, and completed the books of Judges, Ruth, and 1 Samuel. This last scenario was similar to Moses writing out the Pentateuch.

Even when Israel by way of their elders sought a king to lead and defend them, God commended Samuel in 1 Samuel 8:7 saying, *"... Hearken unto the voice of the people in all that they say unto thee: for they have not rejected thee, but they have rejected me, that I should not reign over them."* Samuel remained faithful. Later in life Samuel challenged Israel to bring any charge against him in 1 Samuel 12:3.

> Behold, here I am: witness against me before the Lord, and before his anointed: whose ox have I taken? or whose ass have I taken? or whom have I defrauded? whom have I oppressed? or of whose hand have I received any bribe to blind mine eyes therewith? and I will restore it you.

Because of his faithfulness before all the tribes of Israel they trusted Samuel and granted him access to their individual family and tribal written records. From his communications with Israelites at the tabernacle and their written records Samuel could assemble the material for the book of Judges and put the accounts of the judges into proper sequential order. He could also assemble and present the early material of 1 Samuel.

Years later, when David fled to Samuel at Ramah he could have given the details of the book of Ruth to all who were at the school of the prophets. During the nine years that David was hunted by Saul Samuel could have written Ruth. The earlier events of the book of 1 Samuel were most likely written by Samuel and finished later with David, Nathan (1 Chronicles 29:29; 2 Chronicles 9:29) and Gad, adding appropriate parts with a prophet's insight and historian's perspective under God's guidance. Subsequent writers in 1 Samuel 25:1 reported Samuel's death within two years of the death of Saul and his sons in 28:3 in battle with the Philistines. This was just prior to the sixteen months (1 Samuel 27:7) that David and his band dwelt in southwestern Israel in the area of Philistine occupation by Ziklag before he returned to Judah and became king.

The meaning of "judge"

What was meant by the term, "judge," when used in the books of Judges and 1 Samuel? Earlier under Moses in Exodus 18:20-25 and Deuteronomy 1:15 God gave direction for Moses to appoint judges over the people to deal with their conflicts, disagreements, and application of the laws and commandments God had given to Israel. These numerous judges were placed over tens (of families, not individuals), fifties, hundreds, and thousands with increasing spheres of responsibility.

These became known as the elders of Israel (Exodus 18:21-25; 21:6, 22; 22:8-9; Numbers 25:5; Deuteronomy 1:16-18; 17:9; 21:2; 25:1; Joshua 8:33; 23:2; Judges 2:16; 1 Samuel 8:1-2; Hosea 13:10). These elders of Israel were described in various places.

> These were the renowned of the congregation, princes of the tribes of their fathers, heads of thousands in Israel. (Numbers 1:16);

> That the princes of Israel, heads of the house of their fathers, who were the princes of the tribes, and were over them that were numbered. (Numbers 7:2);

> And if they blow but with one trumpet, then the princes, which are heads of the thousands of Israel, shall gather themselves unto thee. (Leviticus 10:4);

> And Moses spake unto the heads of the tribes concerning the children of Israel, saying, This is the thing which the Lord hath commanded. (Numbers 30:1);

> And Moses, and Eleazar the priest, and all the princes of the congregation, went forth to meet them without the camp. (Numbers 31:13);

> And the chief fathers of the families of the children of Gilead, the son of Machir, the son of Manasseh, of the families of the sons of Joseph, came near, and spake before Moses, and before the princes, the chief fathers of the children of Israel. (Numbers 36:1);

> And these are the countries which the children of Israel inherited in the land of Canaan, which Eleazar the priest, and Joshua the son of Nun, and the heads of the fathers of the tribes of the children of Israel, distributed for inheritance to them. (Joshua 14:1);

> And with him ten princes, of each chief house a prince throughout all the tribes of Israel; and each one was an head of the house of their fathers among the thousands of Israel. (Joshua 22:14)

Then in Deuteronomy 17:9 and 19:17 Moses spoke of the high priest as the judge to whom these judges or elders were to bring difficult cases.

> If there arise a matter too hard for thee in judgment, between blood and blood, between plea and plea, and between stroke and stroke, being matters of controversy within thy gates: then shalt thou arise, and get thee up into the place which the Lord thy God shall choose; And thou shalt come unto the priests the Levites, and unto the judge that shall be in those days, and enquire; and they shall shew thee the sentence of judgment: And thou shalt do according to the sentence, which they of that place which the Lord shall choose shall shew thee; and thou shalt observe to do according to all that they inform thee: According to the sentence of the law which they shall teach thee, and according to the judgment which they shall tell thee, thou shalt do: thou shalt not decline from the sentence which they shall shew thee, to the right hand, nor to the left. (Deuteronomy 17:8-11)

> If a false witness rise up against any man to testify against him that which is wrong; Then both the men, between whom the controversy is, shall stand before the Lord, before the priests and the judges, which shall be in those days; And the judges shall make diligent inquisition: and, behold, if the witness be a false witness, and hath testified falsely against his brother; Then shall ye do unto him, as he had thought to have done unto his brother: so shalt thou put the evil away from among you. And those which remain shall hear, and fear, and shall henceforth commit no more any such evil among you. (Deuteronomy 19:16-20)

Judges as deliverers

The book of Judges only used the term "judge" for various deliverers of the people of Israel. This name was introduced in Judges 2:11-19 to describe Israel's conduct and the purpose for this type of rescuer.

> And the children of Israel did evil in the sight of the Lord, and served Baalim: And they forsook the Lord God of their fathers, which brought them out of the land of Egypt, and followed other gods, of the gods of the people that were round about them, and

bowed themselves unto them, and provoked the Lord to anger. And they forsook the Lord, and served Baal and Ashtaroth. And the anger of the Lord was hot against Israel, and he delivered them into the hands of spoilers that spoiled them, and he sold them into the hands of their enemies round about, so that they could not any longer stand before their enemies. Whithersoever they went out, the hand of the Lord was against them for evil, as the Lord had said, and as the Lord had sworn unto them: and they were greatly distressed. Nevertheless the Lord raised up judges, which delivered them out of the hand of those that spoiled them. And yet they would not hearken unto their judges, but they went a whoring after other gods, and bowed themselves unto them: they turned quickly out of the way which their fathers walked in, obeying the commandments of the Lord; but they did not so. And when the Lord raised them up judges, then the Lord was with the judge, and delivered them out of the hand of their enemies all the days of the judge: for it repented the Lord because of their groanings by reason of them that oppressed them and vexed them. And it came to pass, when the judge was dead, that they returned, and corrupted themselves more than their fathers, in following other gods to serve them, and to bow down unto them; they ceased not from their own doings, nor from their stubborn way.

Judges 3:1-7 was specific when stating God was going to test them.

Now these are the nations which the Lord left, to prove Israel by them, even as many of Israel as had not known all the wars of Canaan; Only that the generations of the children of Israel might know, to teach them war, at the least such as before knew nothing thereof; Namely, five lords of the Philistines, and all the Canaanites, and the Sidonians, and the Hivites that dwelt in mount Lebanon, from mount Baalhermon unto the entering in of Hamath. And they were to prove Israel by them, to know whether they would hearken unto the commandments of the Lord, which he commanded their fathers by the hand of Moses. And the children of Israel dwelt among the Canaanites, Hittites, and Amorites, and Perizzites, and Hivites, and Jebusites: And they took their daughters to be their wives, and gave their daughters to their sons, and served their gods. And the children of Israel did evil in the sight of the Lord, and forgat the Lord their God, and served Baalim and the groves.

After Joshua and the elders died and another generation arose Israel's first punishment came in Judges 3:8-11.

Therefore the anger of the Lord was hot against Israel, and he sold them into the hand of Chushanrishathaim king of Mesopotamia: and the children of Israel served Chushanrishathaim eight years. And when the children of Israel cried unto the Lord, the Lord raised up a deliverer to the children of Israel, who delivered them, even Othniel the son of Kenaz, Caleb's younger brother. And the Spirit of the Lord came upon him, and he judged Israel, and went out to war: and the Lord delivered Chushanrishathaim king of Mesopotamia into his hand; and his hand prevailed against Chushanrishathaim. And the land had rest forty years. And Othniel the son of Kenaz died.

In the book of Judges this term "judge" was only applied to a person who delivered Israel or a portion of Israel from oppression (Ruth 1:1; 2 Samuel 7:11, and perhaps in 1 Chronicles 17:6, 10 and Isaiah 1:26). A functional definition covering all three types of judges was this, individuals raised by the Lord to be godly leaders who served for the well-being of God's covenant people. This included the office of high priest and explained why Eli was called a judge (1 Samuel 4:15-19) who had served for forty years. Every high priest was a judge from Aaron onward, even reaching to Caiaphas before whom Jesus stood in Matthew 26:57.

This information prompted a question. Why of all the high priests that lived during the books of Judges and 1 Samuel was Eli alone pointed out as a "judge?" The answer might be that Eli was brought into the text due to Samuel's connection with his family. But that answer was insufficient.

Eli was given a specific time frame of priestly service, point of death, age at death, length of time as judge, messages of warning from God, and punishment. Those details were recorded to establish chronological information. Moreover, Eli had numerous offspring named and various people mentioned that directly connected with him or were connected to those connected to him. That gave all of the individuals a limitation to the time range for their lives. Eli became the vital key to resolve connecting 1 Samuel with Judges.

This general definition of a judge explained why the Levite Samuel was called a judge, *"And Samuel judged Israel all the days of his life"* (1 Samuel 7:15). It also explained why Joel and Abiah were called judges (1 Samuel 8:1-2). Only some of those broadly called "judges" were deliverers and those deliverers were the type of individuals specifically pointed out in the book of Judges.

The term judge was used in that way in 1 Samuel 15:11 when Samuel chastened the elders, *"And the Lord sent Jerubbaal, and Bedan, and Jephthah, and Samuel, and delivered you out of the hand of your enemies on every side, and ye dwelled safe."* By this connection with *"Jerubbaal, and Bedan* [Jair, 1 Chronicles 7:17], *and Jephthah,"* Samuel named himself a delivering judge.

He served at the same time as some other judges, whether they were Israel's elders, high priests or delivering judges. A distinct case of delivering judges overlapping will be demonstrated with Samuel. As explained later, Samuel was born under judge Tola, was at age twenty when judge Jair began, at age sixty when judge Jephthah began, at age eighty-three when judge Abdon began, and died about two years before judge Abdon finished his eight years.

The periods of service of this specific type of judge and of Israel's oppressions interspersed between them, as given in the book of Judges, are shown in Tables 7 and 8. Together these two sets of periods, 276 and 74 years, summed to 350 years. The forty-year period of Judges 13:1 when Israel did evil again and served the Philistines was not an additional period, but was a concurrent period. Likewise, with Samson's twenty years as judge. Both are explained in detail below in Section V. (See Table 7 and Table 8)

During this lengthy time Israel had some renewals interspersed between periods of idolatry and disobedience. After many years this period of sporadic leadership began to transition with the lengthy service of Samuel and the anointing of king Saul. Now, the text in 1 Kings 6:1 was explicit. *"And it came to pass in the four hundred and eightieth year after the children of Israel were come out of the land of Egypt, in the fourth year of Solomon's reign over Israel, in the month Zif, which is the second month, that he began to build the house of the Lord."*

Table 7. These judges were given in order and their periods summed to 276 years.

Scripture	Period description
Jdg 3:7-11	Judge: Othniel, son of Kenaz; land had rest forty years
Jdg 3:15-30	Judge: Ehud the son of Gera, a Benjamite; rest eighty years
Jdg 3:31	Judge: Shamgar the son of Anath, see: Jdg 5:6; no time given
Jdg 4:4-24; 5:31	Judges: Deborah; then Barak, son of Abinoam of Kedesh-naphtali; rest forty years
Jdg 6:7–8:28	Judge: Gideon, of Joash the Abi-ezrite of Ophrah; rest forty years
Jdg 10:1-2	Judge: Tola the son of Puah, son of Dodo, of Issachar in Shamir in Mt Ephraim; twenty-three years
Jdg 10:3	Judge: Jair, a Gileadite; twenty-two years
Jdg 11:1–12:7	Judge: Jephthah, son of Gilead; six years
Jdg 11:8-10	Judge: Ibzan of Beth-lehem; seven years
Jdg 12:11-12	Judge: Elon, a Zebulonite; ten years
Jdg 12:13-15	Judge: Abdon the son of Hillel, of Pirathon; eight years

This summed the separate periods of the Judges to 276 years.

Table 8. The oppression periods were given in this order and summed to 74 years.

Scripture	Period description
Jdg 3:8	under Chushanrishathaim, king of Mesopotamia; six years
Jdg 3:12-14	Israel did evil again; Eglon the king of Moab, Ammon, Amalek; eighteen years
Jdg 4:1-3	under Jabin king of Canaan; twenty years
Jdg 6:1	Israel did evil again seven years
Jdg 8:33–9:57	*"Israel turned again, and went a whoring after Baalim, and made Baal-berith their god;"* Abimelech attempted three year reign
Jdg 10:6-8	Israel did evil again; served: Baalim, Ashtaroth & served gods of: Syria, Zidon, Moab, Ammon, Philistines; eighteen years

This summed the periods of the oppressions to 74 years.

This meant that this period included: the wilderness wandering, the

Overview of Judges, Ruth and 1 Samuel

interval of conquering and dividing the land, the period of Israel's cyclic waywardness and rescue under numerous judges, the reign of Saul (Numbers 34:17; Joshua 13–19 chpts.; and Acts 13:16-22), the reign of David (2 Samuel 2:11; 5:4; 1 Kings 2:11), the beginning three years of Solomon's reign, and fifteen days into the fourth year which ended the month Abib. The sixteenth day started Zif 1 and on the second day, Zif 2, the temple building formally began (2 Chronicles 3:2).

Start at the exact day of the exodus from Egypt on Abib 15. Add forty years for the wilderness, add six years for conquering, add one year for dividing the land^P, add 350 years of waywardness and judges as summed just above, add forty years for David's reign, add three years into Solomon's reign which equaled 440 years. That left thirty-nine years from the land division up to Judges 3:8 under the first oppression by Chushanrishathaim [479 - 40 - 7 - 350 - 40 - 3 = 39]. Then add fifteen days to get from Abib 15 to the end of Abib (day 30). The next day was Zif 1, exactly 479 years and the sixteenth day of the 480th year counting from the very day of departure from Egypt (1 Kings 6:1). 1. On the seventeenth day, Zif 2, the temple construction formally began according to 2 Chronicles 3:2.

The thirty-nine-year time period that followed after the year of the division of the land (or, if you prefer, forty years from the end of conquering) included these five pieces.

P. The time to conquer and divide the land was seven years which was consistent with the seventh year rest cycle mandated when they entered the land (Leviticus 25:1-18) and God's promise for provision (Exodus 23:11; Leviticus 25:4, 19-21). For six years they labored to defeat the inhabitants and in the seventh year the land was distributed to the tribes. Then they dispersed and took ownership of their own portions. God promised to feed them for the seventh year from the increase of the sixth year (Leviticus 25:21). While they traveled and spread out they must of necessity eat from the land, as God outlined.

Since they could not immediately arrive at their own plot, much of that year passed to disperse, travel, and survey the land to subdivide it for each tribe. Each tribe apportioned their tribal allotment to the major family units and in turn these subdivided the land to the subunits from these families. All of this took time. By the end of this process it was too late in the year to plant crops, so God promised in Leviticus 25:20-22, "And if ye shall say, What shall we eat the seventh year? behold, we shall not sow, nor gather in our increase: Then I will command my blessing upon you in the sixth year, and it shall bring forth fruit for three years." That meant that year six would grow enough to last through Joshua and Eleazar apportioning the land to the tribes, the tribal travel to their allotment, the further land divisions to their families and their subunits. God promised the land's produce would carry them into the eighth year until the harvesting of that year was brought in to eat and sufficient to reach beyond that. [See also: http://www.rcyoung.org/papers.html]

1) Joshua 13:1, *"Now Joshua was old and stricken in years; and the Lord said unto him, Thou art old and stricken in years, and there remaineth yet very much land to be possessed."*;
2) Joshua 14:7-11, where Caleb stated he was eighty-five years old;
3) Joshua 23:2, when, *"Joshua called for all Israel, and for their elders, and for their heads, and for their judges, and for their officers"*;
4) Joshua 24:29, *"And it came to pass after these things, that Joshua the son of Nun, the servant of the Lord, died, being an hundred and ten years old."*; and
5) Joshua 24:31, *"And Israel served the Lord all the days of Joshua, and all the days of the elders that overlived Joshua, and which had known all the works of the Lord, that he had done for Israel."* This was repeated in Judges 2:7, *"And the people served the Lord all the days of Joshua, and all the days of the elders that outlived Joshua, who had seen all the great works of the Lord, that he did for Israel."*

This placed the end of the eight years of judge Abdon the son of Hillel of Pirathon (Judges 12:13-15) when David began to reign as king over Judah. During those thirty-nine years following the division of the land (or, if you prefer to think this way, forty years from the end of the six-year period conquering the land) during which Joshua died and the elders died, *"there arose another generation after them, which knew not the Lord, nor yet the works which he had done for Israel"* (Judges 2:10-13). Then came the first oppression by the king of Mesopotamia (Judges 3:8) which lasted eight years.

Table 9. Lists the time periods after the land division across Israel's oppressions and judges through Abdon and sums the total.

Scripture	Period description	Years	Summed
Jdg chpts. 1–2; 3:1-5	(start at land division, [A-552]) *"And there arose another generation after them who did not know the Lord or the work that he had done for Israel. They took foreign wives, and gave their own daughters to their sons, and they served their gods; served Baalim and the groves."* [part of the thirty-nine years, below]	-	0

Jdg 2:7	"*the people served the Lord all the days of Joshua, and all the days of the elders that outlived Joshua,*" thirty-nine years	39	39
Jdg 3:8	under Chushanrishathaim, king of Mesopotamia; six years	8	47
Jdg 3:7-11	Judge: Othniel, son of Kenaz; land had rest forty years	40	87
Jdg 3:12-14	Israel did evil again; Eglon the king of Moab, Ammon, Amalek; eighteen years	18	105
Jdg 3:15-30	Judge: Ehud the son of Gera, a Benjamite; rest eighty years	80	185
Jdg 3:31	Judge: Shamgar the son of Anath, see: Jdg 5:6; no time given	-	185
Jdg 4:1-3	under Jabin king of Canaan; Judge: Deborah, twenty years	20	205
Jdg 4:4-24; 5:31	Judges: Deborah; then Barak, son of Abinoam of Kedesh-naphtali; rest forty years	40	245
Jdg 6:1	Israel did evil again seven years	7	252
Jdg 6:7–8:28	Judge: Gideon, of Joash the Abi-ezrite of Ophrah; rest forty years	40	292
Jdg 8:33; 9:1-57	"*Israel turned again, and went a whoring after Baalim, and made Baal-berith their god*"; Abimelech attempted three year reign	3	295
Jdg 10:1-2	Judge: Tola the son of Puah, son of Dodo, of Issachar in Shamir in Mt Ephraim; twenty-three years	23	318
Jdg 10:3	Judge: Jair, a Gileadite; twenty-two years	22	340
Jdg 10:6-18	Israel did evil again; served: Baalim, Ashtaroth & served gods of: Syria, Zidon, Moab, Ammon, Philistines; eighteen years	18	358
Jdg 11:1–12:7	Judge: Jephthah, son of Gilead; six years	6	364
Jdg 11:8-10	Judge: Ibzan of Beth-lehem; seven years	7	371
Jdg 12:11-12	Judge: Elon, a Zebulonite; ten years	10	381
Jdg 12:13-15	Judge: Abdon the son of Hillel, of Pirathon; eight years	8	389

This summed the whole period of the book of Judges to 389 years.

The next 342-year period [389 - 39 - 8 = 342] included the judges service to Israel until David became king. This began sequentially with Othniel and ended after Abdon. Saul was anointed and began as king over Israel halfway through the eighteen years of oppression given in Judges 10:6-18.

This made Saul's service as king concurrent with the last four judges for thirty-one years. Saul's reign was concurrent with Jephthah for six years, Ibzan for seven years, Elon for ten years, and Abdon for eight years [9 + 6 + 7 + 10 + 8 = 40; see Table 9]. After Saul and Abdon died, in the same year David became king over Judah. (See Table 9.)

Only thirty-nine years occurred for the time period between the division of the land unto Judges 3:8 (or, if you prefer, forty years from the end of conquering). This clearly made the span from when Joshua finished the land division [A-552] until Saul began as king [A-901] a period of 349 years (if you prefer, from the end of conquering [A-551] to [A-901] was 350 years). The time up to David began his reign in [A-941] was a period of 389 years, and up to Solomon began the temple in [A-984] a period of 432 years. When the forty years of the wilderness journey, the seven years of conquering and dividing the land, the thirty-nine-year period up to the first oppression, the 350 years across the service of the judges, David's forty-year reign, and the three years of Solomon's reign was summed the total met the criteria of 1 Kings 6:1. Then the temple construction began after 479 years had transpired [40 + 7 + (39 + 350) + 40 + 3 = 479].^{Q}

Q. The Temple building started in 1 Kings 6:1 (and 2 Chronicles 3:1-2) by counting from the first year as stated in Exodus 12:2. That same year in the same or first month on the 15th day (Abib 15) was the day of departure from Egypt. (See: Esther 3:7, Exodus 12 ch.; Numbers 28:16; 33:3; 2 Chronicles 35:1; Ezra 6:19; Ezekiel 45:21)
The text of 1 Kings 6:1 read, *"And it came to pass in the four hundred and eightieth year after the children of Israel were come out of the land of Egypt, in the fourth year of Solomon's reign over Israel, in the month Zif, which is the second month, that he began to build the house of the Lord."*
This Scripture text meant start counting from the 15th day, the day of departure. The first month Abib (later known as Nisan) of the first year of the Hebrew calendar aligned with Exodus 12:2. Then count off 479 years to get to the start of the Temple building. In simpler terms take the 480th year minus the first year = 479 complete years transpired.
When Adonijah rebelled (1 Kings 1:1-53) David installed Solomon as co-ruler, so that as David lost his health and died Solomon was in place to lead. This made a shorter time period in which Solomon reigned in his first Hebrew calendar year. He was installed later in the year in the month Tishri** of calendar year [A-981]. The second year, using the same calendar as 1 Kings 6:1, started with Abib 1 of [A-982] (Exodus 13:4). The third year started on Abib 1 of [A-983]. The fourth calendar year started on Abib 1 of [A-984]. As quoted

Overview of Judges, Ruth and 1 Samuel

Can other pieces be brought to show that this was true? Can this time period be solved by just a few quick verses and comments? The answer to the first question was yes, and the answer to the second was no, not at all.

The complete key needed was to align the age or time marker of one significant individual's life in the book of 1 Samuel with the age or time marker of another person's life in the book of Judges. A large amount of material was required to present the necessary pieces, thoroughly consider all aspects, and adequately support that alignment. Only this brought a fully satisfactory and quite defendable solution.

What we learned:

1. The puzzle of the period of the judges must be resolved by fitting Samuel together with Meraioth (Eli) and their Levitical service. The two sons Hophni and Phinehas (Amariah) must fit into God's condemnation against Eli and his progeny in 1 Samuel 2:31. These lives and their progeny must in turn intersect with others.

2. Samuel was not able to write the whole of the book of Judges or 1 Samuel since he died before their events were completed. The prophets Gad and Nathan that served before David in conjunction with David finished each after Samuel's death.

3. All high priests that lived during the period covered by the books of Judges, Ruth, and 1 Samuel were judges, but not like those judges who rescued Israel. They were the highest judge for difficult court cases and interpretation of the law.

4. The book of Judges covered the time period from the division of the land up to king David.

---

above, "*in the fourth* [calendar] *year of Solomon's reign over Israel*" the Temple construction began "*in the month Zif, which is the second month*" (Zif 1) in [A-984]. This was the 16th day into "*the four hundred and eightieth year*" from departure since a full 479 years and fifteen days transpired after Israel's exodus from Egypt. Starting from the very day of departure for Egypt on the fifteenth day count off fifteen more days into the 480th year. This was the last day of Abib which had thirty days [15 + 15 = 30]. The sixteenth or next day began the second month or Zif 1. On Zif 2 formal construction began.

** "When Did Solomon Die?", Rodger C. Young, www.rcyoung.org/frame5.html, or at www.etsjets.org/files/JETS-PDFs/46/464/46-4p p589-603_ JETS.pdf, accessed 10/7/2017. For validation of the placement of Solomon's reign which started before the end of David's forty-year reign see: Rodger Young's Papers on Chronology, www.rcyoung.org/papers.html, accessed March 26, 2017.

5. The periods of individual judge's service began thirty-nine years after the land division (or forty years after conquering) and after eight more years under the oppression of Chushanrishathaim and then ended when David became king over Judah.

6. Samuel served as prophet and Saul served as king while the delivering judges helped Israel.

7. How to apply all of the Scriptures to fully understand and use 1 Kings 6:1.

SECTION V

Connections between Judges and 1 Samuel

Simultaneous judges

These two books cover some of the same time period from different perspectives. The book of Judges was the record of the ongoing story of Israel in their promised land. The text of 1 Samuel went farther in detail and gave necessary time related clues, not really hidden, but presented in unique ways.

Samuel was born at least seventy or more years before David became king since he died about two years before Saul died (1 Samuel 25:1; 31:6). That placed his lifetime in the period of many later judges. This also made Eli, who died at ninety-eight years, live through even more years of the judges.

For a general perspective, by calculating backwards from the end of the last judge Abdon, Eli was born somewhere during the forty-year period in which Gideon served Israel. Samuel was born during the twenty-three-year-long service of judge Tola of Issachar. These two men, each named as a judge in 1 Samuel, lived and served during the time periods that other notable judges had served.

Specific events and time periods in the book of Judges overlap other events and time periods given in Scripture. The first example for the concurrence of judges was stated in Judges 3:31 when Shamgar was not given any type of time duration that he served as judge. This was followed by Judges 5:6 which said, *"In the days of Shamgar the son of*

Anath, in the days of Jael, the highways were unoccupied, and the travellers walked through byways." The only Jael given in Scripture was, *"the wife of Heber the Kenite,"* from Judges 4:17 who lived before and during the period of Deborah and Barak and helped with the victory over Sisera.

This text implied that Shamgar, Deborah, and Barak served at the same time; therefore, perhaps others also did. For a second example, Eli served as judge forty years (1 Samuel 4:3-5, 11-18) concurrently with Samuel (1 Samuel 7:6, 15), while in turn Samuel was judge over Israel concurrently with the reign of Saul (1 Samuel 9:1–10:13). And Samuel lived through David's earlier years.

Very likely Saul's forty-year reign was not God's intended program of protection and was only obtained by the special pleading of the elders of Israel (1 Samuel 12:17-18). Samuel stated that plainly in his speech chiding the elders of Israel.

> And when ye saw that Nahash the king of the children of Ammon came against you, ye said unto me, Nay; but a king shall reign over us: when the Lord your God was your king. Now therefore behold the king whom ye have chosen, and whom ye have desired! and, behold, the Lord hath set a king over you. (1 Samuel 12:12-13)

Then Saul's reign as king was not additive, but occurred simultaneous to the last forty years of the period of the judges and, of course, with Samuel who anointed him. This was implied in the text of 1 Samuel 8:4-7.

> Then all the elders of Israel gathered themselves together, and came to Samuel unto Ramah, And said unto him, Behold, thou art old, and thy sons walk not in thy ways: now make us a king to judge us like all the nations. But the thing displeased Samuel, when they said, Give us a king to judge us. And Samuel prayed unto the Lord. And the Lord said unto Samuel, Hearken unto the voice of the people in all that they say unto thee: for they have not rejected thee, but they have rejected me, that I should not reign over them.

The premature request for a king was directly addressed in 1 Samuel 12:17-18. This meant that Saul had served much of his forty years as king during the periods of the last four sequential judges: Jephthah, Ibzan, Elon, and Abdon. These multiple pieces revealed that the Scriptures had some form of overlap across this time span.

The concurrence with other judges helped explain why Samuel took Saul and renewed his kingship in 1 Samuel 11:14, *"Then said Samuel to the people, Come, and let us go to Gilgal, and renew the kingdom there."* Saul was unable to wholly defend Israel without other special help. Many despised him as king and even opposed him since he was not fully effective as king, at least in their eyes, not wholly capable in defending Israel (1 Samuel 10:27; 11:12).

Saul was slowly building the general acceptance of a national leader over all twelve tribes. The men of Israel were gradually being unified through their assembly together for various battles under one captain (1 Samuel 9:16; 10:1; 13:14; 22:2). This explained the words in 1 Samuel 14:47-48.

> So Saul took the kingdom over Israel, and fought against all his enemies on every side, against Moab, and against the children of Ammon, and against Edom, and against the kings of Zobah, and against the Philistines: and whithersoever he turned himself, he vexed them.

If Samuel's lifetime can properly be placed in connection with one or more judges from the book of Judges, then the second book overlaid upon the first and formed one longer account given in two different methods. Or, if one or more events from Eli's ninety-eight years match with one or more of the judges, the two books can also be interconnected in time. That would resolve and wholly connect the oppression and deliverance events in the book of Judges to the events given in the other books of Scripture.

The divisions of 1 Samuel

The book of 1 Samuel was primarily structured in topical order. Inside each topic the material was given in sequential order. That structure explained the historical difficulty to discern and understand the interconnections between individuals' lives.

The book of 1 Samuel started with the topic of Samuel covering his placement in time and circumstances (1:1–2:11). Then 1 Samuel followed various individuals surrounding Samuel while he grew and served at the tabernacle. The book also noted God's warnings and prophecies against the corrupt priests (2:12-32).

Then the book's author went back and took up the topic of Samuel's core ministry at the tabernacle (3:1-21). Next, 1 Samuel jumped to a much later time period, detailed the fulfillment of the prophecies against Eli and his sons, closed their account (4:1-22), finished the topic of the captured ark (5:1–7:2), and spoke of the punishment to the Philistines (7:3-14) finishing their forty-year oppression. This special defeat of the Philistines was seventy years after Samuel was called at age twelve. It was Samuel's greatest feat as a delivering judge over the Israelites.

After this the next topic was about the national circumstances where Samuel: appointed his sons as judges; interacted with the elders; selected, anointed, and installed Saul; and reported on the early years of Saul as king (7:15–11:15). The topic of Samuel's ministry to the elders and to Saul continued until God rejected Saul (12:1–15:35). One portion of that broader topic of Samuel's ministry to the elders and to Saul gave the effects of Saul's reign and his work with Jonathan to defend Israel (13:1–15:35).

Then the book of 1 Samuel followed the selection of David, his great victory over Goliath when he won the hearts of the people, and David's long journey to become king (16:1–30:31). This part of the book of 1 Samuel included David's interactions with Saul, Jonathan, and Michal, revealed Saul's jealousy, detailed Saul's pursuit of David, and presented various other conflicts. During these last two topics the book of 1 Samuel named various individuals that interconnected with Saul and/or David. Then the book concluded with the battle, death, and burial of Saul and three of his sons (28:1–31:13).

Samuel lived with Eli (Meraioth), anointed and directed Saul, anointed David, hosted David at Ramah, and died shortly before David became king. Samuel's period as a judge in Israel should match those facts, and align with other named contemporary individuals. From this overview the major authorship and details of Judges, Ruth, and 1 Samuel were consistent with the Levite Samuel (1 Chronicles 6:33-38; Exodus 6:24; 1 Samuel 1:1, 21). Those portions that transpired latest in time both in the book of Judges and in the book of 1 Samuel must of necessity have been completed after his death.

The beginning of 1 Samuel

The first part of 1 Samuel was about introducing Samuel. This account began with the individuals and events surrounding Samuel that were interconnected with him. Because Samuel's name means "son of God," 1 Samuel was written to give us information about him, his dedication to serving God, his work before Israel, along with other necessary details. Note the similarity to where Jesus said the Scriptures were about Himself in John 5:39, *"Search the scriptures; for in them ye think ye have eternal life: and they are they which testify of me."*

Samuel as the primary author did not express any of the information in a self-focusing or self-centered manner. In fact, most of the information interwove other individuals that were significant to God's larger plans. Using that filter of what was necessary, Samuel wrote limited information about himself. But he wrote enough to bring the connections to align his life with numerous other lives.

The second topic of 1 Samuel detailed the spiritual climate of Eli, his sons, and the elders. Samuel's words showed that all of them had rejected the Lord, His word, and His ways. So much so, that later Samuel wrote in the topic about the national circumstances, the elders sought out a king to lead them instead. But Saul did not lead Israel toward God.

Saul rejected God's word conveyed through Samuel in his ministry to the elders and to Saul. Saul disobeyed God's specific directions, was impatient under stress, destroyed God's priests who served before the tabernacle, sought to kill the Lord's anointed, and more. The results were more oppression and numerous battles of war to hold back the incursions of Israel's enemies. When the Israelites rejected God personally and by way of their king they also rejected God's rule and protection over them.

The later part of the book of 1 Samuel was mostly about David and the surrounding events that interconnected with him. Samuel did not write all of this part of the book of 1 Samuel, but had collected material for that topic and kept those pieces at the school of the prophets he had started. Since much of the later part of 1 Samuel was about David, his words with Saul, his discussions and covenants with Jonathan, his work, marriage, movements, and more, David probably had a significant part in dictating or writing this part of the book. After Samuel's death, the

SECTION V

prophets that served before David in conjunction with prophet David wrote some of the later text (1 Samuel 22:5; 2 Samuel 7:2-17; 12:1-15, 25; 24:11-19). The most fitting conclusion was that the book of 1 Samuel was prepared and primarily written by Samuel and completed soon afterwards by those who knew many intimate facts about the actions, conversations and effects of those named.

The keys

The first key passage that opened up interconnections between Samuel, Eli, Saul, Jonathan, and David was the significant discovery of the meaning of the expression, *"when Samuel was old,"* from 1 Samuel 8:1. Note well the primary reason the elders gave for asking for a king, *"Behold, thou art old"* (1 Samuel 8:5). A second key was resolving when David brought the ark to the prepared tent at Zion and using that time minus twenty years and seven months (1 Samuel 6:1; 7:2) to establish when the ark was captured. The third key was to place the death of Eli at that time, as Scripture stated in 1 Samuel 4:18, and use his age at death (v.15) to go back to his birth year.

The fourth key was applying the textual minimum age to go to war to Samson (Numbers 1:3; Judges 14:1-4) then add to this his twenty years of judging Israel (Judges 15:20; 16:31) to get forty years for his life span. This twenty-year minimum age for war was also used to establish Jonathan's age and Saul's age. Another key was recognizing the concurrence of when Israel did evil again and served the Philistines for forty years (Judges 13:1) with Eli as judge forty years (1 Samuel 4:18), and later with Samson's lifetime.

The sixth consequential key was discerning the underlying cause for the ark carried into battle. The seventh key was figuring out the context of the event for which Israel repented and Samuel prayed that brought a miracle and a significant routing of the Philistines. This allowed for the placement of Samson's death.

Then by recognizing the connection of the start of the eighteen years of Judges 10:6-18 with the start of the forty years of Judges 13:1 all parts aligned. Other insights were revealed along the way, such as with Jonathan, Jesse, the book of Ruth, et cetera. These seven major keys provided the primary intersections between the lives of Eli (Meraioth), Samuel, Saul, Jonathan, Samson, and David, given in birth order. Other

Connections between Judges and 1 Samuel

verses that described events and named an individual participant under specific circumstances brought precise intersections to further align and validate the time placement of their lives.

How can Judges Eli, Samuel, and Samson be accounted for? When were their lives and when did they serve as judges? How do we resolve the dilemma of the information in the account of the early years of Samuel's life, especially in connection with Eli, Hophni, and Phinehas?

The period of Eli and Samuel

Elkanah (and his son Samuel) was not of the tribe of Ephraim by blood, but a Levite who lived in Ephraim (1 Chronicles 6:16, 22-28). Elkanah could be named after both his home area and his lineage, hence an Ephrathite-Levite of the hill country of Ephraim. The Bible stated in 1 Samuel 1:1, *"Now there was a certain man of Ramathaim-zophim, of mount Ephraim, and his name was Elkanah* (1 Samuel 1:1-2; 1 Chronicles 6:27, 34), *the son of Jeroham* (1 Samuel 1:1-2; 1 Chronicles 6:27, 34), *the son of Elihu* (Eliel / Eliab, 1 Samuel 1:1-2; 1 Chronicles 6:27, 34), *the son of Tohu* (Toah / Nahath, 1 Samuel 1:1-2; 1 Chronicles 6:26, 34), *the son of Zuph* (Zophai, 1 Samuel 1:1-2; 1 Chronicles 6:26, 35), *an Ephrathite."*[R]

R. The text in 1 Chronicles 6:1-38 gave Samuel's Levitical ancestry from Levi (23rd generation) to Samuel (42nd generation). Across the 604 years from Levi's birth to Samuel [A-246 to A-850] there were nineteen generations for an average of 31.8 years from one generation to another. [The generations presented are counting Adam as the first generation proceeding from God.]

23rd: Levi (1 Chronicles 6:16, 33-38)} 1st born: Gershon, 2nd born: Kohath* (1 Chronicles 6:2, 16, 38), 3rd born: Merari (Genesis 46:11)];
24th: Kohath*} sons: 1st born: Amram, 2nd born: Izhar (aka: Amminadab*, Exodus 6:18; 1 Chronicles 6:22, 38), 3rd born: Hebron, 4th born: Uzziel (Exodus 6:18; 1 Chronicles 6:2, 18; 23:12);
25th: Amminadab*} 1st born: Korah* (Numbers 16:1-49; 1 Chronicles 6:37), 2nd born: Nepheg, 3rd born: Zichri (Exodus 6:21);
26th: Korah*} 1st born: Assir, 2nd born: Elkanah, 3rd born: Abiasaph / Ebiasaph* (Exodus 6:24; 1 Chronicles 6:37);
27th: Abiasaph / Ebiasaph*} to Assir (1 Chronicles 6:37);
28th: Assir (1 Chronicles 6:37);
29th: Tahath (1 Chronicles 6:37);
30th: Zephaniah (1 Chronicles 6:36);
31st: Azariah (1 Chronicles 6:36);
32nd: Joel (1 Chronicles 6:36);
33rd: Elkanah (1 Chronicles 6:36); 1st born: Amasai* (1 Chronicles 6:25, 35), 2nd born: Ahimoth (1 Chronicles 6:25);
34th: Amasai* (1Chronicles 6:25, 35);

SECTION V

This showed that Samuel was a Levite by lineage already. He was dedicated to serve God at the tabernacle simply by birth into this family. Hannah and Elkanah then also gave him over to God uniquely by giving him into another family, a preview of Jesus entering into this world.

Earlier this assertion was made, the book of 1 Samuel was not primarily constructed in sequential order, but in topical order. In the introduction the topical sequence of 1 Samuel was presented and that format was subsequently used throughout. This information became evident in parsing the statements about Eli and his family.

All of the information about Eli and his sons was given at the beginning, in one focused topic. Their lives were not laid out interspersed within the actual event sequence of linear time. To place when their life events had occurred they needed to be aligned to other events with great care.

Who is Eli?

Here was a good place to demonstrate again the use of a parenthetical insertion. The high priest was responsible for all conduct of the priests in their Levitical service at the tabernacle, the maintenance of the holy anointing oil, the incense burned in the holy upon the golden altar, the rotation of the shewbread, maintenance of the oil for the lamp stand, trimming of the lamps twice each day, the orderly execution of all sacrifices and offerings (daily, monthly, and holy day along with any spontaneous or required offerings from the people), successive inaugural ceremonies and sacrifices, the receipt of the priests' portion of the sacrifices and offerings, and the rotation of the priests and Levites through their required service period from age twenty-five to fifty,

---

35th: Nahath / Mahath (1 Chronicles 6:26, 35);
36th: Elkanah (1 Chronicles 6:35);
37th: Zuph / Zophai (1 Samuel 1:1-2; 1 Chronicles 6:26, 35);
38th: Toah / Tohu / Nahath (1 Samuel 1:1-2; 1 Chronicles 6:26, 34);
39th: Eliel / Elihu / Eliab (1 Samuel 1:1-2; 1 Chronicles 6:27, 34);
40th: Jeroham (1 Samuel 1:1-2; 1 Chronicles 6:27, 34);
41st: Elkanah (1 Samuel 1:1-2; 1 Chronicles 6:27, 34);
42nd: Shemuel / Samuel (1 Samuel 1:1-2, 8; 1 Chronicles 6:32-34) [19th generation after Levi]} 1st born: Joel / Vashni* [A-873-?] (1 Samuel 8:2; 1 Chronicles 6:28, 33), 2nd born: Abiah [A-875] (1 Samuel 8:2; 1 Chronicles 6:28 [~A-875-?]);
43rd: Joel / Vashni*} Heman [~A-893–905-???];
44th: Heman, a temple singer (1 Chronicles 6:33).

Connections between Judges and 1 Samuel

maintenance of the tabernacle and equipment, and general overseer of the distribution of the Israelite tithes for the Levites (Numbers 3:32; 4:16). This service also included teaching, seeking God's guidance by the Urim and Thummim (Numbers 27:21), and serving as the highest judge in difficult matters (Deuteronomy 17:8-9).

To make sense of apparently opposing texts, examine carefully and discern who was meant by Eli. The high priest who died at ninety-eight years of age after falling over backwards had a birth name, Meraioth, but he was commonly known as *"Eli,"* (1 Samuel 14:3; 1 Chronicles 6:6-7). This was from the Hebrew word (H5941,`Eliy {ay-lee'}; meaning: ascension or lofty) which could have been used as a title of position and/or respect. Probably each high priest in turn was known as "Eli" across this period.

If Eli was a title and not a name, then the priest to whom Hannah spoke in 1 Samuel 1:9 was the older Eli (1 Samuel 2:22), the current high priest (Zerahiah, 1 Chronicles 6:6, 50-53), *"Now Eli the priest sat upon a seat by a post of the temple of the Lord."* This older Eli gave the blessing recorded in 1 Samuel 1:17, *"Go in peace: and the God of Israel grant thee thy petition that thou hast asked of him."* The blessing upon Hannah did not come from Meraioth, the next high priest who was also titled Eli. This made much better sense of the dialogue, blessing, and Hannah's determination to give Samuel over to early Levitical service at the tabernacle as described in 1 Samuel chapter 1 through 2:11.

This removed Zerahiah's last son, Meraioth, from the initial responsibility for Samuel. Meraioth (1 Chronicles 6:6) was way too young at age fifteen to even begin as a priest (the minimum age to start training was twenty-five, Numbers 8:23-25; Numbers 4). The time difference in age between Meraioth and Samuel was only sixteen years as shown later. The descriptive text of 1 Samuel 2:12-17 referred to Zerahiah, his sons, and grandsons (all those old enough to be priests) when the narrative described their conduct.

> Now the sons of Eli were sons of Belial; they knew not the Lord. And the priest's custom with the people was, that, when any man offered sacrifice, the priest's servant came, while the flesh was in seething, with a fleshhook of three teeth in his hand; And he struck it into the pan, or kettle, or caldron, or pot; all that the

fleshhook brought up the priest took for himself. So they did in Shiloh unto all the Israelites that came thither. Also before they burnt the fat, the priest's servant came, and said to the man that sacrificed, Give flesh to roast for the priest; for he will not have sodden flesh of thee, but raw. And if any man said unto him, Let them not fail to burn the fat presently, and then take as much as thy soul desireth; then he would answer him, Nay; but thou shalt give it me now: and if not, I will take it by force. Wherefore the sin of the young men was very great before the Lord: for men abhorred the offering of the Lord.

That meant that God was about to intervene. Even though Zerahiah chided his sons he did not hold his sons accountable. Eli's ineffective attempt was recorded in 1 Samuel 2:22-25.

Now Eli was very old, and heard all that his sons did unto all Israel; and how they lay with the women that assembled at the door of the tabernacle of the congregation. And he said unto them, Why do ye such things? for I hear of your evil dealings by all this people. Nay, my sons; for it is no good report that I hear: ye make the Lord's people to transgress. If one man sin against another, the judge shall judge him: but if a man sin against the Lord, who shall intreat for him? Notwithstanding they hearkened not unto the voice of their father, because the Lord would slay them.

This expression, *"Now Eli was very old,"* used in 1 Samuel 2:22 only fit with the former high priest Zerahiah while Samuel was young as stated, *"And the child Samuel grew on, and was in favour both with the Lord, and also with men"* (1 Samuel 2:26). The older Eli (Zerahiah) would also better explain these words in 1 Samuel 3:2, *"and it came to pass at that time, when Eli was laid down in his place, and his eyes began to wax dim, that he could not see,"* i.e. as well as earlier in life.

One will not require as much time to make sense of many interconnected pieces by reading and considering these pieces as an introduction or preview before many more supportive details are shown. This insightful information about two sequential high priests (father and son) named Eli and about the use of parenthetical statements was valuable to interpret the text. This was the only manner in which all large or small statements about either Eli could be understood as true and be reconciled to each other.

If the second Eli (Meraioth) was old when Samuel was presented at the tabernacle, then the twenty-year period for the ark of the covenant to dwell in the house of Abinadab was false (1 Samuel 6:1; 7:2; 1 Chronicles 13:7; 2 Samuel 5:7; 6:16-17). And if Meraioth was old at that moment, many statements about Meraioth's third and fourth generation descendants as active priests at specific events were false. These stated events will be carefully examined to reveal their time connections and provide the chronological alignment for individuals.

The sons of Eli

How can we account for these words from 1 Samuel 1:3, "*And the two sons of Eli, Hophni and Phinehas, the priests of the Lord, were there?*" The expression, "*the priests of the Lord*," was a parenthetical insertion and can only refer to when they served later in life as priests since they were way too young yet. The text should be understood this way when Samuel used a parenthetical insertion. "*And the two* [grand]*sons of Eli, Hophni and Phinehas,* ([who became] *the priests of the Lord* [when old enough]), *were* [already] *there.*"

This will be shown to be true later and make much more sense when many other connections are made. Samuel wrote this much later in his life and respectfully used the title of their positions of service, i.e. high priest (Eli) and priest of the Lord, when speaking of their earlier years. Samuel probably wrote this after all three had died when the ark was captured.

The remaining part of the text, "*And the two sons of Eli, Hophni and Phinehas ... were there,*" told us that they were already born when Samuel arrived. The younger Eli (Meraioth) at age eighteen and nineteen had an early birth of his own two sons, Hophni [A-852] and Phinehas (Amariah, 1 Samuel 14:3; 1 Chronicles 6:7, 52, [A-853]). They were about two and three years younger than Samuel at age four and all three boys were reared in close proximity. Even when living and serving near to the younger Eli's family Samuel was effectively a "firstborn" to be dedicated to God.

SECTION V

Closely examine 1 Samuel 2:11-22 after Samuel was given to God at the tabernacle by way of the older Eli (1 Samuel 1:21-25). The textual statements revealed context and said that years were passing in verse 19. Then verse 22 added that *"Eli was very old."* This expression was used later in time for both Jesse and Barzillai and meant the older Eli, the current high priest, had attained eighty years or more of age. [See also: The lineage of the high priests]

The younger Meraioth (later titled Eli) cannot be old at that moment in time and have grown sons as priests since he died about seventy-eight years after Samuel arrived, at ninety-eight years of age, just after the ark was captured. Nor did Samuel imply that Hophni and Phinehas were priests at that moment. They could only start training at age 25. But when Samuel wrote down the account all three had served as priests.

Meraioth had served as priest and high priest, and each possessed that title which Samuel conveyed in the text. The same thing occurs today. We speak of the President's younger years but he was not a president then, he was so titled retroactively. Likewise, we say a Queen was born in a certain year. She was not a queen then, but she was a precious baby.

This background and Samuel's tool pointed us to look at the older Eli's sons and grandsons along with their conduct in life. This method indicated or at least prompted us to discern what manner of man the older Eli (Zerahiah) was in raising his sons. Two statements in 1 Samuel 2:12 and 22 called our attention to this: *"Now the sons of Eli were sons of Belial; they knew not the Lord."* and *"Now Eli was very old, and heard all that his sons did unto all Israel; and how they lay with the women that assembled at the door of the tabernacle of the congregation ..."* These two statements were also given to help each reader contrast the strikingly different outcome between the older Eli's natural born sons and this "adopted" child, a son from God.

Meraioth was the youngest of Zerahiah's natural sons. And like the child of David died for David's sin (2 Samuel 12:15-18) Zerahiah was told that his older sons (and grandsons) would die early by the hand of the Lord. This punishment also extended through Meraioth to his two sons when the older Eli was told that his two grandsons would die early, in the same day (1 Samuel 2:34), *"And this shall be a sign unto thee, that shall come upon thy two [grand]sons, on Hophni and Phinehas; in one day they shall die both of them."* Note that both sons of Meraioth, Hophni and Phinehas (1 Samuel 14:3; 1 Chronicles 6:7, 52), were under this generational condemnation. [Compare this with Psalm 69:22-24 and 2 Peter 2:14.]

Notice and apply the details

Several useful statements in the text of 1 Samuel 2:22-25 appeared. First, Zerahiah had sons verified by the expression, *"all that his sons did."* Zerahiah could have had older sons (only two are necessary) born much earlier than Meraioth as the last son. The older sons served as priests already and were included in the Lord's words of condemnation in verses 22-25.

They in turn were to die early for their wicked conduct, *"because the Lord would slay them."* Second, both or all of these earlier sons were fornicators and/or adulterers which required the death penalty (Leviticus 20:10). These priests were much more culpable for their actions since they were to know, live out, and teach God's laws.

Third, the surviving son was Meraioth, who was not slain. That would allow for Meraioth as a late born son to become the subsequent high priest. If this message from *"a man of God"* to the elder Eli occurred when Meraioth had served as a priest for two years, he would have been at age twenty-seven. With Meraioth born in [A-834, his birth time is detailed later] when he was old enough to become a priest at age twenty-five the year was [A-859]; then add two more years to prove his character by his conduct to reach age twenty-seven [A-861].

Fourth, this visit by a prophet of God occurred when Samuel was less than twelve years old as shown by the descriptive expression, *"child,"* he used about himself in verse 26, *"And the child Samuel grew on, and was in favour both with the Lord, and also with men."* Samuel will be shown later in this document to have been born in [A-850]. This birth time for Samuel made him serve alongside the older Eli and the younger Eli during the time period of Judges.

That expression, *"child,"* suggested that Samuel was eleven years of age [A-861 - 850 = 11] and seven years into his time living at the tabernacle when this prophet's message was given to the older Eli, his sons, and Meraioth's sons. Then God gave these individuals enough

SECTION V

time, one whole year (same length as Nebuchadnezzar, Daniel 4:29), to contemplate the message, become repentant, show repentance with a character and behavior adjustment, and carry out the Levitical mandates for personal transgressions and sins of priests. These sin offering sacrifices were given in Leviticus 4:3-12.

The next year [A-862] was the event of 1 Samuel 3 when Samuel was called, heard God's voice, and became age twelve. With Zerahiah at age eighty or more at this warning from God in [A-861] as given in 1Samuel 2:22, *"now Eli was very old,"* his birth year was in or before [A-781, 861 - 80 = 781]. Because Meraioth died at age ninety-eight and judged Israel for forty years (1 Samuel 4:15-18) he became high priest at age fifty-eight [98 - 40 = 58; A-834 + 58 = 892].

Zerahiah died about the age of 111 years [A-892 - 781 = 111]. Other than Joshua's age at death given in Judges 2:8, Meraioth's age at death was the only other age directly given in the books of Judges, Ruth, and 1 Samuel. But that did not mean other life spans or ages of individuals at declared events were indiscernible.

The lengthy passage in 1 Samuel 2:27-34 was not only directed to Meraioth's father but also toward Meraioth since God spoke of *"the arm of thy father's house."* More importantly this passage was also intended for Meraioth because he must be the person who lived to be a witness of the *"sign unto thee"* that was to come upon both Hophni and Phinehas in the same day. Zerahiah would have been dead forty years when they died. Zerahiah would witness the death of his other sons and grandsons over the next thirty years from [A-862-892]. This account in 1 Samuel 2:12-36 was concerned with generational sins recompensed with a generational punishment. The larger text read as follows.

> And there came a man of God unto Eli, and said unto him, Thus saith the Lord, Did I plainly appear unto the house of thy father, when they were in Egypt in Pharaoh's house? And did I choose him out of all the tribes of Israel to be my priest, to offer upon mine altar, to burn incense, to wear an ephod before me? and did I give unto the house of thy father all the offerings made by fire of the children of Israel? Wherefore kick ye at my sacrifice and at mine offering, which I have commanded in my habitation; and honourest thy sons above me, to make yourselves fat with

the chiefest of all the offerings of Israel my people? [referring back to the text given in 1 Samuel 2:12-17] Wherefore the Lord God of Israel saith, I said indeed that thy house, and the house of thy father, should walk before me for ever [referring back to the promise given to Phinehas, son of Eleazar, Numbers 25:6-14, detailed earlier]: but now the Lord saith, Be it far from me; for them that honour me I will honour, and they that despise me shall be lightly esteemed. Behold, the days come, that I will cut off thine arm, and the arm of thy father's house, that there shall not be an old man in thine house. And thou shalt see an enemy in my habitation, in all the wealth which God shall give Israel: and there shall not be an old man in thine house for ever [i.e. throughout succeeding generations]. And the man of thine, whom I shall not cut off from mine altar, shall be to consume thine eyes, and to grieve thine heart: and all the increase of thine house shall die in the flower of their age. And this shall be a sign unto thee, that shall come upon thy two [grand]sons, on Hophni and Phinehas; in one day they shall die both of them.

More about Samuel

Samuel was the primary focus in 1 Samuel 2:11, 18, 21 and 26. All other contextual information was added into this part of the historical account to present information that was not addressed elsewhere. This approach to present the material gave Samuel's placement in both time and circumstances (1 Samuel 1:1–2:11).

In this manner the early text of 1 Samuel gave pertinent insightful information about the people surrounding him while he grew and served at the tabernacle. The author detailed God's warnings and prophecies against those wicked priests (1 Samuel 2:12-36). This illustrated that the early part of 1 Samuel was laid out topically and set the pattern for the subsequent parts of this book.

Samuel reported that as a child he wore a linen ephod (1 Samuel 2:18). The ephod was the name of a one-piece linen garment akin to Jesus' seamless garment (John 19:23-24). According to the statutes about the tabernacle, a linen ephod was required to be worn by the priests (Exodus 29:5) in their service before the Lord. When Abiathar fled Nob when the priests were killed by Doeg he had with him a linen ephod (1 Samuel 22). Therefore, he could serve as a priest before David when David enquired of the Lord through him (1 Samuel 23:1-12; 30:6-8), especially since he was the next high priest (1 Kings 2:26-27, 35).

But Samuel stood in contrast to those natural born sons of the older Eli who became wicked priests at the tabernacle (1 Samuel 2:13-17). The child Samuel grew and matured girded with a linen ephod, a symbol of righteousness (1 Samuel 2:18-19). This was remarkably parallel to Jesus' experience with priests at the temple and for which he cleansed the temple, twice (first: John 2:15, second: Matthew 21:12; Mark 11:15; Luke 19:45-46)[17].

These three pieces in 1 Samuel 1:3 and chapter 2 brought, from a prophet's and historian's perspective, an insertion of pertinent information to the text. If the expression in 1 Samuel 1:3 meant that Hophni and Phinehas were currently priests, that contradicted the later passage (1 Samuel 4:3-5, 11-18) that stated that Eli died at ninety-eight years when the ark of the covenant was carried into the camp of Israel by Hophni and Phinehas where it was captured by the Philistines. This allowed the proper placement for the younger Eli's (Meraioth) birth and death [A-834-932].

Meraioth was born 243 years after the first oppression over Israel started in [A-591] which clearly made his birth occur in the latter half of the book of Judges during Gideon's forty years of service. The book of Ruth occurred in the middle period of the judges and connected Salmon to David. Obed was born halfway between Othniel through Abdon. When the high priest lineage and other pieces are examined these time placements will be validated.

After this the book of 1 Samuel took up the topic of Samuel again and his core ministry at the tabernacle (1 Samuel 3:1-21). God called Samuel while *"the child Samuel ministered unto the Lord before Eli,"* the elder Zerahiah (1 Samuel 3:1-21). This previewed Jesus' submission to his parents in Luke 2:41-51, *"And when he was twelve years old, they went up to Jerusalem after the custom of the feast. ... And he said unto them, How is it that ye sought me? wist ye not that I must be about my Father's business? ..."*

This suggested that Samuel was specially called about the same age. Verse two spoke of the literal dimming of Eli's eyes saying his *"eyes began to wax dim."* The choice of words were not only about Zerahiah's physical capacity but also strongly suggested the decrease of spiritual vision toward God. This was shown when compared to 1 Samuel 1:17, *"Then Eli answered and said, Go in peace: and the God of Israel grant thee thy petition that thou hast asked of him."* and to 2:20, *"And Eli blessed Elkanah and his wife, and said, The Lord give thee seed of this woman for the loan which is lent to the Lord."* (See Isaiah 44:18 and Romans 11:8)

This concept of a parenthetical insertion also applied to 1 Samuel chapters four through seven because those chapters were given out of chronological sequence. The events detailed in those chapters did not transpire when Samuel was young, but occurred when he was much older (1 Samuel 7:5). David was a twenty-one-year old when the ark was captured. Note that Samuel died (1 Samuel 28:1) about two years before David was inaugurated as king over Judah at age thirty (2 Samuel 5:4). That triumphant victory over the Philistines was seven years short of Samuel's death, seventy years from his calling in [A-862], and Samuel's greatest miracle.

In 1 Samuel 7:9-14 Samuel prayed and the result was the Philistines were routed (vv. 10-11), subdued (v.13), and the Ebenezer stone was placed as a memorial (v.12). The defeat of the Philistines came shortly after the capture of the ark, i.e. the next battle. This event also made an excellent placement for the end of the forty years of Philistine oppression that began in Judges 13:1 and concluded in this account at 1 Samuel 7:1-14. This alignment is explained more fully later. [See: The ark was taken]

Note three more parenthetical insertions. After David had killed Goiliath 1 Samuel 17:54 spoke of David taking Goliath's head to Jerusalem which was captured after he became king at age thirty. The second parenthetical insertion given in 1 Samuel 18:5-7 described David in a summary statement which was only learned after sufficient time had transpired for David to prove himself before Saul and the people. The text of 18:5-7 gave a result of what was prophesied about David (2 Samuel 3:18) and fulfilled by David.

The whole prophecy was completed in steps over a longer time frame as shown in 1 Samuel 17:49-51; 18:27; 23:5; 2 Samuel 5:17-25; 8:1; 21:15-22; 1 Chronicles 14:16; 18:1, etc. A third summary statement was the text of 1 Samuel 18:14 which could only be known after more time transpired and the facts were gathered. These pieces showed that 1 Samuel was written some years later when these parenthetical insertions were known, understood, and emplaced to fill in necessary material not dealt with anywhere else.

The man named Meraioth

The older Eli's grown sons had demonstrated the truth of 1 Samuel 2:12, *"Now the sons of Eli were sons of Belial; they knew not the Lord."* For this reason, *"there came a man of God unto Eli,"* (1 Samuel 2:27-36) and spoke prophecies of destruction and death against him and his progeny. The older brothers of Meraioth died under this penalty and he became the next high priest when Zerahiah died. This behavior was summarized with Jesus' words in Luke 13:3 and 5, *"I tell you, Nay: but, except ye repent, ye shall all likewise perish."*

This penalty was entirely consistent with Exodus 20:5, *"Thou shalt not bow down thyself to them, nor serve them: for I the Lord thy God am a jealous God, visiting the iniquity of the fathers upon the children unto the third and fourth generation of them that hate me."* The next Eli, priest Meraioth, the last son of Zerahiah had the two sons named Hophni and Phinehas (Amariah, 1 Samuel 14:3; 1 Chronicles 6:6-7, 52). Both were grandsons to Zerahiah and under that generational penalty. This was affirmed again in 1 Samuel 3:11-14 as multi-generational, i.e. that the age limitation of the prophecy applied to all of Zerahiah's grandsons and continued throughout their succeeding generations.

Hophni and Phinehas were only ten and nine years old in [A-862], but had already sufficiently shown no heart to obey their father or God to be included by name in that prophecy. Remember, traditional Judaism held that the age of accountability was puberty. If a person was old enough to procreate and, therefore, be responsible for another life, they were also old enough to be responsible for their individual choices in life. Hophni and Phinehas were approaching that age.

The message of verses 27-36 was also addressed to Meraioth their father and spoke against wicked behavior. Some years later, both Hophni and Phinehas actively served as priests, each starting at twenty-five years of age, first under Zerahiah and later under Meraioth. Many years later Hophni and Phinehas were cut off before they became *"an old man,"* cut off for their generational sins when the ark was captured, *"in the flower of their age,"* (1 Samuel 4; Exodus 20:5). This fulfillment was within a few weeks after many other priests were killed by Doeg (1 Samuel 22:9-23).

With the phrase, *"that there shall not be an old man in thine house,"* added to the clues provided in 1 Samuel 3 we can establish that this Eli's (Meraioth) sons died before their birth anniversary. Hophni died at seventy-nine [A-852-932], quite near Saul's age at death, and Phinehas at seventy-eight years [A-853-932] (1 Samuel 4:15-22). The two sons' deaths occurred when they carried the ark of the covenant into battle against the Philistines and were killed. Upon hearing the news about them and the loss of the ark their father Eli (Meraioth) also died. Further events with the offspring of Phinehas will be shown to verify these birth and death years for Meraioth, Hophni, and Phinehas.

The deaths of Hophni and Phinehas partially fulfilled 1 Samuel 2:33, *"and all the increase of thine house shall die in the flower of their age."* Three things need explanation. This prophecy did not apply to any priests descending from Ithamar or other family lines from Eleazar. The increase of his house meant succeeding generations descending from Zerahiah starting after the time it was spoken, which explained why Meraioth reached ninety-eight years.

Meraioth was already age twenty-seven and this limitation proceeded through every subsequent generation descending from him and his older brothers. However, only priest Meraioth's ongoing lineage was recorded in the Scriptures. Note therefore, all of Meraioth's male descendants, even Ezra, died before they became *"an old man,"* in biblical terms, from this period of 1 Samuel and onward.

The flower of their age was an agricultural expression derived from observing plants. Flowering plants grew for a significant period before they were mature enough to bloom. After the flower fell off, these plants continued to live. This expression, *"in the flower of their age,"* meant that Zerahiah's offspring would grow, mature, and die somewhere in their later years. Each would die before the age of eighty with none living past their most productive years, i.e. after the bloom. Carefully stated, from the day of that prophecy in [A-861] and beginning with the two named grandsons no male progeny born thereafter descending from the older Eli (Zerahiah) would attain eighty years of age.

SECTION V

Seventy years had transpired from God calling Samuel in 1 Samuel 3 until the four chapters in 1 Samuel 4–7 occurred with the loss of the ark of the covenant. This insertion of chapters in 1 Samuel concluded the information about Meraioth (Eli), Hophni, and Phinehas and showed a partial fulfillment of the prophecy of the Lord spoken against Zerahiah, his sons, and grandsons. This concept was necessary to grasp and correctly use since Scripture authors often finished the account about one individual's life or progeny before starting another.

This was shown with Noah's descendants post flood, with Ishmael and his descendants, the sons of Keturah, Isaac and his family, etc. The same concept occurred with Abimelech, the son of Gideon. A parenthetical insertion, was also employed in 1 Samuel 14:3 where Ichabod was named as a brother, but he was not born until much later in time when Phinehas had died before age eighty and Eli at age ninety-eight had died (1 Samuel 4:19-21).

The text in 1 Samuel 4:18 said that Eli (Meraioth) judged Israel for forty years which gave us the time period he was high priest, from age fifty-eight to ninety-eight. This helped mark off other events with greater certainty. The former high priest Zerahiah had died and this Eli began that office and by default was considered a judge as a national leader up until his death.

When this younger Eli's death was correctly established, Meraioth's forty years as judge aligned with the same forty-year period given in Judges 13:1. Samuel called our attention to that forty-year period in Judges 13:1 when he repeated the expression, *"forty years,"* and meant for us to look back to the last stated forty-year period and connect these two time periods together. These two forty-year events were simultaneous, they started and ended together.

All of this information when taken together showed that Meraioth was not *"very old"* at Samuel's birth. Meraioth (Eli) was born [A-834] in 1117 BC. Meraioth was age sixteen at Samuel's birth, and age twenty when God's gift of Samuel at age four was received at the tabernacle from Hannah and Elkanah. He was twenty-seven years old when the prophecy was spoken in [A-861] and twenty-eight when Samuel was called in [A-862].

This special gift of "God's son" was calling the younger man Meraioth, the next Eli, to walk and lead in truth and righteousness. [See:

Numbers 1:3, 18, 45; 8:24; 26:2, 4] At age twenty Meraioth may have been spiritually minded, but he also appeared to let the light in him go out (Matthew 6:23; Luke 11:34). He had a high calling ("Eli" meant lofty) and heard a prophetic warning to serve as a Godly judge and noble high priest for those forty years.

This generational punishment was applied to the account of every priest descending from Meraioth hereafter. That age limit of less than eighty years for all of Meraioth's descendants helped resolve events in David's and Solomon's lifetime, allowed for the general time placement for Zadok's descendants through Jehozadak, and even applied to Ezra much later. This forced somewhat earlier births of sons to correctly reach to Johanan and fulfill the criteria of 1 Chronicles 6:9-10, and somewhat later births from Johanan to reach to Jehozadak as noted below. [See: The lineage of the high priests]

The early descendants of Meraioth

Meraioth's first son was Hophni (1 Samuel 14:3; 1 Chronicles 6:7, 52) who was born in [A-852] with no descendants given; and his second son was Phinehas [A-853]. Phinehas' two sons were Ahitub (1 Chronicles 6:8) and much later Ichabod [A-932]. Ahitub's three sons were Ahimelech (firstborn, 1 Samuel 22:9, 11, 20), Ahiah (1 Samuel 14:3), and Zadok (2 Samuel 8:17; 1 Chronicles 6:8). Ahimelech's son was Abiathar (1 Samuel 22:20), nephew to Zadok. This young priest Abiathar (at age 25) was the only survivor who fled to David when the priests and their families at Nob were killed by Doeg (1 Samuel 22:9-23) just before the battle when the ark was captured.

Ahitub's much younger brother was Ichabod. He was born to Phinehas' wife after both his father's death by the Philistines and grandfather Eli's death in 1019 BC (1 Samuel 4:16-22; 14:3). Ichabod [A-932-<=1012] died before Solomon died in [A-1020, 931 BC]. After Ahitub, Ahimelech, Ahiah, and many other priests were killed by Doeg, both Hophni and Phinehas were killed by the Philistines, and Eli had died, then Abiathar (son of the first Ahimelech) became high priest. He was ceremonially inaugurated at the tabernacle when David took office in Judah, since he was in flight with David from Saul for about nine years [A-932–941].

SECTION V

Zadok (1 Samuel 14:3; 1 Chronicles 6:8) was born quite near [A-904], 1047 BC. Note here that Zadok must have been born early enough to be a priest serving with David and born late enough for Solomon to establish him as high priest in ([A-981], 970 BC). Zadok died at less than eighty years of age, which was before or early in [A-984, 967 BC].

Abiathar (1 Samuel 22:20, who fled to David) in turn had a son born, Ahimelech (2 Samuel 8:17; 1 Chronicles 24:3-6), and named him after his grandfather. This Abiathar was the high priest that was removed (1 Kings 2:26-27; 4:4) in [A-981, 970 BC] when Solomon in 1 Kings 2:26-27 inaugurated Zadok as the new high priest (1 Kings 2:35). Abiathar was removed from the high priest office because he had aligned with David's son Adonijah in rebellion in [A-981, 970 BC] against God's appointment of David as king (1 Kings 1).

Zadok, born in [A-904], served as a regular priest at the tabernacle from [A-929-954] with the ark missing from late in [A-932] and returned early in [A-953] to Jerusalem. In 2 Samuel 8:17 (1 Chronicles 18:16; 24:31) it stated that Zadok served as priest alongside the second Ahimelech (his great-nephew, born earliest in [A-924 to latest in A-929] the son of the Abiathar who fled to David). If this later Ahimelech was born when Abiathar was age seventeen, then their longest possible overlapping period for regular formal service at the tabernacle was from [A-949-954].

That meant that 2 Samuel 8 occurred in late [A-953] to very early in [A-954]. Another son Jonathan was born to Abiathar around [~A-932 or later, 1019 BC] (2 Samuel 15:27; 1 Kings 1:42-43) who was also aligned with Adonijah (1 Kings 1:42-43). [For perspective, David's forty and one-half year reign was from late [A-941] to early [A-982] 1010-969 BC and the Temple was built over seven years from [A-984-991] 967-960 BC (1 Kings 2:26-27; 7:1; 9:10; 2 Chronicles 8:1).]

Then the high priest's lineage proceeded from Zadok to Ahimaaz to Azariah to Johanan (1 Chronicles 6:9-10) who was born about [A-961] 990 BC. Note that *"he it is that executed the priest's office in the temple that Solomon built in Jerusalem"* (vs 10). Johanan was required to be thirty years of age to independently serve as a priest. His full term of twenty years would have been in the finished temple (A-991 to A-1011; 960 BC to 940 BC].

In turn Johanan about age forty-three had a son Azariah (1 Chronicles 6:9-10, grandson of Azariah) born around 947 BC. All of these priests can be placed in time during the period from David (1040-969 BC) through Solomon (~1000 BC-931 BC) when Meraioth's lifetime was correctly placed from [A-834-932] 1019-1117 BC and other biblical texts were applied as shown above and below. [See below: The lineage of the high priests]

Samuel was old

After filling in necessary information from the later event about Eli, Hophni, and Phinehas in 1 Samuel chapters four through seven, the text returned in chapter eight to focus again upon Samuel. First Samuel 8:1 gave us in one simple statement unique, valuable, and highly specific information about time, *"when Samuel was old."* The key term *"old"* did not mean an "old man" implying Samuel was worn out over many years of life. That unique term *"old"* referred back to the Levitical upper age limit of fifty years to formally serve at the tabernacle (Numbers 8:23-26; 4:3, 23, 30, 35, 47).

Compare this "old" expression in verse one with 1 Samuel 12:1-2. Together they showed that Samuel had aged out of his formal tabernacle service, that he was age fifty [A-900]. That key time stamp for Samuel aligned his age with Eli who was serving as high priest at age 66. Likewise the event of 1 Samuel 4:3-5, 11-18 with the ark of the covenant captured (1 Samuel 4–7 chpts.) aligned their ages, especially with the twenty years and seven months (1 Samuel 7:2) until the ark was moved again by David to Zion. [See below: The ark was taken]

The next topic in the book of 1 Samuel was about the national circumstances: establishing the school of the prophets; appointing his sons as judges; interacting with the elders; selecting, anointing, and installing Saul; the beginning of Saul; and Samuel's ongoing service as judge (1 Samuel 7:15–11:15). When understood correctly, Numbers 8:23-26 required ongoing service from all Levites, including priests, who had aged out of formal tabernacle duties. This became the opportunity for Samuel to fulfill his duties and requirements in other ways as noted in other texts. The Levites were to help priests teach God's law to all Israel (Deuteronomy 6:4-6; 17:8-11, 18-20; Numbers 3; 2 Chronicles 30:22; 35:30; Psalm 1:2; Nehemiah 8:9, 11, 13).

About the time that Samuel turned fifty years of age he started the school of the prophets (1 Samuel 10:5-12; 19:20-24) which he maintained until his death. Those student prophets would have also been able to validate the records that Samuel recorded and were used to write Judges, Ruth, and much of 1 Samuel. Plus they were probably witnesses to David when he gave the information for the book of Ruth and recounted his early experiences before Saul to Samuel (1 Samuel 19:18). The school of the prophets was carried on later by Elijah and Elisha (2 Kings 2:1-18; 4:38, 6:1; 9:1; etc.).

After he finished his formal duties at the tabernacle Samuel set up his two sons Joel (Vashni, 1 Chronicles 6:28) and Abiah as judges in Beersheba (1 Samuel 7:15-17). If Joel was born in [~A-873] and Abiah in [~A-875], they were about twenty-seven and about twenty-five years in age, respectively. Both would have already entered their Levitical service when made judges by Samuel at age 50.

Moreover, this time placement for their births completely fit with David in year [A-953] calling Joel as a head of the Levites, about eighty years old, in 1 Chronicles 15:11-12 to help bring the ark of God to Jerusalem. But Joel and Abiah were unfaithful judges (1 Samuel 8:2-3), *"And his sons walked not in his ways, but turned aside after lucre, and took bribes, and perverted judgment."* Joel and Abiah had grown up around a corrupted priesthood and had not learned or wanted to learn to walk faithfully before God.

Start marking time with the appointment of Joel and Abiah as judges. For the elders of the twelve tribes to hear about their corruption, be convinced of this by more than two reports for each out of deference to Samuel, communicate amongst themselves to formulate and decide upon a plan, and come to Samuel as a group would take almost one year. Then *"all the elders of Israel gathered themselves together, and came to Samuel unto Ramah"* for his approval and help to establish a king when Samuel was late age fifty or age fifty-one. After seeking God's direction, Samuel anointed Saul (1 Samuel 9:1–10:13, [A-901], 1050 BC).

This event of anointing Saul was about one year from the formal end of Levitical service with the school of the prophets already active. This would explain the circumstances when Saul *"prophesied among the prophets"* in 1 Samuel 10:11-12, when *"the Spirit of God was upon the messengers of Saul, and they also prophesied"* in 19:20, and Saul *"stripped off his clothes also, and prophesied before Samuel in like manner, and lay down naked all that day and all that night"* in 19:24. After this the text in 1 Samuel followed the topic of Samuel's ministry to all Israel, to the elders, and to Saul (1 Samuel 12:1–15:35).

Since Samuel was a Nazarite from conception (1 Samuel 1:11) he had extremely long hair. The expression, *"grayheaded,"* Samuel used meant that he had obviously grown out gray hair (1 Samuel 12:2). Here Samuel asked the people of Israel to bring any charge against him for dishonest conduct in carrying out his duties. He was cleared of any wrong-doing.

Then Samuel recounted before Israel God's historic faithfulness and recent help to them, *"And the Lord sent Jerubbaal, and Bedan, and Jephthah, and Samuel, and delivered you out of the hand of your enemies on every side, and ye dwelled safe."* (1 Samuel 12:11). He spoke of how they had feared king Nahash and pled for a physical king to lead in battle. Samuel admonished and urged the Israelites to hold fast to the worship of the true God.

All of this was similar to the character and work of Jesus. Then Samuel called to God for a miracle of nature (not the rain season) to emphatically drive home the point and validate his teaching in verses 12:17-18.

> I will call unto the Lord, and he shall send thunder and rain; that ye may perceive and see that your wickedness is great, which ye have done in the sight of the Lord, in asking you a king. So Samuel called unto the Lord; and the Lord sent thunder and rain that day: and all the people greatly feared the Lord and Samuel.

From here the next sub-topic was the work of Saul and Jonathan to defend Israel after Saul was made king (1 Samuel 13:1–15:35). The earlier text of 1 Samuel 12 occurred just before David's birth and 1 Samuel 13:14 transpired when David was over age four. Recall that Samuel was presented to God when he was only four years of age.

Much later in time, about twenty-two years into Saul's reign [~A-923], Samuel told God's message in chapter 15 to king Saul to utterly destroy the Amalekites. But Saul disobeyed God's command again. Samuel obeyed God and killed Agag. Since Saul rejected God's commands God rejected Saul's kingdom. Samuel's prophetic words in 1 Samuel 13:14 were fulfilled, *"But now thy kingdom shall not continue: the Lord hath sought him a man after his own heart, and the Lord hath commanded him to be captain over his people, because thou hast not kept that which the Lord commanded thee."*

This event ended one topic and marked the start of a new topic in 1 Samuel 16. Saul's refusal to slay Agag came just before God selected and Samuel anointed a shepherd boy named David [A-923]. The setting of both of these texts (1 Samuel 13:3-23 and 1 Samuel 15:1-35) will be explored more fully and validated for their time placement when we examine Saul.

In 1 Samuel 16:1-13 God directed Samuel, who was approaching age 73, to anoint David. He returned again to Ramah, continued his work with the school of prophets, and maintained his work as judge over Israel. Later David fled from Saul and came to Samuel (age 82, 1 Samuel 19:18-19, [A-932]) where David would have been given training to become king (1 Samuel 10:25) along with much more training in the Mosaic law and the formal process of the tabernacle service, as demonstrated in 1 Chronicles 9:22. David used this information to set up the expanded temple services and formal duties later.

Samuel died

More time passed until Samuel died (1 Samuel 25:1) at eighty-nine years of age just before David's rejection by Nabal. Samuel's death was between one and one-half to two years before Saul, Jonathan, and two other sons died in war with the Philistines. Samuel was given to the Lord before birth, and he served as a Nazarite until his death.

Samuel lived his whole life from his childhood service starting at age four, to his formal calling at age twelve, to his death faithfully before God and the people of Israel. *"And Samuel judged Israel all the days of his life."* (1 Samuel 7:15, [A-850-939]). He was God's prophet for seventy-seven years.

His death was while Saul sought David in southern Israel. David was in *"the hold"* (1 Samuel 24:22), but David *"went down to the wilderness of Paran,"* as reported in 1 Samuel 25:1, and sought provisions from a man named Nabal (1 Samuel 25:1-9). Here he met Abigail whom he later married (1 Samuel 25:39-42). From there the Ziphites reported to Saul, and he came out against David again.

Then David when to Philistine occupied territory in southwest Judah and the time *"David dwelt in the country of the Philistines was a full year and four months"* (1 Samuel 27:7). While there David and his men recovered from the Amalekites their families that were captured at Ziklag.

> And David recovered all that the Amalekites had carried away: and David rescued his two wives. And there was nothing lacking to them, neither small nor great, neither sons nor daughters, neither spoil, nor any thing that they had taken to them: David recovered all. (1 Samuel 30:18-19).

The reign of Saul

Saul was anointed by Samuel (1 Samuel 9:1–10:13) in [A-901, 1050 BC] when Samuel was almost or just fifty-one years old. Saul reigned forty years (possibly one or two months longer, if anointed when Samuel was a late fifty) as the first king of Israel (1 Chronicles 10:1-14; Acts 14:21). Somewhere from his anointing to the assembly in chapter 10 Ishbosheth was born (2 Samuel 2:8-10).

Saul's youngest son Ishbosheth was forty years of age or late in his fortieth year when he succeeded Saul as king over the twelve tribes of Israel (2 Samuel 2:8-15). Samuel had gathered the people of Israel to formally cast lots to demonstrate that Saul was selected by God to be the new king (1 Samuel 10:17-25). Contrast Saul's lifelong conduct with Deuteronomy 17:14-20 where God described limitations and requirements of any king over Israel.

In Saul's first year Nahash the Ammonite came against Jabeshgilead and they sought help from Saul. He then mustered his first army by threat of punishment for not assembling. Saul's reign started by threats of tyranny though he defeated Nahash's army by a 3-pronged attack in chapter 11.

Because Israel was slow to respond to a king and his leadership, Samuel asked the people, essentially the Israelite soldiers from all of the tribes, after the very first battle to go to Gilgal and renew the kingdom. *"[T]here they made Saul king before the Lord in Gilgal; and there they sacrificed sacrifices of peace offerings before the Lord; and there Saul and all the men of Israel rejoiced greatly"* (1 Samuel 11:15).

The words about *"Saul took the kingdom over Israel"* (1 Samuel 14:47) told us that from the beginning of his reign he had nay sayers who rejected him as recorded in 1 Samuel 10:27, *"But the children of Belial said,*

How shall this man save us? And they despised him, and brought no presents." This was brought up later by some people of Israel in 1 Samuel 11:12, *"And the people said unto Samuel, Who is he that said, Shall Saul reign over us? bring the men, that we may put them to death."*

David also had resistance to his installation as king. This still festered among the Benjamites and resurfaced late into David's life when he fled Absalom (2 Samuel 16:13). After this the text in 1 Samuel followed the topic of Samuel's ministry to all Israel, to the elders, and to Saul (1 Samuel 12:1–15:35).

Saul's time marker at David's birth

Samuel's speech in 1 Samuel 12:5-11 had a notable inclusion. Verse eleven said, *"And the Lord sent Jerubbaal, and Bedan, and Jephthah, and Samuel, and delivered you out of the hand of your enemies on every side, and ye dwelled safe."* This speech occurred in Saul's reign when Samuel spoke to Israel's elders.

For Jephthah to have already turned back the Ammonites [A-910, more fully explained later] this event and speech was in the year [A-911], the same year that David was born. Samuel had listed recent judges, but not Samson, he was too young yet to serve since he was about nineteen years of age. This placed Samuel's speech before the elders and the miracle that followed early in Saul's eleventh year near to David's birth and one year before Samson's service as a unique judge in Israel.

Earlier the fifth key to solving the book of Judges and 1 Samuel was introduced. That key was "recognizing the concurrence of when Israel did evil again and served the Philistines for forty years (Judges 13:1) with Eli's period as judge (1 Samuel 4:18), and then with Samson's lifetime." Eli (Meraioth) was high priest from [A-892-932]. In his twentieth year, Samson began his twenty-year period of service [A-912-932]. [See below: The period of Samson]

Saul's age at David's birth

David was born when Saul was about forty-nine years old. This was inferred by several methods. First, Israel had been rescued by various judges in the past and led by Joshua, Aaron, and Moses all of whom were older in age. They would not accept a leader who was perceived as too young since they were substantially ruled by elders. He had to be old enough to be a "father figure" over the younger men of Israel. They would not serve as a soldier under an untested individual.

Second, his own son would need to be at twenty years of age to go to war according to Numbers 1:3. If Saul was about age eighteen to twenty-one for Jonathan's birth, add twenty more years to reach age thirty-eight to forty-one when Jonathan was able to become a soldier. With Saul at age thirty-nine, in his fortieth year, when he started to reign for forty years (2 Samuel 2:8-10), Saul would have been almost forty-one in his second year when Jonathan was first described as a soldier (1 Samuel 13:1-2).

Note that Saul was not yet eighty years old at his death. He was neither described as *"very old"* in age nor titled an *"old man."* Take 2 Samuel 19:32 and Barzillai's description of reaching *"a very aged man"* to establish that Saul did not reach this title of eighty years.

One method to establish the length of Saul's reign was the forty-year age of Ishbosheth (2 Samuel 2:8-15) when he took over the kingdom of Saul in [A-941]. Perhaps Ishbosheth was born to Saul's concubine (2 Samuel 3:7-8, [A-901]). Saul's first wife and children were given in 1 Samuel 14:49-50.

David was thirty when he began to reign over Judah. After seven years and six months he began to reign over all Israel (2 Samuel 2:11; 5:5; 1 Chronicles 11:1-9). That started after Ishbosheth [A-901-948] had been murdered (2 Samuel 4:5-7) by two wicked men.

With Saul at age seventy-nine at his death minus David at thirty, Saul was age forty-nine at David's birth and born in [A-862], the same year Samuel was called to be a prophet. If we take 1 Samuel 14:49 strictly, Merab was the firstborn and Jonathan was born the next year or so. But much more likely, she was the first of Saul's much younger daughters because both Merab and her sister Michal were later offered to David as a wife (1 Samuel 18:17-27).

From there the book of 1 Samuel followed the ongoing work of Saul and Jonathan to defend Israel after Saul was made king (1 Samuel 13:1–15:35). This was given in parts. Saul had set up a standing army (1 Samuel 13:1-2) just like Samuel foretold in 1 Samuel 8:11-12. Various parts from chapter 13:3 through 15:35 occurred at different later times. The brief summary in 1 Samuel 14:46-48 listed all the nations he fought against throughout his forty-year reign. That made this statement either another parenthetical insertion filled in after all the facts were known or this text portion was completed after Samuel and Saul died.

> Then Saul went up from following the Philistines: and the Philistines went to their own place. So Saul took the kingdom over Israel, and fought against all his enemies on every side, against Moab, and against the children of Ammon, and against Edom, and against the kings of Zobah, and against the Philistines: and whithersoever he turned himself, he vexed them. And he gathered an host, and smote the Amalekites, and delivered Israel out of the hands of them that spoiled them.

Verse 52 reported Saul's work in these words, *"And there was sore war against the Philistines all the days of Saul: and when Saul saw any strong man, or any valiant man, he took him unto him."* These verses affirmed that Saul was engaged in numerous conflicts, skirmishes, and battles during his forty-year reign, often with the Philistines during their forty-year oppression. This also showed that Saul gradually gained acceptance and status as king, i.e. he *"took the kingdom"* over a long period.

Jonathan's age range

Jonathan must have been at least twenty years of age after the second year of Saul (1 Samuel 13:1; Numbers 1:3) to be described as a soldier. Start with Saul at age thirty-nine, in his fortieth year when installed, add two years as king, subtract twenty years for Jonathan's minimum age for war and arrive at twenty-one years of age for his son's latest birth time [39 + 2 - 20 = 21]. Jonathan was even older when he commanded an Israelite garrison of one thousand soldiers (1 Samuel 13:2-4).

After Saul's forty-year reign Jonathan was at least fifty-eight (79 - 21 = 58) or up to three years older, if born earlier. With David at age thirty to start his reign there was twenty-eight to thirty-one years difference between Jonathan and David. This information showed that Saul [A-862-941] was about twelve years younger than Samuel [A-850-939], about twenty-eight years younger than Eli [A-834-932], eighteen to twenty-one years older than Jonathan [A-(880-883)-941], and about forty-nine years older than David [A-911].

Connections between Judges and 1 Samuel

Philistine rule during Saul's reign

The main part of 1 Samuel chapter 13 did not follow immediately in time with chapter 12. Chapter 13 started the sub-topic of the work of Saul and Jonathan to defend Israel and the effects of Saul's reign (1 Samuel 13:1–15:35). Saul began his reign with the battle against the Ammonites, and after two years Saul had a standing army. Samuel's words about the king taking their sons was fulfilled fairly rapidly. No amount of time was given between verse 2 and verse 3.

"Jonathan smote the garrison of the Philistines that was in Geba" (1 Samuel 13:3). This significant assertion of Israelite resistance caused the Philistines to muster a large army to suppress and control Israel. Saul acted quickly, *"And the people were called together after Saul to Gilgal."* The Philistines assembled a formidable army, *"thirty thousand chariots, and six thousand horsemen, and people as the sand which is on the sea shore in multitude."* Saul's small army was fearful and scared, *"and all the people followed him trembling"* (1 Samuel 13:5-7). Because of Samuel's arrival late in the day to join Saul and his men (1 Samuel 13:8-9), Saul hurriedly offered the planned burnt offering. When Samuel arrived he rebuked and rejected Saul for his actions in 1 Samuel 13:13-14.

> And Samuel said to Saul, Thou hast done foolishly: thou hast not kept the commandment of the Lord thy God, which he commanded thee: for now would the Lord have established thy kingdom upon Israel for ever. But now thy kingdom shall not continue: the Lord hath sought him a man after his own heart, and the Lord hath commanded him to be captain over his people, because thou hast not kept that which the Lord commanded thee.

David was at least age four or even older when the Lord sought *"a man after his own heart"* in chapter 13. Recall that Samuel was age four when he was presented by his parents to Zerahiah at the tabernacle. Note what had occurred eight years later for Samuel and will occur for David.

This event certainly was during the forty-year period of Philistine oppression because of the statements about only two swords were available and every man had to go to the Philistines to sharpen their farming and herding equipment. Thus Israel was greatly controlled or at least significantly oppressed by the Philistines like Judges 13:1 stated. First Samuel 13:17-22 made this obvious.

> And the spoilers came out of the camp of the Philistines in three companies: one company turned unto the way that leadeth to Ophrah, unto the land of Shual: And another company turned the way to Bethhoron: and another company turned to the way of the border that looketh to the valley of Zeboim toward the wilderness. Now there was no smith found throughout all the land of Israel: for the Philistines said, Lest the Hebrews make them swords or spears: But all the Israelites went down to the Philistines, to sharpen every man his share, and his coulter, and his axe, and his mattock. Yet they had a file for the mattocks, and for the coulters, and for the forks, and for the axes, and to sharpen the goads. So it came to pass in the day of battle, that there was neither sword nor spear found in the hand of any of the people that were with Saul and Jonathan: but with Saul and with Jonathan his son was there found.

Saul's request of Ahiah marked time

Chapter 14 occurred some years later and its timing was revealed when Samuel gave to us an exceptionally helpful clue by naming a specific individual, whose life fit into narrow time parameters. During this period the book of 1 Samuel named individuals that interconnected with Saul. Setting these people in time also confirmed the placement of Saul's reign while other judges served.

One of these individuals was introduced in 1 Samuel 14:3, *"And Ahiah, the son of Ahitub, Ichabod's brother, the son of Phinehas, the son of Eli, the Lord's priest in Shiloh, wearing an ephod."* Ahiah was actively serving as a priest and called upon by Saul to *"[b]ring hither the ark of God"* (1 Samuel 14:18). This meant that Ahiah was at least twenty-five or more years of age, most likely at thirty years and past priest training and direct supervision.

This was the first time recorded that Saul called for the ark to be brought to the battle scene. Nothing said the ark was actually brought out at that time. During the second event with the elder priests Hophni and Phinehas, the ark was brought out and captured.

If both Phinehas born [A-853] and Ahitub had their sons when they were from seventeen to twenty years of age, that would place Ahiah's earliest birth range from [A-887-893]. Then this event of Saul occurred no sooner than [A-912; 853 + 17 + 17 = 887, 887 + 25 = 912; for confirmation see below: The alignment of numerous priests]. Because it followed both chapter 12 and 13 in chronological time a good preliminary fit was from [~A-916-921].

Saul was anointed and started as king in [A-901] and this event with priest Ahiah in chapter 14 would fall into the period from fifteen to twenty years into his reign. Saul's twentieth year [A-921] was halfway through his forty years as king. If Jonathan was born as suggested from [A-880-883] and this event was in the year of [A-921], then Jonathan was forty years of age, if born at [A-881].

Perhaps this was part of the purpose of marking out this event in such detail. It validated Jonathan as a mature godly leader and presented him as another deliverer of Israel, just like many judges before him. Jonathan's excellent character was proven again in his conduct with David some years later.

There were three separate pieces that pointed to the midpoint of Saul's reign as king. Jesse was shown to reach age 80 that year [See: Can Rahab of Jericho be the wife of Salmon? Narrowing Jesse's age], Ahiah was called upon by Saul, and Jonathan reached age 40. Each of these fit best in year [A-921]. One more large detail was recorded. This time placement must also match the earthquake reported in 1 Samuel 14:15, *"And there was trembling in the host, in the field, and among all the people: the [Philistine] garrison, and the spoilers, they also trembled, and the earth quaked: so it was a very great trembling."*

Saul's disobedience and rejection

In 1 Samuel certain events must precede others to make sense of the passages. Samuel must be approached by the elders, Saul was anointed [A-901], David was born [A-911], and Saul impatiently made a sacrifice after which he was told, *"the Lord hath sought him a man after his own heart."* After that event Saul requested Ahiah to bring the ark [~A-916-921]. When some time had passed from God's help in chapter 14 these words were recorded in 1 Samuel 15:1-3.

SECTION V

Samuel also said unto Saul, The Lord sent me to anoint thee to be king over his people, over Israel: now therefore hearken thou unto the voice of the words of the Lord. Thus saith the Lord of hosts, I remember that which Amalek did to Israel, how he laid wait for him in the way, when he came up from Egypt. Now go and smite Amalek, and utterly destroy all that they have, and spare them not; but slay both man and woman, infant and suckling, ox and sheep, camel and ass. (1 Samuel 15:1-3)

This was based upon a former text where God spoke to Moses in Exodus 17:14, *"Write this for a memorial in a book, and rehearse it in the ears of Joshua: for I will utterly put out the remembrance of Amalek from under heaven."* Here Saul was directly commissioned to fulfill this directive given either in the last month in the year [A-922] or early months in the next [A-923]. And because Saul disobeyed, *"Samuel said unto Saul, I will not return with thee: for thou hast rejected the word of the Lord, and the Lord hath rejected thee from being king over Israel."* (1 Samuel 15:6).

Saul rebelled from following directions to slay Agag [A-923], Samuel was sent and David was anointed about age twelve in [A-923], David served as musician for Saul, killed Goliath [A-928], became old enough at twenty years to lead soldiers [A-931], paid the dowry, and married Michal [A-931]. Saul sought to kill him before witnesses, David fled for his life [A-932], and Saul hunted for David for almost nine years until Saul's own death in [A-941]. These events were aligned in sequence as presented by event year. During these years in the book of 1 Samuel individuals were named that interconnected with Saul and/or David. These people, recorded in specific scenarios, became complementary markers of time.

Subsequent to Saul's rejection by the Lord (1 Samuel 15:1-35) the book of 1 Samuel immediately turned to another topic. This included the selection and anointing of David (chapter 16, [A-923]), his early time in Saul's court (chapter 16), his great victory over Goliath when he won the hearts of the people (chapter 17), and his long journey to become king (1 Samuel 18:1–30:31). The last topical part included David's interactions with Saul, Jonathan, Michal and Saul's jealousy and pursuit of David, and various other conflicts.

Across this time period Jonathan had established three covenants with David in 1 Samuel 18:1-30; 20:12-17; and 23:1-29 in spite of his father Saul's disposition toward the Lord's anointed. Saul at age seventy had already shown his evil disposition toward David before many witnesses (1 Samuel 18:8-12). Therefore, David fled to Samuel at Ramah. While there David received from Samuel God's counsel and training to be a king (1 Samuel 19:18, [A-932]).

Saul's rage against David and death

One thing noted earlier was that Saul needed to be old enough to be accepted as a king and then prove himself to be accepted as a military leader. But David was accepted as a leader because he was brave enough to go out alone against Goliath in mortal combat. His conduct was commendable and he won the hearts of the people as affirmed in 1 Samuel 18:7 and 21:11.

> And the women answered one another as they played, and said, Saul hath slain his thousands, and David his ten thousands.

> And the servants of Achish said unto him, Is not this David the king of the land? did they not sing one to another of him in dances, saying, Saul hath slain his thousands, and David his ten thousands?

"*Saul eyed David from that day and forward. And it came to pass on the morrow, that the evil spirit from God came upon Saul.*" (1 Samuel 18:9-10). From that day onward Saul feared David (18:12) and sought to destroy him, "*And Saul spake to Jonathan his son, and to all his servants, that they should kill David.*" (1 Samuel 19:1). Hereafter Saul decreased and David increased. He sought to destroy David even at prophet Samuel's home (1 Samuel 19:19-24). After this David continually fled from king Saul's hatred and venom (1 Samuel 20:1–30:31) for almost nine years from [A-932] until Saul's death in the middle of [A-941].

Jonathan spoke to David one more time in 1 Samuel 23:16-18 before his own death along with his father and his two younger brothers. Then 1 Samuel 31:2 recorded, "*Now the Philistines fought against Israel: and the men of Israel fled from before the Philistines, and fell down slain in mount Gilboa. And the Philistines followed hard upon Saul and upon his sons; and the Philistines slew Jonathan, and Abinadab, and Melchishua, Saul's sons.*" Within about two months David ascended to reign as king over Judah.

The post Samuel author(s) concluded the events and lives of Samuel, Saul, and his sons (1 Samuel 28:1–31:13; 14:49). Jonathan was a minimum age of fifty-eight years, if born in [~A-883; ~A-883-941, best fit A-881]. Ishui was probably around age fifty-six [~A-885-941] or more, and Melchishua somewhere near age fifty-four [~A-887-941] or more. The subsequent author(s) also wrote about David's last several years before he was made king over Judah (2 Samuel 2:4).

The alignment of numerous priests

Ahimelech the priest was at the tabernacle at the Levite city named Nob. David had some young soldiers with him when he fled Saul. David spoke with Ahimelech and asked for food, "*give me five loaves of bread in mine hand, or what there is present,*" (1 Samuel 21:3, 1-6). This Ahimelech was the son of Ahitub and the older brother of Ahiah. The birth range of Ahiah was determined before, the best fit was [~A-891-896], with both Phinehas and Ahitub having an early birth of their respective sons. Since Ahimelech served as a priest, and had a son Abiathar who had begun priest training in [A-932], he would have been older than Ahiah who was at least age twenty-five at the time of Saul's request.

Phinehas [A-853] by age eighteen had Ahitub [A-871]. Ahitub about age eighteen had Ahimelech [A-889] and then Ahiah about [~A-891-896; from above: Saul's request of Ahiah marked time]. In turn Ahimelech by age eighteen had Abiathar [A-907-<987]. This would meet the age criteria of Abiathar at age twenty-five [907 + 25 = 932] when David fled Saul in [A-932] and explain why he brought a newly obtained priest's ephod when he fled from Doeg the Edomite's rampage.

Under Saul's directive Doeg killed Ahitub, Ahimelech, Ahiah, and many others. In all "*fourscore and five persons that did wear a linen ephod*" died (1 Samuel 22:18-22). This fulfilled more of God's warnings and prophecies spoken against Zerahiah and Meraioth detailed above (1 Samuel 2:12-36).

David called Abiathar a priest and accepted him in that position in 1 Samuel 23:9, "*And David knew that Saul secretly practised mischief against him; and he said to Abiathar the priest, Bring hither the ephod.*" This affirmed that Abiathar was born at least twenty-five years earlier in [A-907]. Again he was called a priest in 1 Samuel 30:7, "*And David said to Abiathar the priest, Ahimelech's son, I pray thee, bring me hither the ephod. And Abiathar brought thither the ephod to David."*

This time placement for Abiathar also agreed with the text of Mark 2:26. Jesus stated there that David ate the shewbread during the days of Abiathar's service as a priest. Jesus called him, *"the high priest,"* using the title he possessed weeks later, i.e. after Eli had died.

Since Abiathar was with David in flight from Saul (1 Kings 2:26), the other priests were dead, and Eli would die a week or two later (1 Samuel 4:3-5, 11-18, [A-932]), Abiathar would not have been able to go through the lengthy formal ceremony at the tabernacle to be installed as the next high priest until Saul was dead (1 Samuel 22:20-23). The twelve tribes of Israel were without an inaugurated high priest leading required services at the tabernacle for almost nine years, which was longer than the eight-year period of the last judge, Abdon the son of Hillel, who started to serve in [A-933]. The branched candlestick was not serviced, the shewbread was not replaced, the incense was not burned. Neither were their any day of atonement sacrifices, nor blood sprinkled upon the missing ark, nor inauguration ceremonies for any subsequent priests across this time period. But the high priest Abiathar was with *"the light of Israel"* (2 Samuel 21:17) and received messages from God.

The lineage of the high priests

[Author's note: For detailed information about Aaron and the timing of the birth of his four sons (Nadab, Abihu, Eleazar, and Ithamar) see: Section II, Part 1.]

The placement of Meraioth's ninety-eight year lifetime at [A-834-932] was emphatically affirmed by the scriptural information presented about Meraioth, Hophni, Phinehas, Ahiah, Ahimelech, and Abiathar along with the subsequent information about his descendants including Zadok and Johanan. The Scriptures gave us the lineage of Aaron, the first high priest, (1 Chronicles 6:1-15) leading up to the Eli whose birth name was Meraioth (1 Samuel 14:3; 1 Chronicles 6:6), onward through his progeny past the temple destruction, up to the temple reconstruction with Ezra and Jehozadak. Some of these were specifically named as high priest or chief priest (marked with an asterisk *). Here is that list:

26th: Aaron* [A-422-545] begat Eleazar [A-487 or >] Exodus 28:1; Numbers

SECTION V

           3:2; 1 Chronicles 6:3; 24:1-2; {and Ithamar born last [~488 or >] Exodus 28:1; Numbers 3:2; 1 Chronicles 6:3; 24:1}; *Exodus 28:1-4, 41;

27th: Eleazar* begat Phinehas [~A-519] Exodus 6:23-25; *Numbers 31:13, 21, 26;

28th: Phinehas begat Abishua [~A-590] 1 Chronicles 6:4-5, 49-53;

29th: Abishua begat Bukki [~A-656] 1 Chronicles 6:4-5, 49-53;

30th: Bukki begat Uzzi [~A-722] 1 Chronicles 6:3-5;

31st: Uzzi begat Zerahiah [~A-781-892] 1 Chronicles 6:3-5;

32nd: Zerahiah begat Meraioth (Eli, [A-834-932]) 1 Samuel 14:3; 1 Chronicles 6:6, 52;

33rd: Meraioth* (Eli) begat Phinehas (Amariah, 1 Chronicles 6:7, 52; 1 Samuel 14:3, [A-853-932]) who died when the ark was captured;

For every subsequent generation the age at death is always less than eighty [<80] full years due to God's punishment upon the sons of Zerahiah and Meraioth.

34th: Phinehas (Amariah, 1st) begat Ahitub [<=A-871-932] 1 Chronicles 6:7-8;

35th: Ahitub begat Zadok [A-904-983] 1 Chronicles 6:8; 18:16; 2 Samuel 8:17 because Solomon, after inauguration as king in Tishri of [A-981], removed Abiathar* and made Zadok high priest before he died at <80 years of age; *1 Kings 2:26-27; Mark 2:26. Ahitub was comparable to Solomon of Matthew 1:7 and his brother Nathan in Luke 3:31; all three were in the 35th generation.

36th: Zadok* begat Ahimaaz [~A-923] 1 Chronicles 6:8; *1 Kings 2:26-27, 35; 1 Chronicles 29:22, [Note Ezekiel 44:15; 48:11];

37th: Ahimaaz begat Azariah [~A-942] 1 Chronicles 6:9-10;

38th: Azariah begat Johanan [A-961] 1 Chronicles 6:9-10, "[Johanan] he it is that executed the priest's office in the temple that Solomon built in Jerusalem," who had Levitical service from twenty-five to fifty years of age from [A-986-1011] with twenty years in Solomon's Temple ([A-991-1011]);

(*The following birth years in italics were subjective and only provide an approximate time of birth for perspective.*)

39th: Johanan begat Azariah (grandson of Azariah) born [?~A-1004] 1 Chronicles 6:9-10;

40th: Azariah begat Amariah [?~A-1047] Ezra 7:1-5; 1 Chronicles 6:11;

41st: Amariah begat Ahitub [?~A-1091] Ezra 7:1-5; 1 Chronicles 6:11;

42nd: Ahitub begat Zadok [?~A-1134] Ezra 7:1-5; 1 Chronicles 6:12;

43rd: Zadok begat Shallum (Meshallum, Ezra 7:1-5; 1 Chronicles 6:12; 9:11; Nehemiah 11:11, [?~A-1177-~1188)];

44th: Shallum begat Hilkiah [?~A-1231-~1241] Ezra 7:1-5; 1 Chronicles 6:13;
45th: Hilkiah* begat Azariah [?~A-1264-~1284] Ezra 7:1-5; 1 Chronicles 6:13; *2 Kings 22:4; *2 Chronicles 34:9
46th: Azariah* begat Seraiah [?~A-1313-~1330] Ezra 7:1-5; 1 Chronicles 6:14; *2 Chronicles 26:20; 31:10;
47th: Seraiah* begat Jehozadak (Jozadak, Ezra 3:2; 10:18, Josedech, Haggai 1:1, [?~A-1339-~1344]) Ezra 7:1-5; 1 Chronicles 6:14-15. His younger brothers were Meraiah (Nehemiah 12:10-12, 22, 26) and Ezra (Ezra 7:1-5). (Babylonian captivity, 1 Chronicles 6:15 [A-1364] 587 BC.); *2 Kings 25:18; Jeremiah 52:24; Seraiah, the 47th generation, was comparable to Josias of Matthew 1:11 and for Eliezer in Luke 3:29.
48th: Jehozadak* begat Joshua (Ezra 3:2, 8; 5:2; 10:18; Nehemiah 12:26), [Jehozadak, Meraiah, and Ezra of the 48th generation were comparable to Jechonias of Matthew 1:12 and to Jose in Luke 3:29.] Jehozadak also begat Maaseiah, Eliezer, Jarib, and Gedaliah (Ezra 10:18).
49th: Joshua* (Jeshua, Ezra 10:18) the son of Josedech (*Haggai 1:1, 12-14; 2:2-4; *Zechariah 3:1, 8; 6:11) begat Joiakim (Nehemiah 12:10-11, 26). The 49th generation was comparable to Salathiel of Matthew 1:12 and Er of Luke 3:28. [Salathiel (Shealtiel, Ezra 3:2; 5:2) was the legal father of Zorobabel (Zerubbabel, Ezra 3:2; 5:2; Haggai 1:1) conceived through Pedaiah (1 Chronicles 3:19; Deuteronomy 25:5) because Salathiel died childless.]
50th: Joiakim begat Eliashib (Nehemiah 12:10).
51st: Eliashib* (*Nehemiah 3:1, 20; 13:28) begat Joiada (Nehemiah 12:10; 13:28) and Johanan (Ezra 10:6).
52nd: Joiada begat Jonathan (Nehemiah 12:11) and more sons (Nehemiah 13:28).
53rd: Jonathan begat Jaddua (Nehemiah 12:11, 22).
54th: Jaddua. [*No further sequential generations of the high priest were given in the Old Testament of Holy Scripture. However, the New Testament gave the last two recorded Levitical priests: Zacharias and his son John. It also gave the last recorded daughter of a priest, Elisabeth. (Luke 1:5)*]

The ark was taken

The ark of the covenant (Numbers 14:44), often called *"the mercy seat"* (Exodus 25:17-18), held the two cherubim between which the "shekinah" glory and God's voice emanated (Numbers 7:89). The account in 1

Samuel 4:1–6:21 about the capture and absence of the ark of the covenant from the tabernacle conveyed how long the ark was separated from the tabernacle. This was used to connect to the time in 2 Samuel 6:17 when David brought the ark to the tabernacle in Zion.

This was a significant event and potent time marker when the ark was captured (1 Samuel 4:1–7:2). The text carefully stated that the Philistines had the ark for just seven months and upon its return to Beth Shemesh the lowlands were in wheat harvest (1 Samuel 6:1, 13). The day of Pentecost when the first ripe wheat was offered to the Lord came fifty days after the first ripe barley was offered, usually about Abib 16 of the Jewish calendar (Leviticus 23:15-17). Thus Pentecost was about the sixth day of the third month Sivan when the earliest wheat from the lowlands was harvested. That meant seven months prior to 1 Samuel 6:13 was the time of the capture of the ark by the Philistines, i.e. in the previous year early in the eighth month of Bul.

The capture by the Philistines set in motion for over twenty years temporary dwelling places for the ark. The ark of the covenant was returned by David and all Israel in two sessions (2 Samuel 6:1-23; 1 Chronicles 13:1-14; 15:1-29), beginning in the third month of Sivan twenty years and seven months after capture as Scripture declared (1 Samuel 7:2). After an additional three month pause in the house of Obededom (2 Samuel 6:10-19) the ark arrived at the Zion tabernacle in the sixth month of Elul.

David with the Israelites had the ark carried from the house of Abinadab (1 Samuel 7:1; 2 Samuel 6:1-18) and placed in Zion (2 Samuel 5:7; 6:16-17, [A-953]). That made the ark arrive prior to the seventh month of Tishri atonement day sacrifices for high priest Abiathar to officiate. Taking into account David's thirty year age at his ascension, the capture of the stronghold of Zion, completion of his own house, and other events in this time period, David was forty-two years of age (2 Samuel 5:7; 6:16-17, [A-953]).

The time frame when the ark was captured was not stated directly, but obtained by calculation from David at forty-two years minus twenty years and seven months to twenty-one years of age in the eighth month of Bul in [A-932]. This event fit together with 1 Samuel 20:42 after David departed (1 Samuel 18:9, 29; 20:31) from Saul's evil hatred and fled his relentless pursuit. Saul's jealousy of David and multiple attempts to kill him caused David to flee to Samuel (1 Samuel 19:18–20:1).

Saul was angry that David fled and was given food as recorded in 1 Samuel 21–22. Doeg the Edomite, under Saul's command, wrecked havoc upon the city of Nob and killed eighty-five priests living there, except Abiathar (1 Samuel 22:9-20). This attitude of Saul's active opposition to God's directives accounted for the ark of the covenant carried into battle by Hophni and Phinehas when that conflict with the Philistines did not proceed as anticipated. Saul had previously asked Ahiah to bring the ark of the covenant to a battle (1 Samuel 14:18).

Saul did not act alone. The elders of the twelve tribes of Israel had rejected God, refused his methods, and wanted a king. Now they sought their own method of solving this Philistine conflict saying, "*Let us fetch the ark of the covenant of the Lord out of Shiloh unto us, that, when it cometh among us, it may save us out of the hand of our enemies.*" (1 Samuel 4:3-5; see also 12:12-25).

The elders had asked for and brought the physical ark into the battle camp, that "*it may save us*"—hoping for victory. This was a form of carrying an idol or a talisman around, attempting to force "God" to serve them. Transporting the physical ark of the covenant to this battle scene became a man-made substitute for the worship of and faithful obedience to the God of heaven and earth.

With that background and prevailing attitude of rejection of God and his anointed there were serious consequences. The literal ark was taken into battle as requested by the elders, carried by the wayward sons of Eli, then captured by the Philistines in [A-932] (1 Samuel 4:3-5, 11-18; 4–7 chpts.). Previously the primary clues provided in 1 Samuel 3 established that Eli's two sons Hophni and Phinehas died at seventy-nine and seventy-eight years of age, respectively, near Saul's age of death. This had explicitly fulfilled 1 Samuel 2:31, "*there shall not be an old man in thine house,*" i.e. who reached eighty years of age.

"The light of Israel"

Consider this about David: he was the son of an aged father (1 Samuel 17:12), he was anointed (1 Samuel 16:1-13), was a sweet musician (1 Samuel 16:14-23), killed the giant Goliath (1 Samuel 17:48-50), defeated the Philistines in battles (1 Samuel 18:25-27, etc.), walked in the spirit of the Lord before all Israelites (1 Samuel 18:16), held high the value of the Lord's anointed (1 Samuel 24:6, 10; 26:23), made just judgments (2 Samuel 1:16), established the design of the temple (1 Chronicles 28:11), set the courses of the temple servants (1 Chronicles 23:6), was the sweet psalmist of Israel (2 Samuel 23:1), etc. This made David a type of Christ, whose presence was manifested in the ark of God.

David was even called *"the light of Israel"* (2 Samuel 21:17) by his men. This implied that David was a kind of substitute for or representative of the presence of God in spiritual and physical battle. He was even recognized to be so by the Philistine prince, *"Achish answered and said to David, I know that thou art good in my sight, as an angel of God."* (1 Samuel 29:9). This was parallel to the Roman centurion recognizing Jesus as the Son of God (Matthew 27:54).

The Scriptures were clear that in every battle that David had early and later in life, where David went, and by extension his army captain, victory proceeded — David ALWAYS won! (1 Samuel 13:14; 2 Samuel 8:6, 14; 1 Chronicles 11:9; 18 chpt.; 19 chpt.; 20 chpt.; 23:1-5; 29:12-13; Psalm 33:16) For these and other reasons he was a type, a picture or preview, of the presence of the Lord bringing victory to his people, a type portraying the living presence of God as represented in the shekinah radiance.

Another point was that the Israelites were defeated in this battle with the Philistines, but every battle that David fought he won. The anointed David (who represented Christ) was not wanted, so that the ark was lost due to the Israelites' unbelief and disobedience. Now, David fled Saul because Saul sought to kill him (1 Samuel 19:5; 24:2; 26:2) which in symbol was the rejection of the presence of God. Plus David departed from Saul reflecting that God's spirit had already departed from Saul (1 Samuel 16:14; 28:6).

Since David had departed physically and in type, there was no victory, only loss. [Another parallel event was presented in Ezekiel's vision when God in symbol lifted up above the ark, the temple tabernacle, the city, and then departed (Ezekiel 10–11 chpts.).] The slaughter of the priests at Nob and the subsequent capture of the ark of the covenant portrayed the spiritual import of Saul's rejection (and of the Israelites' national rejection) of God. Saul's refusal to submit to God in obedience (1 Samuel 28:18), jealousy against God's appointed leadership

(1 Samuel 18:7-8), and continued hatred of righteousness (1 Samuel 19:1-2, 10; 23:14) was manifested in Saul's efforts to hunt and kill David.

Saul was completely at variance with his son, Jonathan, who upon meeting David was so moved by the spirit in David that Jonathan immediately gave to David four categories of items: his robe, armor, sword and bow, and his belt. In the order listed these delineated that Jonathan surrendered all claims to become the next king, his military position as leader and defender of the twelve tribes of Israel, his talents and skills, and dedicated himself to David in submission to God's anointing upon him (1 Samuel 18:1-5).

Their twenty-eight to thirty-one year age difference made even more striking, *"that the soul of Jonathan was knit with the soul of David, and Jonathan loved him as his own soul,"* (1 Samuel 18:1). As a much older man Jonathan was noteworthy, remarkable, even quite unusual in yielding to David as God's appointed king. His actions previewed John the Baptist with Jesus (John 3:26-32).

Placing this event with the loss of the ark of the covenant at this time period when David had fled from Saul made complete sense. The one priest with an ephod, who later heard the word of God and told forth God's messages to David, had also fled from Saul. Saul no longer had God's spirit (1 Samuel 16:14), most of the twelve tribes of Israel were not seeking God very well under Saul's leadership (1 Samuel 22:18-22; 23:19).

Many men of valor and their families had already begun to assemble unto David (1 Samuel 22:1-2). It was David who in a manner portrayed or previewed the real spiritual ark, Christ Jesus, and lived openly before God, whom Abiathar served. This revealed a lamentable, dismal period, but God raised up other Godly men to serve. Samson and Jephthah will be shown to fit within the forty-year period when Saul was king from [A-901-941].

Where was Jonathan?

When examining this account in 1 Samuel chapters 4–7 a significant question came to mind, "Where was Jonathan?" The answer to that was not the same as for Samuel when he had attained fifty years of age. Earlier Jonathan was shown to have died in his final battle at a minimum age of fifty-eight. His brothers were most likely also over fifty years of age at their death. Perhaps at this event Jonathan was caring for other civic duties or involved in another conflict with Israel's enemies. Or he was not involved in this conflict due to some other reasons, one of which could be surprising.

Two more reasons appeared credible using the information provided in the writings of Moses. The directive in Deuteronomy 20:7 stated, *"And what man is there that hath betrothed a wife, and hath not taken her? let him go and return unto his house, lest he die in the battle, and another man take her."* Additionally, the text of Deuteronomy 24:5 commanded, *"When a man hath taken a new wife, he shall not go out to war, neither shall he be charged with any business: but he shall be free at home one year, and shall cheer up his wife which he hath taken."*

If Jonathan had been busy with military conflicts and matters of civic service for his father Saul for the last thirty years, then he may not have married. This was consistent with his affection for David which could be stronger when not having any children of his own. This provided an excellent time for Jonathan to marry and supply the reason that he was not involved in this conflict.

The third and less likely reason pertained to matters of care surrounding the possible death of his wife's parent or even his mother in which case Jonathan was in a period of mourning and excused from assembling with the other Israelites for this battle due to uncleanness for contact with the dead. Numbers 19:11 stated, *"He that toucheth the dead body of any man shall be unclean seven days."* This passage in Numbers conveyed more information through verse 16.

The reason was not that, *"Jonathan Saul's son arose, and went to David into the wood, and strengthened his hand in God."* There David and Jonathan entered into their third covenant (1 Samuel 23:16-18). That event was much later in time and nearer to Samuel's death in 1 Samuel 25:1. Samuel had died about one and one-half to two years before Saul and Jonathan died in their final battle with the Philistines.

At some point Jonathan married. If he married earlier, then Jonathan and his wife were barren of children until shortly before his death. This might be another circumstance where an aged mother in Israel had a child under the Lord's blessing.

Jonathan was about fifty-eight [up to sixty-one] when he died. He was only about fifty-three [up to age fifty-six or a 0.66 to 0.70 ratio to an eighty-year life expectancy] for the birth of his son. If he was married around his early twenties, this would make his wife barren, in Scripture terms, for twenty-five or more years.

If Jonathan became betrothed or married at this later time about when the ark was captured in [A-932], he would have been about forty-nine years of age [up to age fifty-two, when using A-880-883 for his birth range]. With Jonathan's best fit birth year in A-881 he was at age fifty-one. Jonathan could not serve in the army of Israel for one whole year from marriage. Either way, Jonathan had only one child, a son Mephibosheth was born in [A-936] five years before Jonathan died (2 Samuel 4:4, [A-941]).

> And Jonathan, Saul's son, had a son that was lame of his feet. He was five years old when the tidings came of Saul and Jonathan out of Jezreel, and his nurse took him up, and fled: and it came to pass, as she made haste to flee, that he fell, and became lame. And his name was Mephibosheth.

The period of Samson

Samuel's speech before Israel in 1 Samuel 12 came about ten years after Saul was anointed because of the people named in it. Note again in Samuel's speech in 1 Samuel 12:5-11 that he did not mention Samson as having served to defend Israel in his list of recent judges. "*And the Lord sent Jerubbaal, and Bedan, and Jephthah, and Samuel, and delivered you out of the hand of your enemies on every side, and ye dwelled safe*" (1 Samuel 12:11). Perhaps Samuel brought his own name into this because he was already over 50, had completed his Levitical tabernacle service, and was fulfilling God's purpose for him as judge. Or the later author(s) put his name there since he was a life-long judge-deliverer.

Samson was not mentioned there because he was not of sufficient age to "*begin to deliver Israel out of the hand of the Philistines*" (Judges 13:5). His period as judge did not start before this, but came after this event of 1 Samuel 12:1-25. Hebrews 11:32 had not only a subtle but also an extremely powerful confirmation when its author said, "*And what shall I more say? for the time would fail me to tell of Gedeon, and of Barak, and of*

Samson, and of Jephthae; of David also, and Samuel, and of the prophets." Note carefully that the order of delivery was in three couplets: Gedeon and Barak, Samson and Jephthae, David and Samuel. Each couplet placed the second person in time first in order in the text.

However, for real time progression reverse the individuals named in each couplet. Barak [A-757] came before Gideon [A-804], Jephthah [A-910] came before Samson [A-912], and Samuel [A-850] came before David [A-911]. This placed Samuel's speech before the elders and all Israel (1 Samuel 12:1-25) plus the miracle that followed (verses 16-18) in Saul's tenth year [A-911] prior to Samson's service as a unique judge in Israel from [A-912-932]. That confirmed Samuel's speech occurred early in [A-911], the same year that David was born.

This was exactly how they worked out in a timeline. The multiple periods of Judges 3:8 through 12:13-15 were sequential. Only Judges 13:1 was given out of order and repeated a significant statement. That meant Judges 13:1 had quoted previous text, referred back to it, and started at the same time as Judges 10:6-8.

Since the account in Judges 13 explicitly began with the forty years of Philistine oppression and immediately followed with Samson's life story this implicitly directed us to join these two things together. It gave the clue to align both time periods at that point. That meant Samson's lifetime also started the same year as Judges 10:6-8. Both overlaid upon the same forty-year period.

In the account of Judges, finishing the main chronological sequence of the oppressions and the delivering judges was consequential to the author(s) before beginning a new subject, the topic of Samson. The details about Samson followed after finishing the main framework of the judges and their periods of service, from Othniel through Abdon. It was laid out this way to give the outer boundaries of those time periods of oppression and deliverance so that they would be properly connected sequentially and their individual time durations summed. Both Judges 10:6-8 and 13:1 started with the same phrase, *"And the children of Israel did evil again in the sight of the Lord."* Each text related that Israel was sold or delivered, *"into the hands of the Philistines."*

Therefore, Judges 13:1 started the same year as Judges 10:6-8 and both periods followed right after the twenty-two years of judge Jair given in Judges 10:3. Inside the full sequence of Judges 3:8 through 12:15 the six years of Jephthah began in [A-910] or 1041 BC and the twenty years of Samson as judge started in [A-912] or 1039 BC.

Noting that the men of the twelve tribes of Israel were counted in Numbers 1:3, *"from twenty years old and upward, all that are able to go forth to war,"* Samson was almost twenty years of age, in his twentieth year, when he began to afflict the Philistines in Judges 14:4. Then adding twenty years as judge (Judges 16:31) brought Samson to year forty at death [A-932]. Therefore, that forty-year period of Philistine oppression aligned exceptionally well with Samson's entire lifetime. His final act with his death was the slaughter of *"the lords of the Philistines"* (Judges 16:23-30), which completed twenty years as judge.

> And Samson called unto the Lord, and said, O Lord God, remember me, I pray thee, and strengthen me, I pray thee, only this once, O God, that I may be at once avenged of the Philistines for my two eyes. And Samson took hold of the two middle pillars upon which the house stood, and on which it was borne up, of the one with his right hand, and of the other with his left. And Samson said, Let me die with the Philistines. And he bowed himself with all his might; and the house fell upon the lords, and upon all the people that were therein. So the dead which he slew at his death were more than they which he slew in his life. (Judges 16:28-30)

Such a great one man slaughter by Samson offended the pride of the Philistines, damaged their image of power, and weakened their control over Israel (specially note God's words in Ezekiel 25:15). Samson's last and overwhelming victory against them provided the reason for another invasion. The parenthetical insertion of 1 Samuel 4:9 recorded that the Philistines encouraged one another, saying, *"Be strong and quit yourselves like men, O ye Philistines, that ye be not servants unto the Hebrews, as they have been to you: quit yourselves like men, and fight."*

The Philistines won that battle and captured the ark of the covenant from Saul and held the ark for seven months (1 Samuel 6:1). Their success emboldened the Philistines to return a little later that same year in battle against Israel. The forty-year Philistine oppression ended when their control was removed by a miracle through Samuel (1 Samuel 7:10-14), *"So the Philistines were subdued, and they came no more into the* [eastern or far] *coast of Israel."*

Their preliminary success in battle and capture of the ark encouraged their prompt return (1 Samuel 7:7) and the subsequent profound event with Samuel ended this Israelite servitude. After defeat, hardship, and disease was inflicted upon the Philistines the majestic ark of the covenant came back again to Israel on a lowly ox cart (1 Samuel 6:6-13), about the time of the feast of weeks (also called Pentecost) in [A-933]. This was seven months from capture (1 Samuel 6:1).

The ark was briefly held until moved into the house of Abinadab where it remained for twenty years (1 Samuel 7:1-2; These two verses belong to the end of chapter 6 and finish the request of verse 21.). The remainder of 1 Samuel 7 occurred quickly after the capture of the ark. After twenty years in the house of Abinadab the ark was transported in 2 sessions by David to the Zion tabernacle (1 Chronicles 13:1-14; 15:1-29, [A-953], detailed above).

The information presented made 1 Samuel 7:9-14 mark the year of Samson's death [A-932] and the end of forty years of Philistine oppression [A-892-932]. Judges 13:5 only stated that Samson would *"begin to deliver." "For, lo, thou shalt conceive, and bear a son; and no razor shall come on his head: for the child shall be a Nazarite unto God from the womb: and he shall begin to deliver Israel out of the hand of the Philistines."* Samuel's miracle finished the task of deliverance.

> And as Samuel was offering up the burnt offering, the Philistines drew near to battle against Israel: but the Lord thundered with a great thunder on that day upon the Philistines, and discomfited them; and they were smitten before Israel. And the men of Israel went out of Mizpeh, and pursued the Philistines, and smote them, until they came under Bethcar. Then Samuel took a stone, and set it between Mizpeh and Shen, and called the name of it Ebenezer, saying, Hitherto hath the Lord helped us. So the Philistines were subdued, and they came no more into the [far or eastern] coast of Israel: and the hand of the Lord was against the Philistines all the days of Samuel. And the cities which the Philistines had taken from Israel were restored to Israel, from Ekron even unto Gath; and the coasts thereof did Israel deliver out of the hands of the Philistines. And there was

peace between Israel and the Amorites. (1 Samuel 7:10-14)

Samson's lifetime entirely fit into the forty years of Philistine affliction and oppression spoken of in Judges 13:1. This forty-year period ended with Samuel's greatest miracle. For about nine years the Philistines neither penetrated to the eastern side of Israel nor made incursions very deep into Israel, i.e. until they came midway into Israel to Jezreel in battle by mount Gilboa where king Saul and his sons died (1 Samuel 29 and 31 chpts.).

Samuel continued the worship of God

The information in 1 Samuel 7 followed in linear time sequence after the loss of the 85 priests at Nob, the transport of the *"ark of the covenant"* into battle (Exodus 25:21-22; Numbers 10:33; 14:44; Deuteronomy 10:8; Joshua 3:11), Israel's defeat in that battle, the death of Hophni and Phinehas, the loss of the *"ark of the covenant,"* and then Eli's death. This meant there was no high priest actively administering the tabernacle system of observances and sacrifices which centered upon the ark residing in the most holy place. [See: Hebrews 5:1-2] Nor was the annual day of atonement sacrifices completed with blood sprinkled before and upon the ark by the high priest across this period since Abiathar, the next high priest, was in flight with David from Saul. Abiathar was a fugitive, but when joined with David he served *"the light of Israel"* (2 Samuel 21:17).

Because the tabernacle worship was disrupted by these events the Scripture text said that Samuel *"was offering up the burnt offering"* (1 Samuel 7:10) and he *"built an altar unto the Lord"* (1 Samuel 7:17). As a leading Levite Samuel knew God had directed the Israelites to use the tabernacle to bring their offerings to God (Deuteronomy 12:5-7, 11, 21; 16:11; Nehemiah 1:9). Due to Saul's attitude and actions as king, the elders' false spiritual leadership, and Israel's willing blindness (Jeremiah 2 chpt.) they were without a place of worship with sacrifices, for the high priest was to superintend all sacrifices and offerings, regular and holy day tabernacle services, and make an annual atonement for Israel upon the ark of the covenant.

Therefore, Samuel became in essence a priest (1 Samuel 7:5-12) when he built an altar of earth stones (Exodus 20:4; Deuteronomy 27:4-7;

Joshua 8:31) to maintain that worship in spirit and in truth. Samuel acted in the same manner that Noah did for his family (Genesis 8:20), Abraham did for Abimelech (Genesis 20:14-18), Job did for his family (Job 1:5) and his three friends (Job 42:7-10), Jethro did for Midian (Exodus 3:1; 18:9-12), and Moses did for the twelve tribes of Israel (Exodus 40:27-29; Leviticus 8:21, 28-29; Psalm 99:6). [In a manner this was followed by David for Israel (2 Samuel 24:25; 1 Chronicles 21:26), Elijah for Israel (1 Kings 18:30-32), and Christ Jesus for mankind (Hebrews 3:1; 4:14; 6:20).] This worship of the LORD, the God of Abraham, Isaac, and Israel, Samuel upheld until he died. First Samuel 7:15-17 explained Samuel's remaining years this way.

> And Samuel judged Israel all the days of his life. And he went from year to year in circuit to Bethel, and Gilgal, and Mizpeh, and judged Israel in all those places. And his return was to Ramah; for there was his house; and there he judged Israel; and there he built an altar unto the Lord.

Where was Samson?

Another essential question must be addressed. Where was the strong man Samson when the big man Goliath challenged Israel in [A-928], four years earlier from [A-932]? This alignment of Samson's lifetime starting at the same time as Judges 10:6-8 fit exceptionally well with this battle scene. When Samson was about thirty-six years of age he was captured by the Philistines as recorded in Judges 16:21, "*But the Philistines took him, and put out his eyes, and brought him down to Gaza, and bound him with fetters of brass; and he did grind in the prison house.*" That occurred just before the Philistines mounted a reprisal for Samson's recent damages to them (Ezekiel 25:15).

The Philistines brought out their own strong man, Goliath, to respond to the challenges of Samson, especially knowing that Samson was already captured and blinded. "*And there went out a champion out of the camp of the Philistines, named Goliath, of Gath, whose height was six cubits and a span.*" (1 Samuel 17:4). The strong man Samson was supplanted by the strong man Goliath to reassert and reestablish Philistine control over Israel. Thus, in arrogance, the Philistine army came out with their brazen challenge to a one man combat and decision for victory.

Connections between Judges and 1 Samuel

This battle scene came about *"at Shochoh, which belongeth to Judah."* To the utter surprise and wondering amazement of the host of Philistines a modest-sized youth came out, stood in defiance against their Goliath, and killed him (1 Samuel 17:40-50). This fully aligned with David before Goliath at age seventeen (in his 18th year [A-928]) and with David fleeing Saul four years later at age twenty-one.

During that four-year period Samson's hair grew out again (Judges 16:22) The Lord heard and honored Samson's last prayer, and the house fell upon the lords and the host of Philistines inside (Judges 16:27-30). That battle when the ark was captured (1 Samuel 4) came after David fled Saul because, 1) Samson in his fortieth year had just destroyed many of the Philistines rulers (Judges 16:27-31), 2) the Philistine populace wanted revenge (Ezekiel 25:15), 3) and they sought to retain control over Israel (1 Samuel 4:9).

The Philistine forty-year oppression ended

As detailed above, this time period which started with Judges 10:6-8 [A-892-910] and aligned with Judges 13:1 [A-892-932] also coincided with Eli as judge [A-892-932]. This forty-year period fell within the lifetime of Samuel and overlapped for thirty-one years [A-901-932] into the forty-year period of the reign of king Saul [A-901-941] who outlived Samson by nine more years. This agreed with the work assigned to Saul in 1 Samuel 9:16, *"To morrow about this time I will send thee a man out of the land of Benjamin, and thou shalt anoint him to be captain over my people Israel, that he may save my people out of the hand of the Philistines: for I have looked upon my people, because their cry is come unto me."*

And when Israel cried unto the Lord there was deliverance. Saul lived after Samson's death and served until the intended king, David, was prepared by God to take office. That occurred when David was age thirty in [A-941].

The end of this forty-year period was emphasized by a miracle from God in 1 Samuel 7:9-14 when the Philistines were routed, subdued, and the Ebenezer stone was placed [A-932]. This multi-piece explanation accounted for the forty years of Philistine oppression, gave that period significant starting and ending points, and correlated multiple events into one cohesive whole. God used six years of judge Jephthah

[A-910-916], seven years of judge Ibzan [A-916-923], nine of the ten years of judge Elon [A-923-933], twenty years of judge Samson, thirty-one years of king Saul, four years of David from Goliath's death, judge Samuel, about thirty-one years of brave Jonathan, and all forty years of Eli as high priest and judge, during this forty-year period.

Six of these individuals were in various ways types of Christ, while Eli (Meraioth) languished and king Saul entirely succumbed to the temptations of this world. That made three remarkably potent victories over the Philistines in four years by God's servants. These included David slaying Goliath and the subsequent routing of the army [A-928], Samson destroying the Philistine lords and temple in [A-932], and then Samuel's climactic defeat of the Philistine army slightly later in [A-932].

During this same forty-year period God used two unique Nazarites to preview the future work of Christ. Consider this: Samson served and sacrificed himself (Judges 16:25-31), Samuel served both as a prophet (1 Samuel 3:20; Acts 3:24) and essentially as a priest (1 Samuel 7:9-10, 17; 10:8; 11:15; 16:2; Psalm 99:6) but not as a Levitical priest descending from Aaron. And Samuel yielded himself to establish another person, David, as God's intended king. God had shown himself strong on the behalf of the twelve tribes of Israel when he raised up Godly men.[18,19]

The placement of Jephthah

The placement in time for judge Jephthah was derived through three separate methods. 1) The last four judges in succession before David became king were Jephthah, Ibzan, Elon, and Abdon. Add their respective years of service [6 + 7 + 10 + 8 = 31]. David was age thirty in [A-941] when he was made king. That made judge Jephthah start one year prior to David's birth year [A-941 - 31 = A-910]. With only simple addition of the years of service given for the last four consecutive judges, the start of the six-year period of judge Jephthah can be placed in [A-910].

Or, if you prefer, start from the year of the land division in [A-552] and add thirty-nine years to get to the first oppression in [A-591]. Add up the sequential time periods, oppressions and deliverances, given in the book of Judges before Jephthah (Section III. Table 9) [8 + 40 + 18 + 80 + 20 + 40 + 7 + 40 + 3 + 23 + 22 + 18 = 319]. Then add 319 to [A-591] and arrive at [A-910] for judge Jephthah to begin his service.

2) Note this from Samuel's speech in 1 Samuel 12:5-11, *"And the Lord sent Jerubbaal, and Bedan, and Jephthah, and Samuel, and delivered you out of the hand of your enemies on every side, and ye dwelled safe."* Jephthah's defeat of the Ammonites east of the Jordan river had recently been completed when Samuel spoke this in Saul's eleventh year. Jephthah had served his first year and Samson started later in [A-912]. As presented earlier, this event and speech occurred in the year [A-911], probably just prior to David's birth.

Set between the chapters of 1 Samuel 12 and 14 was the account of chapter 13 when Saul disobeyed Samuel's directive from God to wait, but then proceeded in *"offering the burnt offering"* (verse 9). To this foolish action Samuel gave God's response, *"But now thy kingdom shall not continue: the Lord hath sought him a man after his own heart, and the Lord hath commanded him to be captain over his people, because thou hast not kept that which the Lord commanded thee."* (1 Samuel 13:14) The expression in verse 14, *"the Lord hath sought him a man after his own heart,"* fit well with David over age four, the age when Samuel was presented before Eli (Zerahiah) at the tabernacle. This was the age when God began to mold David for His purposes.

First Samuel chapter 13 ended describing the oppression of the Philistines in limiting the Israelite use of tools and weapons. This helped explain Saul's first request of Ahiah in 1 Samuel 14:3 and 18 to have the ark brought to the battle scene several years later, i.e. to attempt to get this God on his side, like a lucky device, a charm, or talisman. This time placement of chapter 14 was argued above based upon Ahiah's ancestry, minimum Levitical age, and status as a priest for [A-916-921, see: Saul's request of Ahiah marked time], probably halfway through Saul's reign.

3) The last method was provided in the New Testament with the unusual presentation of the text in Hebrews 11:32 that used three reversed couplets. When the names in each couplet was reordered chronologically Jephthah began to serve before Samson started his twenty years. [This was explained above with Samson]

Three hundred years

Some assert that the 300 years given by Jephthah, son of Gilead, as described in Judges 11:12-26 must start when the twelve tribes of Israel approached Canaan under Moses' leadership. They fought against Sihon, king of the Amorites and took ownership of their territory. King Sihon and the Amorites lived north and west of the Ammonites, and the Ammonites lived north of the Moabites on the east side of the Jordan river.

This led to Jephthah's question in Judges 11:26, "*While Israel dwelt in Heshbon and her towns, and in Aroer and her towns, and in all the cities that be along by the coasts of Arnon, three hundred years? why therefore did ye not recover them within that time?*" He asked why neither Moab, which was far south and east from that territory, nor Ammon (formerly associated under king Eglon of Moab when they captured and "*possessed the city of palm trees,*" Judges 3:8-11) had asserted ownership in the last three centuries — not three hundred years exactly, but about three hundreds of years, commonly expressed as three centuries.

Jephthah used the expression three hundred(s) of years in the same manner that three days and three nights were used in 1 Samuel 30:12; Jonah 1:17, and Matthew 12:40. In each of these occurrences the three day long periods were not meant to be understood as exactly three complete units of twenty-four hours, but to be understood as significant parts of three days. Jephthah did not ask a chronological question, but a rhetorical question. If the territory of land was valuable to own, and it was truly the property of either Moab who led the historical invasion or Ammon who made the current claim, then why did neither Moab nor Ammon assert their own claim earlier and recover ownership of this land during the major part of the past three centuries? [See Section IV. Table 9]

Three hundred complete years prior to Jephthah's service to Israel in [A-910] was in [A-610]. This was eleven years into judge Othniel's forty years of service and rest (Judges 3:9-11, [A-599-639]). His period was followed in Judges 3:12-14 by another oppression of eighteen years under Moab in alliance with Ammon and Amalek [A-639-657].

> And the children of Israel did evil again in the sight of the Lord: and the Lord strengthened Eglon the king of Moab against Israel, because they had done evil in the sight of the Lord. And he gathered unto him the children of Ammon and Amalek, and went and smote Israel, and possessed the city of palm trees. So the

children of Israel served Eglon the king of Moab eighteen years.

This was the era when Ammon and Moab could have begun to contest ownership of some of Gilead because in Judges 3:13 Moab with Ammon, under Eglon king of Moab, had captured *"the city of palm trees."* That was the area near Jericho. Then forty-seven years later from Othniel's eleventh year of service [A-610 to A-657 = 47 years] judge Ehud delivered Israel from the Moabites, not from the Ammonites (Judges 3:15-30, [A-657-737]). Israel had recovered the land 253 years earlier from Moab [A-910 - A-657 = 253]. By asking his question in this way Jephthah completely invalidated any possible claim from Ammon.

Only if the Ammonites had truly begun to assert ownership of the land eleven years into Othniel's period could the three hundred(s) of years that Jephthah gave confirm the exact amount of years that had transpired. Otherwise the stated expression of three hundreds of years remained part of a carefully crafted rhetorical question used to present information and to help argue his case. The answer to Jephthah's question emphasized that neither Ammon's claim nor any potential claim from Moab had moral or legal strength, especially after 253 years or significant parts of three centuries had passed.

The three hundreds of years used by Jephthah was just a rhetorical time period to show the inherent weakness of the Ammonite assertion of ownership over the land. This phrase was not meant to be understood as, nor was it used as, an exact chronological period. Three germane reasons exist: 1) 271 years prior to Jephthah's statement [910 - 639 = 271] Moab captured this territory [A-639], 2) only eighteen years later the ownership was regained from Moab by Ehud [A-657], and 3) Ammon never made any claim for at least 253 years since then [A-910 - A-657 = 253]. To recheck this for yourself, go back to Section IV. Table 9 and sum the years from Jephthah's first year backward.

What we learned:

1. Judges of different types served in Israel at the same time.

2. Eli, whose birth name was Meraioth, died at age ninety-eight when David was twenty-one years of age.

3. Meraioth's progeny through the fifth generation of descendants served as priests while David lived for seventy years.

SECTION V

4. Samuel was fifty-one years of age when he anointed Saul.

5. Saul was most likely thirty-nine years old, i.e. in his fortieth year, when anointed and died before completing eighty years of life, i.e. in his eightieth year. Ishbosheth was forty years old when he began to reign after Saul's death. He was most likely late in his fortieth year and not forty full years old (2 Samuel 2:8-10) since he was not named as Saul's son in the earlier list (1 Samuel 14:49).

6. The placement of David's birth year came between the beginning of service for Jephthah and Samson. That Jonathan and David had twenty-eight to thirty-one years difference in age (best fit at thirty).

7. Named priests' ages for service aligned and fit the context of significant events within Eli's life time and with subsequent events after his death.

9. The spiritual scenario of Israel when the ark was taken into battle and captured. How Eli, Samuel, Samson and David fit into the time when the ark was captured.

10. The year when David brought the ark into Zion.

11. How to connect the lives of Eli and many others named in 1 Samuel with the book of Judges.

Make a visual tool:

Take the third timeline that was constructed earlier. Then measure 2 1/16 inch (5.27 cm) to the left of "Solomon's temple," make another vertical line, label it "Saul-king," and below write "A-901" for the start of Saul's forty years as king. Then measure 3 5/16 inch (8.5 cm) to the left of "Solomon's temple," make another vertical line, label it "Samuel" for his birth time, and below write "A-850." Samuel's death [A-939] two years prior was less than 1/8 inch (<1.2 mm) to the left of "David-king" at "A-941." David was born to the right of "Saul-king" and was thirty years old when he began to reign over Judah. Measure from "Solomon's temple" just under 1 7/8 inches (4.6 cm) to the left, mark it, label it "David born," and below write "A-911."

The beginning of the forty-year period of Samson and of Eli as judge is measured to the left of "Solomon's temple" just under 2 5/16 inches (5.8 cm). Label it "Samson/Eli" and below "A-892." Samson's lifetime ended 1 inch (2.54 cm) to the right; mark and label it "Samson/Eli-died," and below write "A-932." Samson began as judge about twenty years after his birth at "A-912." Measure to the left of "Solomon's temple" 1 13/16 inches (4.6 cm) or measure 1/2 inch (1.27 cm) to the right of "Samson/Eli"and label that mark "Samson-judge." Jephthah began his six years in [A-910] one year before David's birth. Mark and label.

Then measure from "Solomon's temple" to the left 3 3/4 inches (9.5 cm), mark, label it "Eli born" for his birth time, and below write "A-834." Then by the vertical line marked "Samson/Eli" make a label for Judges 10:6-18 and Judges 13:1, write "Jdg 10:6-8; 13:1" since both time periods started there. Then by "Saul-king" write "Samuel-51" for his age when Saul was anointed. The space between "Eli born" to "Samson/Eli" was fifty-eight years, label "58 yrs." This made a simple, accurate, and useful timeline to understand everything written to this point. Fill in other information, if desired.

The method to measure and place any event year that fits within this timeline is to take the event year [relative to Abraham's birth year], subtract from that the initial year on the respective timeline, divide the result by 40 years / inch to get the distance in inches (in decimal point notation) from the start of that timeline. To get the centimeter distance multiply that result by 2.54 cm / inch for the distance in centimeters. Here is an example using Gideon for the second timeline starting at [Abram-505]: start with year [A-804], subtract year [A-505], divide by 40 years / inch and get 7.475 inches, multiply this by 2.54 cm / inch to arrive at 19 cm length to measure from year [A-505] to reach year [A-804]. Use an online converter to get the inches in fraction notation or divide the decimal inches by 0.0625 (per 1/16 inch) to get any fractions of an inch. Example: 0.475 divided by 0.0625 equals 7.6 of the 1/16 inch units which gets rounded to 8/16 or 1/2 inch.

SECTION VI

The books of Judges, Ruth and 1 Samuel have a place in time

Genesis through 1 Samuel

What appeared to be disparate information taken from other Scriptures had a significant bearing upon how to interpret the textual information presented from the books of Genesis, Job, Exodus, Joshua, Judges, Ruth, and 1 Samuel (given in chronological order, especially since the first Eli was born about [A-781, 11 years after Obed). The later author(s) assumed readers would have had a comprehensive knowledge of the Mosaic writings, especially any Levitical requirements. Plus they used key expressions to refer to other statements.

Seven methods demonstrated that the period of the twelve tribes of Israel in Egypt was 215 years. First, the text of Genesis 15:13-16 was shown to be fulfilled by numerous events in the lives of Abraham, Isaac, Jacob, Joseph, and Israel's descendants as given for the next 400 years. Second, the fourth generation was demonstrated to be verified by Eleazar and Ithamar entering Canaan which limited the time from the first generation to the fourth generation to 215 years.

Third, the fact that Jochebed was twice given as the direct daughter of Levi was detailed and her age for the births of Miriam, Aaron, and Moses was limited by prior Biblical templates that God established with Abraham and Sarah. Fourth, Acts 13:16-20 was shown to verify this 215 year period. Fifth, the three texts in Exodus 1, Psalm 105, and Acts 7 established that Aaron was born, Hezron and Hamul died at 133 years in Egypt, the new Pharaoh arose the next year, and the following year Moses was born eighty years before the exodus from Egypt.

Sixth, Exodus 12:40 gave the whole period of sojourning from Abraham entering Canaan to the youngest infant who left Egypt as 430 years. Seventh, Exodus 1:6 established that Job died before Hezron and Hamul, and the other detailed information about the book of Job affirmed the time duration of Israel in Egypt. All of this clearly and carefully established when the twelve tribes of Israel left Egypt to properly connect time from Abraham at age 105 to 1 Kings 6:1 [A-984], a period of 879 years. [A-984 minus A-105 = 879]

The period of the judges from Othniel through Abdon summed to 342 years. Adding that to the prior eight-year period of oppression of Israel under Chushanrishathaim the combination of oppressions and judges summed to 350 years. This came after the period of thirty-nine years for Joshua 24:31 and Judges 2:7.

Therefore, 389 years spanned from the year of the land division [A-552] until king David began in Judah in [A-941]. Or, if you prefer, the time duration was 390 years from the end of conquering Canaan [A-551]. A cohesive bridge of events from Abraham in Genesis through 1 Samuel was given in the text of Scripture.

The broad spectrum of information and the explanations presented resolved numerous pieces such as these. In the book of Genesis it was for Jacob's age at the birth of his sons and for their early offspring. In the books of Genesis and Exodus it was for how long the twelve tribes of Israel were in Egypt and how to resolve Exodus 12:40. Genesis, Exodus, and Job gave the time placement of the book of Job, the connection with Job's experience to that pharaoh arising, and the connections that Moses had to Job. With Exodus, Psalms, and Acts the year the new pharaoh arose that enslaved the Israelites was solved.

The granular details in Joshua, Judges, Ruth, and 1 Samuel revealed that Rahab of Jericho did not marry Salmon. Together, the books of Joshua and Judges gave the length of the period after Joshua died. The two ends of the book of Ruth gave the keys to the birth year of Obed [A-770] whose placement was in the very middle of the 342 year period of the judges service to Israel, exactly midway between the start of Othniel and the end of Abdon [A-599 + 171 = 770]. Plus the book of Ruth had connected the period of the judges to David becoming king.

In the books of Judges and 1 Samuel repetition of information and expressions that referred back to prior material gave the interconnections between individuals and events. They revealed that the forty years of Philistine oppression when Samson lived was the same period when Meraioth (the second Eli) served as high priest. The books of Judges, Ruth, 1 Samuel, and Acts showed that when Abdon's eight-year period ended David began as king.

In 1 Samuel these were given: the restricted age range of Jesse at David's birth, Jonathan's age compared to David, the strategic use of Samuel's speech to mark David's birth year, priest Ahiah marked an event year in Saul's lifetime midway in his kingship, Abiathar's minimum age when he fled Nob allowed the calculation of Ahitub's birth, Zadok's placement as high priest set his birth time, the special statement about Johanan gave his birth time, et cetera. This information reinforced the primary intersections with time placement between the lives of Eli to Samuel and Samson, Samuel to Saul, Jonathan, and David, plus both Saul and Jonathan to David. Meanwhile other verses brought more intersections to further align their lives.

Judges, Ruth, and 1 Samuel integrate

The two books of Judges and 1 Samuel covered some of the same time period from two different perspectives. The book of 1 Samuel went much farther in detail and gave necessary time related clues presented in plain sight and in unique ways. The book of Ruth provided time related clues through its introduction and inheritance puzzle. From both Old and New Testaments unnoticed, under appreciated, or unused material was brought forward and explained that yielded a very satisfactory solution to various riddles of time given in Genesis through 1 Samuel, that is from Abraham to Solomon.

The progression of all time periods given in the book of Judges were sequential except for the Philistine oppression which included Samson's forty years. Both the eighteen years of Judges 10:6-18 and the forty years of Judges 13:1 were concurrent by starting at the same time. That was specially presented by the repetition of the introductory verse of Judges 13:1 linking it to Judges 10:6-18. Samson's placement was emphasized by being the last judge with the most material written along with his twenty year length of service added to the Israelite minimum age for war.

The forty years that Eli was high priest and judge referred back to the last use of forty years from Judges 13:1. Samuel simply repeated previous material to give the correct connections. These two major alignments revealed the primary forty-year intersection of Judges with 1 Samuel.

First, the alignment of Eli's term as high priest and judge with the forty years of Philistine oppression was demonstrated. This was emphatically supported by the details of Eli's descendants and their alignment with the contemporary events with Saul, David and Solomon. The timing of the deaths of the priests at Nob, of Hophni and Phinehas in battle, of Meraioth upon the news of the ark, and the subsequent defeat of the Philistines by Samuel provided an end to those forty years.

Various events with Saul and David were shown to align with Levi's descendants through Kohath beyond Eli to Phinehas, Ahitub, Zadok, Ahimelech, Ahiah, Abiathar, Jonathan, Johanan, etc. Likewise for the Levites through Kohath beyond Elkanah to Samuel, Joel, and Heman. All of these named descendants of Levi intersected in various ways with Judah's descendants through Jesse (David, Solomon, etc). Most of those individuals and/or events were recorded in very specific detailed circumstances that bound them to rigid time constraints.

The second major alignment was that Judges 13:1 began at the same time as the period of Judges 10:6-18. That year also started the forty-year life-time of Samson. This was supported by events in Saul's lifetime and his battles with the Philistines, Samson's capture followed by the strongman Goliath challenging Israel, Goliath's defeat and David's rise, David's age when fleeing from Saul, Samson's death event, the retaliatory battle with the capture of the ark, followed by another battle with Samuel's miracle defeating the Philistines.

Additional support was given by events in prophet Samuel's life, his miracles, and validated by events that aligned with other contemporary individuals. This was verified by the timing of: Samuel's speech in 1 Samuel 12:5-11, David's birth, Saul's disobedience, Saul's request of Ahiah, Saul spared Agag, and David's anointing. This was also supported by Samuel's words about Jephthah.

Those two major components gave the proper overlap of the book of Judges with the book of 1 Samuel. A not so minor piece was the book of

Ruth placed between Judges and 1 Samuel that not only implied, but made the connection between the opening and the closing statements, i.e. the days when the judges ruled were directly connected to David, who became king after the last judge had served. The book of Ruth was an effective tool to bridge the book of Judges to that of 1 Samuel and to introduce the coming king.

This connection of the period of the judges directly to the start of David as king was clearly affirmed in the speech that Stephen gave before Israel's leaders. The text of Acts 7:45 read, *"Which also our fathers that came after brought in with Jesus* [Greek word for Joshua] *into the possession of the Gentiles, whom God drave out before the face of our fathers, unto the days of David."* The part to specially note was this, *"whom God drave out before the face of our fathers, unto the days of David."* The driving out of the Canaanites in the land was done initially by Joshua and then was to have been continued by the various tribes in their own spheres as they grew larger and filled the land promised to them.

Because of the profound waywardness of Israel God provided judges as deliverers to help drive out the land's inhabitants. Both Israel's waywardness and the purpose for the judges were detailed. Stephen's words affirmed that these judges continued *"unto the days of David."*

This expression can only mean David as king. Stephen's expression, *"the days of David,"* cannot mean when he was an early child, recently anointed, had killed Goliath as a youth, or won the hearts of Israel. Nor does it fit with his nine years fleeing from Saul.

It presented the same type of application as *"the days of Saul."* In this manner both the book of Ruth and the text of Acts, as two witnesses, directly connected the period of the judge's service to reach unto when David became king over Judah. The last forty years of the period of the sequential judges were, therefore, concurrent with Saul's reign.

This was consistent with the use of the expression, *"there was no king in those days,"* given in Judges 17:6; 18:1; 19:1; 21:25. Two things were self-evident. The first was that the seventeenth through twenty-first chapters of Judges occurred before Saul was anointed. The second was that using that very expression itself implied that there was a king after *"those days"* while various later judges ruled.

SECTION VI

Judges chapters 17–21

With the correct understanding of the time placement of the material given in the book of Judges for chapters one through sixteen we can return to examine the last five chapters in the book of Judges. The name and lineage given for the sojourning Levite spoken about at length in Judges chapters seventeen and eighteen was *"Jonathan, the son of Gershom, the son of Manasseh"* (Judges 18:30). No further ancestral lineage was discernible unless the expression *"the son of Gershom, the son of Manasseh"* was given in reverse order to the usual form to establish that this person descended from Moses' son Gershom and from his grandson Manasseh.

Moses was a Levite since he descended from Kohath, Levi's second son (Genesis 46:11; Numbers 26:58-59). The names of Moses' two sons were Gershom and Eliezer (Exodus 2:22; 18:3; 1 Chronicles 23:14-15). If the order of descent for this Levite was from Levi, to Kohath, to Amram, to Moses, to Gershom, to Manasseh, to Jonathan, then this Levite could potentially be identified as a descendant of Moses. He would fit across this time span as Moses' great-grandson.

But if the Gershom named was the direct son of Levi (1 Chronicles 6:16) and Manasseh was a later descendant, this Jonathan had an insufficient chain of lineage given to connect to his full ancestry. However, Hebrew scholars assert this name Manasseh was a purposeful and careful misspelling of the real name Moses, hiding that he was "the [grand]son of Moses." This was done to alienate this corrupt grandson of Moses from his noble grandfather Moses, because of Jonathan's conduct.

For this Jonathan to sojourn and be recognized as a qualified Levite he would have been at least old enough to begin Levitical service at age twenty-five to fit the description, *"And there was a young man out of Bethlehemjudah of the family of Judah, who was a Levite, and he sojourned there."* (Judges 17:7) However, when we substitute the limited scriptural use of *"young man"* to be age forty it also fit the text very well. This Jonathan was carefully described as both a "father"as a Levite and a "son" by physical age to Micah in Judges 17:10-11.

The accounts given in Judges chapters 17 through 21 followed the initiation and full sequence of the judges. This later section of text supplied important material to validate and verify the earlier statements of Israel's extreme waywardness and apostasy leading up to their first oppression. The text in Judges 20:28 had placed Phinehas as the high priest, which came after Eleazar had died in or just before [~A-590].

This would have made the battle of the eleven tribes of Israel against the Benjamites occur later in [A-590] just before the first oppression. That meant or at least seriously implied these last five chapters occurred before [A-591] and were part of the basis for the first oppression under Chushanrishathaim [A-591-599]. This description of ugly, sinful events validated the necessity for both the oppressions or punishments and the help of the judges as deliverers or saviors for Israel.

Summary

Since the Scriptures were given by one supreme author they were intimately intertwined and highly interactive in their material. And because God's word was *"profitable"* (2 Timothy 3:16-17) it was: 1) fully consistent with other statements in Scripture, 2) supplied information to supplement many other abbreviated Scripture texts, 3) interconnected or integrated with other Scriptures to help explain specific textual phrases, 4) resolved other apparently contradictory or difficult expressions, and 5) brought them into one cohesive whole. The internal connections or intra-relationship of the Scriptures provided a good way for one topic to cascade out to impact other topics and to have other verses brought to the forefront to integrate with the text under consideration.

Sometimes a puzzling verse only needed one other verse to make sense of it. At other times an array of other Scriptures needed to be brought to bear upon the material to discern what it said and grasp the implications derived from it. Interpreting Scripture always required supplication by prayer and wisdom from God granted through His Spirit.

The inter-relationship of the Holy Scriptures can be illustrated in a manner by the systems in the human body. The human body has a skeletal framework with joints connected by tendons and muscles and then wrapped with a skin. Inside of this covering is a complex set of inter-connecting systems: endocrine, neurological, circulatory, excretory, immune-defense, recycling, etc. The body maintains wholeness by referencing the status of these and other systems, by constantly measuring various metabolic levels and adjusting to them through its built-in pre-programmed responses. The human body uses the inputs from these systems and other monitoring sensors to manage the repair and replacement of injured or aged parts to maintain system health and body wide well-being.

That meant that the information given in one part of the human body (a truth statement made in one location) must be joined to or buffered (i.e. limited in some manner) by information gathered from another part (another truth statement from another location) to derive appropriate responses (i.e. logically processed if-then conclusions). This same thing was true in the Holy Scriptures.

Pieces of information which were often separated and given in another section of the same book or even in another book of the Bible were assembled to draw out or formulate logically processed if-then conclusions. Some of those truth statements were simple and straight forward. But some truth statements were pieces of information that limited or confined other truth statements which brought them into a narrowed or specific time application.

This analysis and deductive process used the Mosaic and Levitical law, time sequence information, connections with other people or events, Scripture to interpret Scripture, and limited application of biblical typology and numerology. The subtle expressions detailed herein which demarcated time in various ways have been interpreted and applied into the text by substitution. These parts converged into a unified set of interconnections. Thus rethinking the whole time period from Genesis through 1 Samuel required discerning how writers in their era would lay out and integrate a lengthy and very complex narrative.

The Scriptures were notably consistent, highly intertwined in their material, and even self-correcting. Thus these solutions for the time periods of Genesis through 1 Samuel fit with and helped to solve many other quandaries. They were consistent with other given time periods stated in Scripture, integrated details of both Levitical and Mosaic law, fit with all of the truth statements given about the lives of each of the numerous individuals named across this period, and brought them into one cohesive whole—presenting "a symphony of harmony."

An invitation to study Holy Scripture

Each reader is invited, encouraged, and urged to reexamine the computations, the various integrated texts and their applicability, the explanations for many connections and conclusions, and any results derived from them. Likewise reexamine the identified parenthetical statements and their applications, the phrases that became time substitutions, the reasoning to correlate pieces, and how all of these converged. The births, events, and deaths of some of these individuals were placed with reasoned certainty, if not a high degree of certainty. Others were placed just as Scripture stated. These were bound by the confines of the scriptural expressions relating to their lives and the events that transpired during their lifetimes.

If these deductions were correct or at least reasonable, then there was a continuous and very detailed record of time related information carefully written and preserved in Scripture from Adam through Noah and Abraham reaching past David unto Solomon and Nathan his brother. [Examine the subsequent indexes.] From Solomon's death secular history has adequate records to validate his death date and subsequent events unto the present.[20,21,22] This solution also meant that there was a known, written, and continuous chain of people carefully detailed in time that lead from Adam through Seth, Noah, Abraham, Isaac, Jacob, Judah, reaching through Jesse and David, and ultimately leading unto Christ Jesus.

The solution to the various riddles of time spanning from Abraham in the book of Genesis through 1 Samuel was carefully demonstrated with explanations for:

1) when Joseph and his siblings were born,
2) the age of Judah's grand-children Hezron and Hamul at entry to Egypt,
3) the time duration of the twelve tribes of Israel in Egypt by seven methods,
4) when the book of Job occurred,
5) when Job died,
6) the year that pharaoh arrived who oppressed Israel,
7) the year of the exodus from Egypt,
8) the meaning and use of 1 Kings 6:1 in connection to the original Passover event,
9) the age of Joshua at mount Sinai,

10) the year of Joshua's death,
11) the time duration of *"all the days of Joshua, and all the days of the elders that outlived Joshua,"*
12) that Salmon did not marry Rahab of Jericho and conceive Boaz,
13) how the book of Ruth helped explain the full lineage of David,
14) when the book of Ruth occurred,
15) the birth and death years of the older and younger Eli,
16) the meaning of *"Samuel was old"* and when Samuel anointed Saul,
17) the year David brought the ark to the prepared tent at Zion,
18) the time placement of the death of Eli as Scripture stated,
19) the use of the textual minimum age to go to war to Samson plus his twenty years as judge to reach forty years,
20) the age range of Jonathan and Saul,
21) the concurrence of when Israel did evil again and served the Philistines for forty years with Eli's period as judge and with Samson's lifetime,
22) the underlying cause for the ark carried into battle and when it occurred,
23) the context of the event for which Israel repented and Samuel prayed that brought a miracle and a significant routing of the Philistines which followed right after Samson's death,
24) the proper time placement of all named judges, including Jephthah and Samson,
25) the specific or approximate birth, death or event years of more than 135 individuals,
26) and more.

This detailed solution to the time placement of individuals and events in these Old Testament books brought fulfillment and harmony with a great many neglected, unused, or underappreciated Scriptures. Perhaps 1) the perplexing riddles of the length of time in Egypt, 2) the narrow time period for the book of Job, 3) the year of arrival of that oppressing pharaoh, 4) the year when Joshua died, 5) the lack of any connection of Rahab of Jericho to Salmon, 6) the longer ancestry of David, 7) the ages of Saul and Jonathan, 8) the proper time placement of Jephthah and Samson, and 9) the alignment between the books of Judges, Ruth, and 1 Samuel that has long plagued scholars and Bible students is finally resolved. You be the judge: examine, evaluate and decide.

Personal Thoughts

This material was the result of numerous parts: years of Bible study, attention to numerous minute Old Testament details from Abraham through David, careful examination of the Mosaic and Levitical law and the tabernacle services, collation of lineages, trust in and application of God's promises and punishments, study of typology, and more. These, for as much value as they impart, were altogether insufficient by my own effort. Grasping this material required God by His Spirit to present "aha" moments and reveal numerous connections in answer to prayer.

Have you ever went to people and asked, "How old was '*old*'?" when God used that expression in the Bible. And then what did "*waxed old and stricken in age*" mean when used in various places? More over what did "*very old*" or "*very aged*" mean in contrast to the expression, "*old?*" That was the key answer needed to align one specific individual's life with another's life, but it was not given by men or women. God showed it in two distinct places. One was with Samuel and the other with Zacharias, both descendants of Levi under the Levitical obligations to serve God as exchanged firstborn sons (Exodus 13:2; 22:29; Numbers 3:12-13, 45-47).

All of these pieces the Lord of heaven revealed slowly after focused study interspersed with many requests in prayer and backed up with tedious text checking. God's help enabled me to recall, find and connect other pieces from Holy Scripture with these events to bring clarity to them. And here I want to express gratitude for my Lord and Savior Christ Jesus in revealing to me and equipping me to grasp and integrate these pieces into a cohesive whole to resolve the longstanding riddles of time given in (chronological order): Genesis, Job, Exodus, Joshua, the early part of Judges, Ruth, and the later part of Judges that aligned with 1 Samuel.

His written word in the *textus receptus* (known as the Received Text), as preserved in the King James translation, was completely reliable and impeccably true (Psalm 12:6-7; 119:160).[23]

> "*O magnify the Lord with me, and let us exalt his name together.*"
> (Psalm 34:3).

SECTION VI

What we learned:
1. God's word as preserved was wholly trustworthy and accurate.
2. The Scriptures were complexly integrated internally which enabled it to correct wrong approaches and validate correct applications in surprising ways.

Make a visual tool:
Now that you know how to make this timeline, do it again with great care. And in the corner cite this work. Then share it with others.[S]

Here are some supplemental footnotes of interest.[T,U]

S. To obtain a printable copy in pdf format of 1) a table of the six ways to establish Israel was in Egypt for only 215 years, and 2) the visual tool timeline go to: www.lookinguntojesus.info/Timeline/. Enter username: Timeline, and enter the password: Psalm 24:3.

T. Numbers 26:21 and 1 Chronicles 2:18 said there were other sons born to Hezron after Aram. David's lineage was through Aram (Ram). After Aram was born to Hezron (~72 years) Hezron fathered Caleb (~75, [~A-364]), Caleb (~58) fathered Hur [~A-422], 1 Chronicles 2:1-5, 18-20. Hur (perhaps ~83) held up Moses' arms with Aaron (age 83, Exodus 7:7) in battle against Amalek before they arrived at Sinai (Exodus 17:10-12; 19:1-2; Deuteronomy 25:17-19).
In turn, Hur (~27) was father of Uri [?~449], then Uri (~27) was father of Bezaleel [?~476] (same generation as Salmon). When Bezaleel was about age thirty he built the tabernacle and its equipment from [A-505-506] (Exodus 31:1-11; 35:50; 38:22; 1 Chronicles 2:20; 2 Chronicles 1:5). Bezaleel with his spirit filled gifts mirrored Jesus' age at the beginning of his ministry.

U. All those twenty or older at the exodus from Egypt, except Joshua and Caleb, died in the wilderness. That meant about one million or so people were buried during those last thirty-eight years in the wilderness (Numbers 11:21, 600,000 men x 2 including spouses). One million averaged to about 26,300 or more people died per year or about 84 or more persons were buried per day, skipping weekly Sabbath days. The sobering solemn evidence of the journey of disbelief for the twelve tribes of Israel was a vast cemetery.

Names With Birth, Death and/or Event Year for 135 individuals
All times given are relative to the birth year of Abraham with the notation [A-xxx] or [A-xxx-yyy].

© 2017-2020 by Brian Kuehmichel

This tilde symbol "~" is used for a careful approximation of the time given. Extra notes are required for some individuals to explain their birth, marriage, event and/or death time range(s). To get the B.C. year that each relative time statement represents take Abram's birth in 1951 B.C. and subtract the relative birth, death, or event time of any individual listed here. [Ex: 1951 B.C. - 932 = 1019 B.C.] Symbols: < means less than the given year, —< means a long time but an uncertain end year, > means greater than the given year, <= or >= means less than or greater than and including the given year.

Aaron [A-422-545], 1529-1406 BC, see page 26.
Abdon [judge to Israel, A-933-941]
Abiah [A-875-~965]
Abiathar, high priest [A-907–<987]
Abigail (married David, [A-939])
Abihu [~A-481-late wilderness]
Abimelech [son of Gideon, false king, A-844-847]
Abinadab (second son of king Saul) [A-~(882-885)–932]
Abinadab (location of Ark for 20 years [A-933-953])
Abishua [~A-590–<=696]
Abraham (Abram) [A-0-175]
Absalom [A-941-968]
Adonijah (son of David) [A-~941-981]
Agag [A-???-923]
Ahiah (son of Ahitub) [A-891-893–932]
Ahimaaz [~A-923–<=1003]
Ahimelech (son of Ahitub) [A-~889-932]
Ahimelech (son of Abiathar born from [A-924 to A-929], priest with Zadok

Names with birth, death and/or event year

Ahitub (son of Phinehas) [<=A-871-932]
Amariah (first, see Phinehas)
Amminadab [~A-387-415 to -<506]
Amram [A-~331-<=488]
Asher [A-249-???]
Azariah (son of Ahimaaz) [~A-942-???]
Barachel (father of Elihu) [?~A-200]
Barak [judge to Israel, land rested A-757-797]
Barzillai [born A-888, age 80 at A-968]
Bedan (Jair) [judge to Israel, A-870-892]
Benjamin [~A-266–<=400]
Bildad the Shuhite [<=A-267, second oldest before Job, age 80 or > at A-347]
Bilhah [~ age 20, A-244]
Boaz [~A-696–~804]
Bukki [~A-656–<=761]
Buz [born ~A-85]
Caleb [A-467-?, age 85 at A-552]
Chushanrishathaim [oppressed Israel, A-591-599]
Dan [A-247-???]
David [~70 1/2 years, A-911-982]
Deborah [prophetess & judge to Israel, land rested A-757-797]
Dinah [born A-251-252-???]
Eglon [oppressed Israel, A-639-657]
Ehud [judge to Israel, land rested A-657-737]
Eleazar [A-~487-~590]
Eli (Meraioth) [A-834-932]
Eli (Zerahiah) [A-781-892]

Elihu (son of Barachel; of Nahor, Abram's older brother, Nahor to Buz to Barachel) [~A-307-???, ~age 40 before Job at A-347]
Eliphaz the Temanite [<=A-267, oldest before Job, age 80 or > at A-347]
Elisheba [best fit birth time, ~A-453-458 or maximum range of ~A-422-459]
Elon [judge to Israel, A-923-933]
Ephraim [A-288-???]
Er [A-259-274]
Esau [A-160-???; >120 years, Genesis 35:29]
Gad [A-248-???]
Gideon (Gedeon, Jerubbaal) [judge to Israel, A-804-844]
Goliath [A-???-928]
Hamul [A-290-423]
Heman [~A-905-~995]
Hezron (Esrom) [A-290-423]
Hophni [A-852-932]
Ibzan [judge to Israel, A-916-923]
Ichabod [A-932-<1012]
Isaac [A-100-280]
Ishbosheth [A-901-948]
Ishmael [A-86-223]
Ishui [~A-(882-885)–941]
Israel (Jacob) [A-160-307]
Issachar [A-249-???]
Ithamar [A-~488-~598]
Jabin [oppressed Israel, A-737-757]
Jacob (Israel) [A-160-307]
Jael [killed Sisera, A-757]
Jair [judge to Israel, A-870-892]
Jephthah (Jephthae) [judge to Israel,

Names with birth, death and/or event year

A- 910-916]
Jerubbaal (see Gideon)
Jesse [~A-841-~939]
Joab died late [A-981]
Job (Jaschub) [born A-270–282, died 410–422; best fit ~A-277-417]
Jochebed [~339->=461]
Joel (Vashni) [A-873-~963]
Johanan [A-961–<1041]
Jonathan (son of Saul) [min age if 883; ~(880-883)–941, best fit 881–941]
Jonathan (son of high priest Abiathar) [A-(932-955)–<=1012]
Joseph [A-251-361]
Joshua [110 years, best fit A-465-575]
Judah [A-247-???]
Keturah [probably > age 25 in A-140 at marriage to Abraham]
Kohath [best fit, A-281-414; latest possible, A-290-423]
Laban [best fit, A-123-???, ~134 at Jacob's departure in A-257]
Leah [best fit, ~A-197-<290]
Levi [A-246-383]
Manasseh [A-287-???]
Melchishua [A-~(884-887)–941]
Mephibosheth [A-936-???]
Meraioth (Eli), high priest [A-834-932]
Michal [late born daughter to Saul, David's wife at A-931]
Miriam [<=420–544]
Moses [A-425-545], 1526-1406 BC, see page 23 or footnote H.
Naaman [~A-285-286–<=418]
Naashon (Nahshon, Naasson) [best fit, A-455-545; ~A-435-455–545]
Nabal [died, A-939]
Nadab [~A-479–late wilderness, ~540]
Nahash [Saul's first battle, A-901]
Nahor [best fit when born about five years before Abram]
Naphtali [A-248-???]
Nathan [prophet, served years before David died A-982]
Obed [best fit, A-770-876]
Onan [A-260-275]
Othniel [A-~530-639; first judge to Israel, land rested A-599-639]
Pharez (Phares) [A-277–<=410]
Phinehas, son of Eleazar [~A-519-<= 627]
Phinehas (Amariah) [A-853-932]
Rachab [best fit, ~A-622-729]
Rachel [best fit, ~A-200–~266]
Rahab of Jericho [latest birth time, A-527; best fit <A-527– <=622]
Ram (Aram, son of Hezron) [~A-361– ~486-488]
Rebekah [best fit: age 20 at A-140 for marriage to Isaac; lived to send Jacob to Haran in A-237, ~age 117; ~A-120->237]
Reuben [A-244-???]
Salmon [~A-545-~655]
Samson [A-892-932, began year 20 as judge to Israel, A-912-932]
Samuel [A-850-939]
Sarah [A-10-137]
Saul [best fit, A-862-941]
Shamgar [pre & post A-757]
Shelah [best fit, A-260-???]

Names with birth, death and/or event year

Shuah [best fit, A-147–(297-307), ~150-160 year life span]

Shuah's daughter (Judah's wife A-258) [born ~A-245 or slightly earlier – died before A-276, Gen 38:12]

Simeon [A-245-???]

Sisera [killed by Jael, A-757]

Solomon [A-951–1020]

Tamar (Thamar) [born ~A-256-259; wife to Er, A-274, then Onan, A-275 (both died); mother to twins Pharez and Zarah from Judah by A-277]

Tola [judge to Israel, A-847-870]

Uzzi [~A-722-<=827]

Zadok, high priest [A-904-<=984]

Zarah (Zerah, Zara) [A-277–<=410]

Zebulun [A-250-???]

Zerahiah, high priest [~A-781-892]

Zilpah [~ age 20, A-244]

Zophar the Naamathite [Zohar from Simeon <=A-267, third oldest before Job, age 80 or > before Job at A-347]

Name Index
from Abraham to Solomon

Aaron xiii, 9, 23, 27-30, 32-35, 37, 39, 46-49, 51, 52, 56, 61, 63, 64, 73, 84, 112, 121, 129, 131, 146, 182, 191, 206, 213, 214, 224, 225, 233

Abdon xii, 2, 121, 122, 136, 138, 147, 148, 150-152, 155, 157, 170, 191, 200, 206, 214, 225, 234, 235

Abiah 147, 162, 178, 225, 234

Abiathar 139, 169, 175, 176, 190-192, 194, 195, 197, 203, 216, 225, 226, 234-236

Abigail 180, 225, 235

Abihu 33-35, 46, 191, 225

Abimelech 75, 148, 151, 174, 204, 225, 234

Abinadab 165, 189, 194, 202, 225

Abishua 192, 225

Abraham i, iii, xiii-xvi, 1-4, 6-12, 15-17, 22, 27, 28, 39, 41, 42, 45, 48, 50, 52-55, 61, 62, 65, 68-73, 75-82, 85-87, 92, 110, 111, 119, 120, 122, 127, 128, 131, 138, 140, 204, 213-215, 221, 223, 225, 233

Abram 10, 11, 16, 38, 40-42, 50, 51, 53, 54, 70, 71, 88, 115, 137, 225, 226, 233

Absalom 182, 225, 235

Achish 189

Adonijah 152, 176, 225, 235, 236

Agag 15, 179, 180, 188, 216, 225

Ahiah 138, 139, 175, 186, 187, 190, 191, 195, 207, 215, 216, 225, 234, 235

Ahimaaz 176, 192, 225, 226

Ahimelech 139, 175, 176, 190, 191, 216, 225, 234

Ahimelech (son of Abiathar) 176

Ahimelech (son of Ahitub) 139, 175, 190, 191, 216, 225

Ahitub 139, 175, 186, 187, 190, 192, 216, 225, 234

Amariah 138, 153, 165, 172, 192, 225, 227

Amariah (son of Azariah) 192

Aminadab 9, 33, 34, 36, 37, 52, 90, 113

Aminadab (Amminadab) 36, 113

Amminadab 9, 33, 34, 36, 111, 113, 161, 225, 235

Amram 27, 28, 33, 34, 38, 46-49, 51, 52, 56, 62, 161, 218, 225, 233

Aram 34, 37, 52, 70, 71, 113, 224, 227

Asher 22, 225

Azariah (aka: Ozias, Uzziah) 98

Azariah (son of Ahimaaz) 176, 192, 236

Azariah (son of Hilkiah) 193, 226

Azariah (son of Johanan) 176, 192

Azariah (son of Zephaniah) 161

Azariah begat Amariah 192

Barachel 70-72, 78, 226

Barak 2, 122, 123, 148, 151, 156, 199, 200, 226, 234

Barzillai 72, 94, 166, 226, 234, 235

Bedan (see Jair) 147, 179, 182, 199,

Name Index

207, 226, 234
Benjamin 22-24, 26, 60, 65, 66, 69, 70, 133, 205, 226
Bildad 68, 69, 72, 73, 78, 84, 226
Bilhah 14, 22, 24, 44, 226
Boaz 8, 89-93, 95, 97-111, 113, 114, 117, 118, 121-123, 222, 226
Bukki 192, 226
Buz 71, 226
Caleb 35, 91, 126, 128, 130, 131, 133, 134, 150, 224, 226
Christ Jesus 4, 5, 24, 109, 114, 125, 138, 197, 204, 221, 223
Chushanrishathaim 119, 126, 133, 136, 146, 148, 149, 151, 154, 214, 219, 226, 234
Dan 22, 133, 141, 226
David xii, 1, 2, 5, 8-10, 25, 29, 34, 56, 90-97, 99, 100, 107-114, 118, 122, 127, 135, 136, 138, 139, 141, 142, 149, 150, 152-155, 158-160, 166, 170, 171, 175-185, 187-191, 194-198, 200, 202-207, 209, 210, 214-217, 221-223, 225-227, 235, 236
Deborah 2, 122, 123, 148, 151, 156, 226, 234
Dinah 14, 22-24, 44, 59, 67, 98, 226
Doeg 170, 173, 175, 190, 195, 235
Eglon 148, 151, 208, 209, 226, 234
Ehud 2, 120, 122, 148, 151, 209, 226, 234
elder 60, 66, 70, 167, 170, 186
elders xiii, 1, 21, 56, 60, 81, 119, 121, 125-127, 130, 132-134, 141, 143, 144, 146, 147, 150, 151, 156, 158-160, 177-179, 182, 187, 195, 200, 222
Eleazar 29, 30, 33, 35-37, 46, 48, 49, 51, 52, 56, 103, 111, 131, 143, 149, 169, 173, 191, 192, 213, 219, 226, 227
Eli (see: Zerahiah and Meraioth) xiii, 2, 94, 101, 110, 121, 123, 138, 139, 146, 147, 153, 155, 156, 158-168, 170-175, 177, 182, 184, 186, 191, 192, 195, 205-207, 209, 210, 213, 215, 216, 222, 226, 227-231, 234, 235
Eli (Meraioth) 2, 101, 110, 121, 139, 146, 147, 155, 156, 158, 160, 163-165, 167, 170, 172-175, 177, 182, 184, 191, 205, 206, 216, 222, 226, 234
Eli (Zerahiah) 138, 162-164, 166, 167, 170-174, 207, 213, 226, 234
Elihu 10, 70-73, 78, 79, 161, 162, 226
Elihu (Eliel / Eliab 161
Eliphaz 66-69, 72, 73, 77, 78, 85, 226
Elisheba 33, 34, 36, 37, 52, 90, 226
Elkanah 161, 162, 171, 174, 216, 234
Elon 68, 148, 151, 152, 157, 206, 226, 235
Ephraim 128, 129, 148, 151, 161, 226
Er 24-26, 69, 193, 226, 227
Esau 6, 7, 11-13, 15, 17, 27, 43, 44, 67, 68, 76-79, 82, 83, 226, 233
Esrom 25, 62, 113, 226
Ezra 52, 112, 173, 175, 191-193
Gad 22, 23, 141, 142, 153, 226
Gideon (Gedeon, see Jerubbaal) 2, 15, 120, 148, 151, 155, 174, 199, 200, 211, 225, 226, 234
Goliath 25, 96, 158, 188, 189, 195, 204-206, 216, 217, 226, 235
Hamul 24-26, 34, 52, 56, 57, 62-64, 66, 67, 74, 82, 84, 214, 221, 226, 233

Name Index

Hannah 162, 163, 174
Heman 162, 216, 226
Hezron 24-26, 34, 52, 56, 62-64, 66, 67, 74, 82, 84, 111, 113, 214, 221, 224, 226, 227, 233
Hilkiah 193
Hophni 138, 139, 153, 161, 165-170, 172-175, 177, 186, 191, 195, 203, 216, 226, 234, 235
Ibzan 148, 151, 152, 157, 206, 226, 235
Ichabod 174, 175, 226, 235
Isaac xiii, 6-8, 11-17, 20, 21, 24, 27, 28, 41-43, 47-49, 53, 54, 68, 76-79, 82, 85, 86, 92, 111, 127, 131, 174, 204, 213, 221, 226, 227, 233
Ishbosheth 139, 181, 183, 210, 226, 234, 235
Ishmael 10-13, 17, 27, 43, 49-51, 75, 85, 174, 226, 233
Ishui 190, 226, 235
Israel xiii, 1, 2, 8, 10, 15, 17, 19, 21, 26, 29-31, 35, 45-47, 51-56, 61, 63, 64, 66, 68, 74, 83, 84, 86, 87, 91, 94, 96, 97, 102, 103, 105-107, 111, 119-122, 125-132, 134, 138, 140-148, 150-160, 163, 164, 166, 168-171, 174, 177-189, 191, 194-210, 213, 214, 216, 217, 219, 221, 222, 224-227
Israelites 1, 5, 8, 45, 48, 54, 60, 63, 64, 74, 82, 83, 86, 115, 126, 132-134, 140, 142, 158, 159, 164, 179, 186, 194, 196, 198, 203, 214, 233
Issachar 22, 23, 65, 66, 77, 79, 148, 151, 155, 226, 233, 234
Ithamar 33, 35, 37, 46, 51, 52, 56, 173, 191, 192, 213, 226
Jabin 122, 148, 151, 226, 234
Jacob xiii, 6, 7, 11-15, 17, 19-27, 38, 39, 42-44, 48, 52-54, 59-62, 65, 68, 76, 77, 82, 84-86, 89, 111, 117, 129, 131, 213, 221, 226, 227, 233
Jael 156, 226, 227
Jair (see Bedan) 147, 148, 151, 200, 226, 234
Jehozadak (Josedech, Jozadak) 175, 191, 193
Jephthah (Jephthae) 2, 147, 148, 151, 152, 157, 179, 182, 197, 199-201, 205-211, 216, 222, 226, 234
Jeroham 161, 162
Jerubbaal (see Gideon)147, 179, 182, 199, 207, 226
Jesse xii, 89-97, 99-102, 107, 110, 111, 113, 114, 117, 118, 122, 138, 139, 160, 166, 187, 215, 216, 221, 226, 234, 235
Jesus (see Christ Jesus) xvi, 4, 5, 24, 31, 32, 89, 97, 100, 108-112, 114, 125, 138, 146, 159, 162, 170, 179, 191, 196, 197, 204, 217, 221, 223
Joab 226
Job iii, 1, 5, 8, 15, 19, 65-88, 204, 213, 214, 221-223, 226, 227, 233
Jochebed 1, 27-29, 33, 34, 38, 48, 51, 56, 213, 226, 233
Joel 147, 161, 162, 178, 216, 226, 234
Johanan 175, 176, 191-193, 215, 216, 226, 236
Jonathan 158-160, 176, 179, 180, 183-190, 193, 197-199, 206, 210, 215, 216, 218, 222, 226, 234, 235
Jonathan (grandson of Moses) 218
Jonathan (son of Abiathar) 176, 216
Jonathan (son of Joiada) 193
Joseph xii, xiii, 8, 12, 14, 15, 20-26, 34, 37, 44, 45, 52, 59-64, 66, 67,

73, 75, 87, 88, 98, 103, 108, 111, 143, 213, 221, 226, 233

Joshua iii, 1, 2, 5, 8, 21, 35-37, 43, 49, 52, 56, 70, 73, 89, 91, 96, 97, 101, 103, 104, 108, 118, 119, 125-135, 137, 140, 143, 146, 149-152, 168, 182, 188, 193, 203, 204, 213, 214, 217, 221-224, 226, 233, 234

Judah 1, 8-10, 15, 19, 22-26, 28, 29, 34, 36, 37, 52, 62, 69, 70, 90, 91, 94, 98, 104, 111, 113, 133, 138, 139, 142, 150, 152, 154, 171, 175, 180, 183, 190, 205, 210, 214, 217, 218, 221, 226, 227, 233, 235

Judge xiii, 2, 40, 72, 118-123, 125, 137, 138, 141, 144-148, 150, 151, 153, 155, 156, 158, 160, 163, 164, 174, 175, 177, 180, 182, 191, 199-201, 205, 206, 208-211, 215-217, 222, 226, 227, 234, 235

Keturah 11, 15, 27, 77, 79, 83, 85, 92, 174, 226, 233

king of Egypt 21, 29, 61

Kohath 26-28, 37, 38, 46-49, 52, 62, 66, 84, 161, 216, 218, 226

Laban 12-15, 21, 23, 43, 44, 53, 98, 227

Leah 13, 14, 22-24, 44, 65, 227, 233

Levi xii, 1, 15, 19, 22-24, 26-29, 33, 34, 37, 44, 46-49, 52, 54, 59-62, 66, 90, 139, 161, 213, 216, 218, 223, 227, 233

Manasseh 103, 129, 143, 218, 227

Melchishua 189, 190, 227, 235

Mephibosheth 199, 227

Meraiah 193

Meraioth (see Eli) 94, 138, 153, 158, 160, 163, 165-168, 170, 172-175, 182, 190-192, 206, 209, 215, 216,

Name Index

226, 234, 235

Michal 158, 183, 188, 227

Miriam 27, 28, 32, 33, 46, 51, 73, 213, 227, 233

Moses xiii, 5, 8, 10, 27-30, 32, 33, 36, 38, 46-48, 51, 54-56, 61, 63, 64, 73, 74, 81-84, 86, 87, 103, 113, 128, 129, 131, 132, 141-143, 145, 182, 188, 198, 204, 213, 214, 218, 227, 233

Naaman 69, 227

Naashon (Naasson, Nahshon) 10, 33, 34, 35, 36, 37, 90-93, 95, 99, 101, 102, 111, 113, 118, 227

Nabal 180, 227

Nadab 33-35, 46, 191, 227

Nahash 156, 179, 181, 227

Nahor 10, 70-73, 79, 82, 83, 226, 227

Naphtali 22, 122, 148, 151, 227

Nathan 141, 142, 153, 192, 221, 227

Nathan (son of David) 192

Obed 89-93, 95, 97, 99-102, 107, 108, 111, 113, 117, 118, 121, 122, 135, 170, 213, 214, 227, 234

Onan 24-26, 227

Othniel 2, 119-122, 136, 146, 148, 151, 152, 170, 200, 214, 227, 234

pharaoh 1, 8, 15, 19-22, 29, 37, 45, 46, 52-54, 59-64, 73-75, 82-84, 86, 87, 214, 221, 222-233

Pharez (Phares) 24-26, 34, 52, 62, 113, 133, 227, 233

Philistine 2, 75, 76, 79, 142, 171, 180, 185, 195, 196, 200-206, 215, 216

Philistines 42, 43, 76, 142, 145, 147, 148, 151, 157, 158, 160, 170, 171, 173, 175, 180, 182, 184-186, 189, 194-196, 198, 200-207, 216, 222, 234, 235

Phinehas (Amariah, son of Meraioth 138, 139, 153, 161, 165, 166, 168-170, 172-175, 177, 186, 187, 190-192, 195, 203, 216, 218, 225, 227, 234, 235

Phinehas (son of Eleazar) 29, 30, 32, 169, 192, 218, 227

Rachab xii, 89, 96-101, 104-111, 113, 114, 118, 227

Rachel 13, 14, 22, 24, 227, 233

Rahab 1, 8, 10, 19, 89-91, 96-98, 100-102, 113-115, 117, 122, 187, 214, 222, 227

Ram 34, 36, 70, 111, 113, 224, 227

Rebekah 11-13, 15, 27, 79, 227, 233

Reuben 22, 24, 44, 227

Ruth 89, 90, 97, 99, 102-114, 117, 118

Salmon xii, 1, 8, 10, 19, 37, 89-93, 95-104, 106-108, 110, 111, 113-115, 117, 118, 122, 123, 170, 187, 214, 222, 224, 227

Samson xiii, 2, 138, 139, 160, 161, 182, 197, 199-202, 204-207, 210, 211, 215, 216, 222, 227, 234, 235

Samuel iii, xiii, xiv, 2, 4, 5, 8, 15, 27, 34, 70, 72, 79, 92-96, 98, 101, 110, 118, 121, 137-143, 146-149, 153-192, 194-208, 210, 213-217, 220-223, 227, 234, 235 – *Levitical ancestry 161*

Sarah (Sarai) 11, 15, 27, 28, 70, 75, 79, 92, 97, 127, 213, 227, 233

Saul xiii, 2, 49, 50, 94-96, 110, 139, 141, 142, 148, 149, 152, 154-160, 171, 175, 177-191, 195-199, 201, 203, 205-207, 210, 211, 215-217, 222, 225-227-232, 234, 235

Seraiah 193

Shallum (Meshallum 192

Shamgar 122, 148, 151, 155, 156, 227

Shelah 24-26, 227

Shuah 24, 25, 27, 68, 69, 78, 92, 122, 227, 233

Shuah's daughter 69, 227

Simeon 22, 24, 44, 69, 70, 73, 227

Sisera 122, 156, 226, 227

Solomon i, iii, xiv-xvi, 1-4, 8, 55, 56, 61, 70, 79, 91, 111, 135, 136, 139, 141, 152, 153, 175-177, 192, 215, 216, 221, 227, 233, 235, 236

Tamar (Thamar) 25, 26, 79, 227

Teman 68, 77

Tohu (Toah / Nahath 161

Tola 65, 147, 148, 151, 155, 227, 234

Uzzi 192, 227

Vashni 162, 178, 226, 234

Zadok 111, 139, 175, 176, 191, 192, 216, 225, 227, 234-236

Zara 25, 52, 227

Zarah 25, 26, 34, 52, 227

Zebulun 22, 227

Zerah 77, 227

Zerahiah (first Eli) 52, 163, 164, 166-168, 170, 172-174, 185, 190, 192, 207, 226, 227, 234

Zilpah 14, 22, 227

Zohar 69, 70

Zophar the Naamathite 69, 70, 72, 73, 78, 86, 227

Zuph (Zophai) 161

Major Event Index
for the twelve tribes of Israel
(years from birth year of Abraham)

Abram entered Canaan [A-75] 10, 39, 49-51, 53, 54, 214

Jacob & family enter Egypt [A-290] 15, 21, 22, 24, 26, 34, 45, 48, 52-54, 59, 62, 65-67, 69, 77, 86, 128, 149

Pharoah arose [A-424] 59, 60, 63, 64, 73, 74, 82, 83

Exodus from Egypt [A-505] 8, 35, 39, 46-50, 52, 55, 61, 63, 66, 91, 117, 126, 129, 130, 137, 138, 149, 153, 214, 224

Wilderness period [A-505-545] 10, 31, 35, 37, 43, 49, 50, 56, 82-84, 87, 90-92, 99, 103, 117, 119, 126, 128, 130-132, 134, 136-138, 148, 149, 152, 180, 186, 224, 227

Israel entered Canaan [A-545] 28, 33, 35, 39, 45, 51, 52, 56, 90-92, 97, 102, 117, 119, 213

Conquer Canaan [A-545-551] 136, 138, 214

Land division [A–552] 50, 51, 115, 126, 133, 136, 138, 149, 150, 152, 206, 214

First oppression 36, 119, 126, 133-136, 149, 150, 152, 170, 206, 218, 219

First judge [A-599-639, See Othniel] 2, 119, 121, 122, 136, 146, 148, 152, 170, 200, 208, 209, 214

Anointing of Saul [A-901] 94, 95, 148, 152, 156, 158, 177, 178, 181, 187, 188, 199, 205, 210, 211, 217

Anointing of David [A-923] 110, 180, 188, 189, 195-197, 216, 217

Last judge [A-933-941, See Abdon]

David became king [A-941] 152, 176, 189, 205, 206, 210, 214, 215, 217

Solomon became king [A-981] 152, 176

David died [A-982] 91, 176

Temple construction [A-984-991] 55, 91, 115, 134, 135, 137, 149, 152, 157, 176, 153, 210

Brief Event Timeline
from Abraham to Solomon
(years from birth year of Abraham)

Abram entered Canaan [A-75]
Ishmael born, son of Abram via Hagar [A-86]
Isaac born, son of Abraham via Sarah [A-100]
Shuah born, last son of Abraham via Keturah [A-147]
Esau and Jacob, son of Isaac via Rebekah [A-160]
Abraham died [A-175]
Ishmael died (age 137) [A-223]
Jacob entered Haran [A-237]
Levi born, son of Jacob via Leah late in [A-246]
Judah born, son of Jacob via Leah late in [A-247]
Joseph born, son of Jacob via Rachel [A-251]
Jacob left Haran [A-257]
Joseph sold into Egypt [A-268]
Job (Jashub) born, son of Issachar, best fit [A-277]
Isaac died (age 180) [A-280]
Joseph became ruler in Egypt (age 30) [A-281]
Hezron and Hamul born, sons of Pharez [A-290]
Israel and family enter Egypt [A-290]
Jacob died (age 147) [A-307]
Job had calamities (age 70) [A-347]
Joseph died (age 110) [A-361]
Levi died (age 137) [A-383]
Job died (age 140) [A-417]
Aaron born, son of Amram via Jochebed [A-422]
Hezron and Hamul died [A-423]
Pharaoh arose [A-424]
Moses born, son of Amram via Jochebed [A-425]
Joshua born, son of Nun [A-465]
Israelites depart from Egypt [A-505]
Miriam died at age 124 early in [A-544] (Numbers 20:1)
Aaron (age 123) and Moses (age 120) died late in [A-544] (Deuteronomy 34:8; Joshua 3:15)

Israelites under Joshua enter Canaan, Abib in [A-545] (Joshua 3:15)
Conquering Canaan [A-545-551]
Division and occupy land [A-552]
Joshua died (age 110) [A-575]
Served under Chushanrishathaim, king of Mesopotamia; 8 years [A-591-599]
Judge: Othniel, son of Kenaz; land had rest 40 years (~age 110) [A-599-639]
Israel did evil; Eglon king of Moab, Ammon and Amalek; 18 years [A-639-657]
Judge: Ehud the son of Gera, a Benjamite; rest 80 years (~age 100) [A-657-737]
Served under Jabin king of Canaan; 20 years [A-737-757]
Judges: Deborah; Barak, son of Abinoam; rest 40 years [A-757-797]
Obed born halfway between Othniel through Abdon [A-599–941; A-770]
Zerahiah born (first Eli in 1 Samuel 3) [A-781-892]
Israel did evil again; 7 years [A-797-804]
Judge: Gideon, of Joash the Abi-ezrite of Ophrah; rest 40 years (age 80) [A-804-844]
Meraioth born, son of Zerahiah (Eli) [A-834]
Jesse born, son of Obed [A-841]
Abimelech, son of Gideon, attempted three year reign [A-844-847]
Judge: Tola the son of Puah, son of Dodo, of Issachar; 23 years [A-847-870]
Samuel born, son of Elkanah [A-850]
Hophni born, son of Meraioth [A-852]
Phinehas born, son of Meraioth [A-853]
God called Samuel (age 12) [A-862]
Saul born, son of Kish, best fit [A-862]
Judge: Jair (Bedan, 1 Chronicles 7:17), Gileadite; 22 years [A-870-892]
Samuel's formal Levitical service at tabernacle (age 25 to 50) [A-875-900]
Ahitub born, son of Phinehas [A-871]
Joel (Vashni) born, son of Samuel [A-873-~963]
Abiah born, son of Samuel [A-875-~965]
Jonathan born, son of Saul [~A-880-883], best fit age 40 at [A-921]
Barzillai the Gileadite of Rogelim born [A-888]
Ahiah born, son of Ahitub, [A-891-893], best fit [A-891]
Begin simultaneous / sequential events:
    Israel did evil again; 18 years oppression: served Baalim, Ashtaroth & the gods of Syria, Zidon, Moab, Ammon, [A-892-910]
    Begin forty years oppression by Philistines [A-892-932]

Brief Event Timeline

   Eli (Zerahiah), the former high priest, died (age 111) [A-781-892]
   Eli (Meraioth) became high priest (age 58 to 98) [A-892-932]
   Samson born to Manoah & his wife [A-892]
Samuel started school of the prophets, end of 50 years [A-900]
Joel and Abiah made judges in Beersheba (ages 26 and 25 respectively) [A-900]
Samuel (age 51) anoints Saul (age 39) to be king early in [A-901]
Ishbosheth born, son of Saul [A-901]
Zadok born, son of Ahitub [A-904]
Abiathar born, son of Ahimelech [A-907]
Judge: Jephthah, son of Gilead; six years [A-910-916][19]
Samuel's speech, 1 Samuel 12:5-11 – Samson not named, early [A-911]
David born, son of Jesse [A-911]
Samson (near age 20) began to afflict Philistines [A-912]
Ahiah, began wearing an ephod as priest [A-916-921], best fit age 30 at [A-921]
Judge: Ibzan of Bethlehem; 7 years [A-916-923]
David (~age 12) anointed by Samuel [A-923]
Judge: Elon, a Zebulonite; 10 years [A-923-933]
Samson (age 36) captured and bound by Philistines [A-928]
David (age 17) slays Goliath in war [A-928]
Begin simultaneous & rapid sequential events:
   Samson died (age 40) destroying Philistines, judged Israel 20 years [A-932][18] while
   David fled Saul (age 21) [A-932].
   Doeg slaughtered 85 priests, by Saul's command [A-932] and
   Abiathar, nephew to Zadok, fled to David [A-932].
   Hophni and Phinehas died at the battle scene [A-932] with
   Ark of covenant lost in battle to Philistines [A-932] early in the eighth month of Bul, held seven months [A-932-933].
   Meraioth (high priest Eli) died age 98 [A-932] followed by
   Ichabod born to Phinehas after his death [A-932], died <80 years of age [A-932–<=A-1012].
   Philistines returned a little later that year, defeated by Samuel age 82 [A-932].
Ark of God returned to Kirjathjearim (after seven months) early in month Sivan, kept twenty years [A-933-953] by Amminadab
Judge: Abdon the son of Hillel, of Pirathon; 8 years [A-933-941]

Jesse (~age 96) and wife taken to Moab by David [~A-937]

Jesse died (~age 98) [~A-939]

Samuel died (age 89) [A-939]

David met, married Abigail [A-939]

David nearby Gath for 16 months [A-940-941], Amalekites burn Ziklag [A-941]

King Saul died (age 79); sons Jonathan (~age 60), Ishui, Melchishua died [A-941]

David (age 30), king over Judah in Hebron, 7.5 years [A-941 Tishri – 949 ~Zif]

Ishbosheth (age 40), son of Saul, made king over Israel [A-941-949]

Absalom born, son of David via Maacah daughter of Talmai king of Geshur [~A-941]

Adonijah born, son of David via Haggith [A-~941]

Ishbosheth murdered (~age 47.5 to 48 early in year ~Zif) [A-949]

David (age 37.5) made king over Israel, 33 years [A-949-982]

Solomon born, son of David via Bathsheba at Jerusalem [A-951]

Ark of Covenant moved in 2 sessions to Zion tabernacle, David age 42, starting at month Sivan with a three month pause by Obededom until the month of Elul before placement in the Zion tabernacle [A-953]

Temple preparations made by David [A-960-981]

Absalom rebelled forty years from David defeating Goliath, and died [A-968]

Barzillai the Gileadite of Rogelim at age 80 years [A-968]

Rehoboam born, son of Solomon via Naamah the Ammonite [A-979]

Adonijah (age 40) rebelled [A-981], and died later [A-981]

Solomon became king in Tishri [A-981]

Abiathar removed as high priest, Zadok established as high priest [A-981]

King David died (age 70.5) by month Nisan and before Tishri [A-982]

Temple building began 17 days after 479th anniversary on 2nd of Zif in [A-984]

Zadok the high priest died <80 years [A-904–<=984]

Temple completed in 11th year of Solomon's reign [A-991]

Johanan born [A-961], son of Azariah, with Levitical tabernacle service from 25 to 50 years of age from [A-986-1011] and with 20 years in Solomon's Temple [A-991-1011], died <80 years [A-961–<=1041]

Rehoboam made king over Israel about Tishri [A-1019] of 932 BC[20]

King Solomon died in his fortieth year of reign, before Tishri [A-1020] of 931 BC[20,21]

Scripture Index
Old Testament

Genesis
3:15 109
8:20 204
10:22-23 70
11:10-13 100
11:26-29 71
11:26-32 10
11:27-32 10
11:29 82
11:29-31 10
11:32 10
12:1 10, 42
12:1-3 50, 120, 137
12:1-8 10
12:2 10
12:2-3 28
12:4 10, 51
12:4-8 10
12:5 71
12:5-10 53
12:10-20 53
12:11, 14 79
13:18 76
14:14 75
14:23 75
15:13 40, 41, 47, 49, 51
15:13-15 39
15:13-16 4, 19, 39, 40, 50, 52, 56, 77, 82, 213
15:16 39, 41, 45, 48, 52
15:18-21 87

16:1 11
16:11-16 11, 13
16:12 43
16:15-16 27
17 chpt. 11, 75
17:4-9 11
17:6 75
17:8 42
17:10-14 11
17:17 10, 28
17:20 12
17:23-26 11
18:11 127
18:14 20
18:19 77, 85
19:35-39 71
20:1 53
20:2-3 75
20:11-12 10
20:14-16 75
20:14-18 204
21:1-5 11, 12, 13, 127
21:5 6
21:5-10 42
21:8-10 11, 51
21:8-10, 21 47, 49
21:8-14 27
21:8-9 11, 43
21:10-14 11
21:21 11
21:22 76
21:22-23, 34 53
21:23 42

21:30-32 76
22:19 76
22:20-22 70
22:20-23 82
22:20-24 71
22:21 71
22:23 12
23:1-2 11, 92
23:3-18 42, 53
24:1 76, 127
24:15, 24-27 82
24:16 76, 79
24:29 12
24:50 76
24:67 11, 12, 27
25 chpt. 27, 92
25:1-10 11
25:1-2 27
25:1-4 11
25:5, 11 76
25:6 27, 77
25:9 12
25:12-16 12
25:17 12, 13
25:20 11, 12
25:24-26 11, 12, 68
25:25-26 6
25:26-28 53
25:30 68
26:1, 6 76
26:1-3 53
26:7 79
26:12-14 76

26:12-18 43
26:16, 27 42, 43, 76
26:17-21 43
26:20-33 24
26:26-31 76
26:32 76
26:34 68
26:34-35 12, 43
27:1-4 12, 13
27:1-42 43, 44
27:5 7, 11, 12
27:5-41 12, 13
27:41 13
27:41–28:8 13
27:46 43
28:1-5 13, 42, 44
28:1-7 12, 13
28:2-5 12
28:5, 7, 10 53
28:9 12, 43
28:10 43, 44
28:12-15 77
29:4 43
29:5 82
29:14-18 12
29:18-21, 27-29 14
29:18–30:25 22, 26, 59
29:20, 27-29 14
29:20-28 13
29:21 14
29:24-26 44
29:31-32 22

Scripture Index

29:33 22
29:34 22
29:35 22
30:4-6 22
30:7-8 22
30:9 23
30:9-11 22
30:13 22
30:14-18 22
30:19-20 22
30:21 22
30:22-24 22
30:24-25 12
30:24–31:20 43
30:24–31:55 12, 15
30:25 14, 23
30:25-31 23
30:25-43 23
30:25–31:55 12
30:25–37:26 43
30:26-34 14
30:27-43 14
30:28 43, 44
30:43–31:1 77
31:1-16, 38-42 43, 44
31:7, 41 14
31:1-36 59
31:16 77
31:22-23 44
31:22-28 98
31:25 53
31:30 44
31:38-41 13
31:41 12, 14, 23
31:53 10, 71
32:13-15 76
32:28 77
32:3-5 76
32:4 53
32:6 76
32:6-8 44
33:1-3 44
33:17 53
33:17-20 43
33:18-20 53
34:1-2 44
34:1-31 24
34:25 24
34:25-26, 30-31 44
34:27-29 77
35:11, 16-20 44
35:11-12, 15 77
35:16-18 22, 23
35:16-20 24
35:22 24, 44
35:24 12
35:27 24, 53, 76
35:27-29 12
36:1-8 68, 76
36:3 12
36:6-8, 20-30 68
36:8 68
36:9-14 77
36:11 68
36:15-17 77
37:1-36 24
37:1 42, 43
37:11, 19-20 44
37:14 24
37:2 24
37:2-31 20
37:23-24 44
37:27-28 44
37:3 12
37:31-32 44
37:36 43-45
38 chpt. 24
38:2, 12 24
38:2-4 25
38:2-5 25
38:5 25
38:6-7 25
38:8-10 25
38:11-27 25
38:11-30 25
38:12 69
38:27-30 25
38–46 chpts. 9
39:1 43-45
39:1-19 20
39:19-20 44
39:20 20
39:20–41:1 20
39:5-6 46
39:7-19 44
40:15 44
40:23–41:1 44
41:1 20
41:1-57 59
41:14-46 20
41:41–42:1 46
41:46 70
41:47-53 21
41:53 21
41:54 21
41:54-57 21
41:56-57 77
43:1-15 26
43:33 xiii
44:18-34 26
45:4-6 21
45:6 15
45:11 77
45:16-18 46
45:17-18 47, 49
45:17-21 45
45:4-8 46
45:6 21, 59
45:6, 11 21
45:6, 11, 24-28 21
46 chpt. 25, 26
46:8-27 27, 48
46:1-7 21, 43
46:10 69
46:11 47, 49, 161, 218
46:12 24-26, 34, 62
46:13 65
46:2-4 53
46:21 69
46:26 65
46:29 44
46:33-34 45
47:4 53, 54, 86
47:4-6 82
47:8-9 21
47:9 15, 21, 44
47:1-11 45
47:28 15
47:5-6 46, 47, 49
47:7-10 21
48:16 129
49:8-10 84
49:33 15
49:33–50:14 60
50 chpt. 82
50:1-14 15

Scripture Index

50:1-14 21
50:20 15
50:22-26 21
50:24 87

Exodus
1 chpt. 8, 62, 213
1:1-05 48, 49
1:1-14 43, 60
1:1-5 27, 43
1:5 27
1:6 8, 52, 62, 63, 66, 67, 214
1:6-24 61, 74
1:8-12 45
1:8-13 48, 49
1:8-14 52, 60
1:8-16 63
1:10-14 74
1:12 43
1:13-14 45
1:15-21 29
1:15-22 45
1:20-21 51
1:22 74
2 chpt. 62, 63
2:1-11 74
2:1-2 61
2:1-7 33
2:1-8 33, 46, 48
2:2 74
2:3 74
2:8-10 33, 51
2:11-15 63
2:15 81
2:22 218
3:1 81, 204

5:1 64
5:6-14 45
6:3-5 53
6:16 26, 52, 59, 62, 66
6:16-18 27, 46, 48
6:18 47, 49, 62, 161
6:20 27, 28, 46-49, 62
6:21 161
6:23 33, 35, 46
6:23-25 192
6:24 158, 161
6:3-5 54
7:1 33, 52
7:7 33, 63, 81, 129, 224
7:7 33, 35, 46, 48, 63
7–8 chpts. 74
8:19 74
11:2-3 46
11:5 75
12 chpt. 152
12:2 152
12:12-13 55
12:2 152
12:29-30 75
12:40 39, 48-50, 53-55, 86, 214
12:40-41 43
13:2 223
13:3-4 55
13:4 152
13:19 21
14:9-28 75

15:20 33, 52
17:10-12 224
17:14 188
18:1-8 87
18:3 218
18:9-12 204
18:20-25 142
18:21-25 143
19:1-2 224
20:4 203
20:5 172, 173
21:6, 22 143
22:8-9 143
22:29 223
23:11 149
23:15 55
23–24 chpts. 49
24:1 46
24:1, 9 33
24:1-9 35
25:17-18 193
25:21-22 203
28 chpt. 24, 35
28:1 33, 35, 36, 46, 48, 90, 191, 192
28:1-4, 41 192
29:5 169
31:1-11 224
33:11 81, 126, 128-130
35:50 224
38:22 224
40 chpt. 24, 35
40:27-29 204
41:50-52 128

Leviticus

4:3-12 168
8 chpt. 24, 35, 46
8:21, 28-29 204
10:1-16 46
10:1-7 35
10:4 143
20:10 167
21:17-23 46
23:15-17 194
25:4, 19-21 149
25:1-18 149
25:20-22 149
25:21 149
29:1-35 46

Numbers
1:1 130
1:1-18 35, 52, 91, 130
1:3 160, 183, 184, 201
1:3, 18, 45 175
1:6-8 10, 34
1:16 143
1:18 35, 130
1:18-19 90
2:3 10, 34, 36, 90
3 chpt. 177
3:2 35, 46, 48, 191, 192
3:4 35
3:12-13, 45-47 223
3:19 27, 46, 48
3:32 163
4 chpt. 139, 163
4:3, 23, 30, 35,

Scripture Index

47 33, 35, 70, 127, 177
4:16 163
7:2 143
7:11-17 36
7:12, 17 10
7:89 193
8:23-25 139, 163
8:23-26 33, 35, 46, 127, 177
8:24 175
10:12 87
10:14 10
10:28-30 87
10:29 87
10:33 203
11:21 224
11:28 126, 128, 129
12:16 87
13:6-8 126
13:8, 16 70, 128
13:1–14:10, 24 126
14:29-31 131
14:30, 38 91
14:33 43
14:33-34 10, 37
14:34-36 35, 131
14:44 193, 203
16:1-49 161
19:11 198
19:11-16 198
20:1 33
21:4-31 87
25:5 143
25:6-14 29, 169
25:11-13 30
26:2, 4 175
26:4 35, 131
26:21 25, 224
26:58-59 218
26:59 27, 46, 48
26:63-65 131
26:64-65 35, 91, 126
27 chpt. 107
27:1-10 103, 113
27:1-11 103, 104, 108
27:8 106, 109
27:8-10 105
27:18 132
27:21 163
28:16 152
30:1 143
31:13 143, 192
32:11-12 35, 131
32:12 91
32:13 10, 37, 43
33:3 55, 152
33:38 35
33:39 33, 63, 64, 225
34:17 49, 126, 149
36 chpt. 103, 104, 108
36:1 143
36:8 103, 104, 106

Deuteronomy
1:15 142
1:16-18 143
2:7 43
2:9 71
4:9 133, 140
6:4-6 177
7:7 10
10:8 203
11:19 133, 140
12:5-7, 11, 21 203
12:8 133
16:11 203
17:8-11 144
17:8-11, 18-20 177
17:8-9 163
17:9 121, 143
17:10-11 140
17:14-20 181
18:15 33
19:16-20 144
19:17 121, 143
21:2 143
24:4-7 203
24:5 198
25 chpt. 107
25:1 143
25:5 193
25:5-6 102, 104, 108
25:7 198
25:17-19 224
34:7 28
34:9 132
34:10 33, 52, 81

Joshua
1:1 126
2:1 97
2:1, 4 97
2:1-24 89, 96
2:12-13, 18 97
2:18 97
3:11 203
5:4-6 35, 131
5:6 37, 43
5:13-15 132
6:2 132
6:17-25 89, 96
6:22 97
6:23 97
8:31 204
8:33 143
13:1 126, 127, 150
13–19 chpts. 49, 126, 149
14:1 35, 49, 52, 143
14:7-11 126, 150
14:7-9 126
14:15 2
15:16-18 119
15:41 70
17:3-6 103, 104, 108
17:4 35, 52
19:51 35, 52
21:21 35, 52
22:14 143
23:1 133
23:1-3 127
23:2 143, 150
23–24 chpts. 134
24:1-29 126
24:29 126, 150
24:29-30 130
24:31 1, 118,

Scripture Index

125, 130, 150, 214
24:32 21
24:33 35, 52

Judges
1:1–3:7 119
1:13 119
1–2 chpts. 150
2:7 1, 118, 125, 130, 138, 150, 151, 214
2:8 126, 168
2:10 133
2:10-13 119, 132, 150
2:11-19 144
2:12 134
2:16 143
2:18-19 120
3:1-5 150
3:1-7 145
3:5-7 132
3:7 133
3:7-11 121, 148, 151
3:8 119, 135, 136, 138, 139, 148-152
3:8-11 146, 208
3:8–12:13-15 200
3:8–12:15 2, 200
3:9-11 119, 208
3:11 2, 120
3:12-14 148, 151, 208
3:13 209

3:15-30 148, 151, 209
3:31 122, 148, 151, 155
4:1-3 148, 151
4:4-24 122, 148, 151
4:11 87
4:17 156
5:6 155
5:6, 31 122
5:31 148, 151
6:1 148, 151
6:7–8:28 148, 151
8:24 15
8:28 120
8:32 120
8:33 151
8:33–9:57 148
9:1-57 151
10:1-2 148, 151
10:3 148, 151
10:6-08 200, 204, 205
10:6-18 2, 151, 152, 160, 215, 216
10:6-8 148, 200
11:1–12:7 148
11:8-10 148, 151
11:11-12 151
11:13-15 151
11:1–12:7 151
11:26 2, 207, 208
12:11-12 148
12:13-15 121,

138, 139, 148, 150
13:1 2, 147, 160, 171, 174, 182, 186, 200, 203, 205, 215, 216
13:5 199, 202
13–16 chpts. 2
14:1-4 160
14:4 201
15:2 79
15:20 160
16:21 204
16:22 205
16:23-30 201
16:25-31 206
16:27-30 205
16:27-31 205
16:28-30 201
16:31 160, 201
17–18 chpts. 218
17:6 133
17:7 218
17:10-11 218
17:6; 18:1; 19:1; 21:25 217
17–21 chpts. 133, 218
18:30 218
20:28 218
21:25 133

Ruth
1:1 106, 121, 146
1:2 103
1:3-5 104
1:4 122

1:6-19 106
1:12 104, 106
1:20 104
2:1 108
2:19-22 106
3 chpt. 106
3:1 106
3:10 108
3:11 108
3:12 103
3:13 104
4:3-4 104, 105
4:6 104, 105
4:7-10 106
4:10 104
4:14-15, 17 107
4:15 108
4:18 24
4:18-22 111, 112
4:19 34
4:20 35, 92
4:20-22 98
4:21 92, 107
4:21-22 92, 114
4:22 95

1 Samuel
1:1 161
1:1, 21 158
1:1-2 161, 162
1:1-2, 8 162
1:1–2:11 157, 163, 169
1:2 179
1:3 2, 165, 170
1:9 163
1:11 179

Scripture Index

1:17 163, 171
1:21-25 166
1:28 141
2 chpt. 170
2:11, 18, 21, 26 169
2:11-22 166
2:12 172
2:12, 22 166
2:12-17 163, 169
2:12-17, 27-36 139
2:12-32 158
2:12-36 101, 168, 169, 190
2:13-17 170
2:18 169
2:18, 28 139
2:18-19 170
2:20 171
2:22 163, 168
2:22 164
2:22-25 164, 167
2:26 164, 167
2:27-34 168
2:27-36 172
2:31 2, 72, 138, 139, 153, 195
2:33 173
2:34 166
3 chpt. 168, 173, 174, 195
3:1-21 158, 170
3:2 164, 170
3:4-14 141
3:11-14 139, 172
3:20 141, 206
3:27-36 172
4 chpt. 173, 205
4:1-22. 158
4:1–6:21 193
4:1–7:2 194
4:3-5 195
4:3-5, 11-18 156, 170, 177, 191, 195
4:9 201, 205
4:15 160
4:15-18 94, 168
4:15-19 146
4:15-22 173
4:16-22 175
4:18 2, 160, 174, 182
4:19-21 174
4–7 chpts. 171, 174, 177, 195, 197
5:1–7:2 158
6:1 160, 165, 201, 202
6:1, 13 194
6:6-13 202
6:13 194
6:21 202
7 chpt. 202, 203
7:1 194
7:1-14 171
7:1-2 202
7:2 160, 165, 177, 194
7:3-14 158
7:5 171
7:5-12 203
7:6, 15 156
7:7 202
7:9-10, 17 206
7:9-14 171, 202, 205
7:10 203
7:10-14 201, 203
7:15 2, 147, 180
7:15-17 178, 204
7:15–11:15 158, 177
7:17 203
8:1 160, 177
8:1-2 143, 147
8:2 162
8:2-3 178
8:4 141
8:4-7 156
8:5 160
8:7 141
8:11-12 183
9:1–10:13 156, 181
9:16 157, 205
9:1–10:13 178
10:1 157
10:5-12 178
10:8 206
10:11-12 178
10:17-25 181
10:25 180
10:27 157, 181
11 chpt. 181
11:12 157, 182
11:14 157
11:15 181, 206
12 chpt. 179, 185, 199
12:1-2 177
12:1-25 199, 200
12:1–15:35 158, 179, 182
12:3 141, 142
12:5-11 182, 199, 207, 216
12:11 179, 182, 199
12:12-13 156
12:12-25 195
12:16-18 200
12:17-18 156, 179
13 chpt. 185, 207
13:1 184
13:1-2 183
13:1–15:35 158, 179, 183, 185
13:2-3 185
13:2-4 184
13:3 185
13:3-23 180
13:3–15:35 183
13:5-7 185
13:8-9 185
13:9 207
13:13-14 185
13:14 157, 179, 196, 207
13:17-22 186
13:19-22 207
14 chpt. 186, 187
14:3 139, 163, 165, 167, 172, 174-176, 186, 191, 192
14:3, 18 207
14:15 187
14:18 186, 195

Scripture Index

14:3, 18-19, 36-42 138
14:46-48 183
14:47 181
14:47-48 157
14:49 183, 190, 210
14:49-50 183
14:52 184
15:1-3 187, 188
15:1-35 15, 180, 188
15:6 188
15:11 147
16 chpt. 180, 188
16:1 95
16:1-13 110, 180, 195
16:1–30:31 158
16:2 206
16:14 196, 197
16:14-23 195
16:15-23 95
16:22 110
17 chpt. 188
17:4 204
17:12 2, 72, 92-94, 98, 110, 195
17:12-20 96
17:40-50 205
17:48-50 195
17:49-51 171
17:54 171
18:1 197
18:1-30 189
18:1-5 197
18:1–30:31 188

18:5-7 171
18:7 189
18:7-8 197
18:8-12 189
18:9, 29 194
18:9-10 189
18:12 189
18:14 171
18:16 196
18:17-27 183
18:25-27 195
18:27 171
19:1 189
19:1-2, 10 197
19:5 196
19:18 178, 189
19:18-19 180
19:18–20:1 195
19:19-24 189
19:20 178
19:20-24 178
19:24 179
20:1–30:31 189
20:12-17 189
20:31 194
20:42 194
21:3, 01-6 190
21:11 189
21–22 chpts. 195
22 chpt. 170
22:1-2 197
22:1-4 93, 96
22:2 157
22:3 93
22:5 160
22:9, 11, 20 175
22:9, 20 139

22:9-20 195
22:9-23 173, 175
22:18 139
22:18-22 190, 197
22:20 175, 176
22:20-23 191
23:1-12 170
23:1-29 189
23:5 171
23:6 139
23:9 190
23:14 197
23:16-18 189, 198
23:19 197
24:2 196
24:6, 10 196
24:22 180
25:1 110, 142, 155, 180, 198
25:1-9 180
25:39-42 180
26:2 196
26:23 196
27:7 142, 181
28:1 171
28:1–31:13 158, 190
28:3 142
28:6 196
28:18 196
29 chpt. 203
29:9 196
30:6-8 170
30:7 190
30:12 208
30:18-19 181

31 chpt. 203
31:2 189
31:6 155

2 Samuel
1:16 196
2:4 190
2:8-10 181, 183, 210
2:8-15 181, 183
2:11 149, 183
2:31 196
3:7-8 183
3:18 171
4:4 199
4:5-7 183
5:4 70, 149, 171
5:5 183
5:7 165, 194
5:17-25 171
6:1-18 194
6:1-23 194
6:10-19 194
6:16-17 165, 194
6:17 194
7:2-17 160
7:11 146
8:6, 14 196
8:11 171
8:17 175, 176, 192
12:1-15, 25 160
12:15-18 166
12:24-25 70
14:27 79
15:27 176
16:13 182
19:32 72, 94,

Scripture Index

183
19:33-37 101
21:15-22 171
21:17 191, 196, 203
24:11-19 160
24:25 204

1 Kings
1 chpt. 176
1:1 127
1:1-53 152
1:42-43 176
2:11 149
2:26 191
2:26-27 139, 176, 192
2:26-27, 35 170
2:35 176
3:4 79
4:4 139, 176
6:1 2, 4, 55, 91, 135, 137, 138, 148, 149, 152, 214
7:1 176
9:10 176
18:30-32 204
18:31 98

2 Kings
1:42-43 176
2:1-18 178
4:38 178
6:1 178
8:25 98
9:1 178
13:1–15:38 98

22:4 193
25:18 193

1 Chronicles
1:17 71
1:34-37 68
2:1-15 98, 111, 112
2:1-5, 18-20 224
2:3 25
2:10 10, 34, 36, 90
2:11 92
2:18 224
2:20 224
3:19 193
6 chpt. 35, 48
6:1-15 191
6:1-38 161
6:2, 16, 38 161
6:2, 18 161
6:3 192
6:3-5 192
6:4-5, 49-53 192
6:6 163, 191
6:6, 50-53 163
6:6, 52 138, 192
6:6-7 163
6:6-7, 52 172
6:7, 52 165, 167, 175, 192
6:7-8 192
6:8 175, 176, 192
6:9-10 175, 176, 192
6:11 192
6:12 192

6:13 193
6:14 112, 193
6:14-15 193
6:15 193
6:16 218
6:16, 22-28 161
6:16, 33-38 161
6:22, 38 161
6:23 27, 48
6:25 161
6:25, 35 161
6:26, 34 161, 162
6:26, 35 161, 162
6:27, 34 161, 162
6:28 162, 178
6:28, 33 162
6:32-34 162
6:33 162
6:33-38 158
6:35 162
6:36 161
6:37 161
7:1 65
7:17 147, 234
7:22-27 70, 128
9:11 192
9:22 180
10:1-14 181
11:1-9 183
11:9 196
12:32 66
13:1-14 202
13:7 165
14:16 171
15:1-29 202

15:11-12 178
16:18-20 10
17:6, 10 146
18 chpt. 196
18:1 171
18:16 176, 192
19 chpt. 196
20 chpt. 196
21:26 204
23:1-5 196
23:3, 24-27 139
23:6 196
23:12 161
23:13 46
23:14-15 218
23:21-22 105
24:1 192
24:1-2 192
24:3-6 176
24:31 176
28:11 196
29:12-13 196
29:22 192
29:29 141, 142

2 Chronicles
1:5 224
3:1-2 152
3:2 55, 149
8:1 176
9:29 142
22–25 chpts. 98
26:20 193
30:22 177
31:10 193
31:16-19 47
34:9 193

Scripture Index

35:1 152
35:30 177

Ezra
2:62 47
3:2 193
3:2, 8 193
5:2 193
6:19 152
7:1, 11 52
7:1-5 112, 192, 193
10:6 193
10:18 193

Nehemiah
1:9 203
3:1, 20 193
8:9, 11, 13 177
9:19-21 101, 132
11:11 192
12:10 193
12:10-11, 26 112, 193
12:10-12, 22, 26 193
12:11 193
12:11, 22 193
12:26 193
13:28 193

Esther
1:11 79
2:7, 17 79
3:1, 10 15
3:7 152
8:3, 5 15

9:24 15

Job
1:1 86
1:2-3 75
1:3 77
1:5 204
1:8 82
1:9-10 73
1:11 73
2:11 69
2:11a 68
4:1 68
8:1 69
11:1 69
15:10 66
19:23-24 81
19:25-27 84
23:8-9 80
23:12 85
32:2 70
32:2-7 71
32:4-6 70
32:6 72, 73
33:1-6 71
33–37 chpts. 72
42:7-10 204
42:10, 13 66
42:11 65, 79, 81, 82
42:12-13 78
42:12-16 66
42:14-15 79
42:15 79
42:16 86
42:14-15 79

Psalms
1:2 177
12:6-7 223
22 chpt. 5, 126
33:16 196
34:3 223
69:22-24 167
77:15 98
78:4-7 133, 140
90:10 91, 101
99:6 204, 206
105 chpt. 213
105:22-27 61, 74
105:26 63
105:37 51
106:10 43
115:12 29, 52
119:160 223

Songs of Solomon
1:15-16; 2:2, 10, 13; 4:10; 5:9; 6:10 79

Isaiah
1:26 146
44:18 171

Jeremiah
2 chpt. 203
32:27 20
49:8 68
52:24 193

Lamentations
4:21 68

Ezekiel
10–11 chpts. 196
20:13, 21 132
25:15 201, 204, 205
44:15 192
45:21 152
48:11 192

Daniel
4:29 168

Hosea
13:10 143

Jonah
1:17 208

Haggai
1:1 193
1:1, 12-14 193
2:2-4 193

Zechariah
3:1, 8 193
6:11 193

Malachi
2:4-7 30
3:6 98

New Testament

Matthew
1:1 193
1:1, 16 108
1:1-16 98, 111, 112
1:5 89, 97-100, 108, 112-114, 118, 122
1:8 98, 107
1:12 193
1:18-20 109
6:23 175
12:40 208
21:12 170
21:23–22:46 108
22:24 102
22:41-46 108
26:57 146
27:46-50 5
27:54 196

Mark
2:26 191, 192
11:15 170
12:9 102
15:34-37 5

Luke
1:7 127
1:18 127
2:41-51 170
3:23 70, 98, 108
3:23-38 24, 98, 111, 112
3:28 193
3:29 193
3:31 192
3:32 98
3:35-36 100
11:34 175
13:3, 5 172
19:45-46 170
20:28 102

John
1:12 109
2:15 170
3:26-32 197
5:39 159
10:35 20
19:23-24 169
19:25-27 109

Acts
3:22 33, 52
3:24 206
7 chpt. 213
7:15-21 61, 74
7:18-21 63
7:20 61
7:20-21 74
7:23-27 129
7:29-30 63
7:37 33, 52
7:45 217
13:16-20 49, 50, 52, 213
13:16-22 49, 149
13:19 49, 126
14:21 181

Romans
4:12-13, 16 79
5:10 109
10:5 132
11:8 171
11:15 109
11:33 20

1 Corinthians
2:3 4

2 Corinthians
5:18 109
5:21 109
11:2 79
11:9 4

Galatians
3:15-17 48, 49
3:15-18 50
3:16 109
3:17 50
4:4, 27-31 109
4:6 109

Philippians
2:5 109

Colossians
1:20 109

2 Thessalonians
2:5 4

1 Timothy
5:8-11 109

2 Timothy
3:16-17 219

Hebrews
2:17 109
3:1 204
4:14 204
4:15 109
5:1-2 203
6:20 204
7:9-10 54
7:26 109
11:8-10 42, 53, 54
11:17-19 85
11:22 21
11:31 89, 96
11:32 199, 207

James
2:25 89, 96

1 Peter
3:18 109

2 Peter
2:14 167

1 John
3:1-2 109

Revelation
22:17 109
22:18-19 112

Notes

Notes

Endnotes

1. Thomas, B., Two date range options for Noah's flood, J. Creation Vol. 31:120 -127, 2017.

2. Wood, B.G., Recent Research on the Date and Setting of the Exodus, www.biblearchaeology.org/post/2009/10/19/Recent-Research-on-the-Date-and-Setting-of-the-Exodus.aspx#Article, accessed March 26, 2017.

3. Young, R.C., "When Did Solomon Die?", www.rcyoung.org/frame5.html, or www.etsjets.org/files/JETS-PDFs/46/46-4/46-4-pp589-603_JETS.pdf, accessed 10/7/2017. For further validation of the placement of Solomon's reign which started before the end of David's forty-year reign see: Rodger Young's Papers on Chronology, www.rcyoung.org/papers.htm l, accessed March 26, 2017.

4. Young, R.C., Evidence for inerrancy from an unexpected source: OT chronology, Bible and Spade 21:Spring 2008, p.54., biblearchaeology.org/research/chronological-categories/exodus-era/2662-evidence-for-inerrancy-from-a-second-unexpected-source-the-jubilee-and-sabbatical-cycles, accessed March 26, 2017.

5. Young, R.C., "Evidence for inerrancy from an unexpected source: the Jubilee and Sabbatical Cycles", Bible & Spade 21:Fall, 2008, biblearchaeology.org/research/exodus-from-egypt/2662-evidence-for-inerrancy-from-a-second-unexpected-source-the-jubilee-and-sabbatical-cycles, p.118., or at www.rcyoung.org/articles/unexpected2.pdf, p.10., accessed March 26, 2017.

6. Young, R.C., "Evidence for inerrancy from an unexpected source: OT chronology", Bible and Spade 21:Spring 2008, p.54., biblearchaeology.org/research/divided-kingdom/3295-evidence-for-inerrancy-from-an-unexpected-source-ot-chronology, accessed March 26, 2017.

7. Khamudi, https://en.wikipedia.org/wiki/List_of_pharaohs, image: https://upload.wikimedia.org/wikipedia/commons/thumb/4/48/CylinderKhondyPetrie.jpg/100px-Cylinder_Khondy_Petrie.jpg, accessed October 7, 2017.

8. Apepi, https://en.wikipedia.org/wiki/List_of_pharaohs, accessed October 7, 2017.

9. Ahmose I, Rensselaer Polytechnic Institute, http://homepages.rpi.edu/~holmes/Hobbies/Genealogy2/ps23/ps23_021.htm, accessed 10/7/2017. Ahmose / Tethmosis rejected the single god belief of Amenhotep IV / Akhenaton. Shortly after his death Egyptians returned to their polytheism.

Endnotes

10. Amenhotep IV / Akhenaton became pharaoh about 1553 BC and ruled for seventeen years. He is known for changing Egypt's religion from polytheism to monotheism and is believed to be the first monotheistic ruler in world history since he closed other temples and elevated the god Aten to the highest position. Akhenaten means, "living spirit of Aten.", www.kyrene.org/cms/lib2/AZ01001083/Centricity/Domain/894/AKHENATEN%20AND%20TUTANKHAMEN%20NOTES.pdf accessed October 7, 2017.

11. "What is proudly advertised as Egyptian history is merely a collection of rags and tatters.", Sir Alan Gardiner. Gardiner, A., *Egypt of the Pharaohs*, Oxford University press, Oxford, p. 53, 1961, 1964.)

12. Morelle, R., *New timeline for origin of ancient Egypt*, BBC News, www.bbc.com/news/science-environment-23947820, accessed October 7, 2017.

13. Mitchell, E., *Doesn't Egyptian Chronology Prove That the Bible Is Unreliable?*, https://answersingenesis.org/archaeology/ancient-egypt/doesnt-egyptian-chronology-prove-bible-unreliable/ , accessed 10/7/2017.

14. Adamthwaite, M., *Perspectives on ancient chronology and the Old Testment-part 1*, Journal of Creation 31(3):61-67, 2017, https://creation.com/ot-ancient-chronology-1, accessed 4/30/2018.

15. Adamthwaite, M., *Perspectives on ancient chronology and the Old Testment- part 2*, Journal of Creation 32(1):76-83, 2017, https://creation.com/ot-ancient-chronology-2, accessed 6/20/2018. Adamthwaite asked for "a re-assesment of the period in question" after presenting numerous conflicts amongst and within the current interpretations of Egyptian chronology. "Rethinking Chronology from Abraham to Solomon," corrected some and revealed new internal connections during this period to validate the time related information given in the Scriptures.

16. Kuehmichel, B., Barren Women, Virginity and Proof of Virtue, www.lookinguntojesus.info /BSTopics/Biblestudies/BarrenWomen-Virginity-ProofOfVirtue.html, accessed September 29, 2020.

17. McDurmon, J., Why Jesus cleansed the temple twice (a long-standing mystery solved), April 14, 2016, www.theaquilareport.com/why-jesus-cleansed-the-temple-twice-a-long-standing-mystery-solved/, accessed April 28, 2017.

18. Kuehmichel, B., Samson Previews Christ, August 22, 2015, www.lookinguntojesus.info/ BSTopics/TypesShadows/SamsonPreviewsChrist.html, accessed April 6, 2020.

19. Kuehmichel, B., Jephthah's Vow and His Daughter, August 22, 2015, www.lookinguntojesus.info/BSTopics/Biblestudies/JephthahsDaughter.html, accessed April 6, 2020.

20. Young, R.C., Three Verifications of Thiele's Date for the Beginning of the Divided Kingdom, AUSS Fall 2007, www.rcyoung.org/papers.html, accessed July 15, 2017. See other applicable papers at: www.rcyoung.org/papers.html.

21. Kitchen, Kenneth A., How we know when Solomon Ruled, Biblical Archaeology Review; Sep/Oct 2001; 27, 5, www.etf.cuni.cz/~prudky/pdf/Kitchen-2001_BAR-How_We_Know.pdf, accessed July 5, 2017.

22. Adamthwaite, M. R., Perspectives on ancient chronology and the Old Testament–part 2, Journal of Creation 32(1):76-83, 2018.

23. Kuehmichel, B., Why we still use – The King James Bible, www.lookinguntojesus.info/BSTopics/Topics/WestilluseTheKingJamesBible.html, accessed April 1, 2020.

www.ingramcontent.com/pod-product-compliance
Lightning Source LLC
Chambersburg PA
CBHW071810080526
44589CB00012B/743